"In this smart and readable book, Snider does the spadework for a theology of preaching after the death of the Christian God shaped by Western metaphysics. Influenced by John Caputo's reading of Derrida, Snider discovers a constructive homiletic emerging from the ashes of philosophical deconstruction . . . His relentlessly positive approach to Derrida is refreshing, and his homiletical ideas encourage a fundamental rethinking of both our reasons for preaching and the messages we preach."

—JOHN S. McCLURE,
author of *Otherwise Preaching*

"There has been a lot of talk about preaching over the past number of years–debates about its viability and vitality in these post-secular, interactive times. But in the midst of all that talk, very little has been said about content. It was assumed that we all knew 'what the message' was, that it was simply a matter of finding the right container. Phil Snider ups the conversation by inviting us to consider the content of the influential and culture-shaping world of continental philosophy and offers us ways to incorporate it into our communicating. Phil doesn't want us to domesticate these ideas, he wants us to use them to inform and frame a new way of preaching, but beyond that, a new way of thinking about life, God, church and everything in between."

—BARRY TAYLOR,
Professor of Culture & Religion at Fuller Theological Seminary and Associate
Rector of All Saints Episcopal Church, Beverly Hills

Preaching After God

Preaching After God

*Derrida, Caputo, and the Language of
Postmodern Homiletics*

Phil Snider

CASCADE *Books* · Eugene, Oregon

PREACHING AFTER GOD
Derrida, Caputo, and the Language of Postmodern Homiletics

Cascade Books
An Imprint of Wipf and Stock Publishers
199 W. 8th Ave., Suite 3
Eugene, OR 97401

www.wipfandstock.com

ISBN 13: 978-1-61097-498-1

Cataloging-in-Publication data:

Snider, Phil, 1973–

    Preaching after God : Derrida, Caputo, and the language of postmodern homiletics / Phil Snider.

    x + 224 p. ; 23 cm. —Includes bibliographical references.

    ISBN 13: 978-1-61097-498-1

    1. Preaching. 2. Deconstruction. 3. Postmodernism—Religious aspects—Christianity. 4. Derrida, Jacques. 5. Caputo, John D. I. Author. II. Title.

BV4211.3 S65 2012

Manufactured in the U.S.A.

Excerpts from *After the Death of God*, by John Caputo and Gianni Vattimo (ed. Jeffrey Robbins), © 2007, Columbia University Press. Reprinted with permission of the publisher. Excerpts from *What Would Jesus Deconstruct?*, by John Caputo, © 2007 (John Caputo), Baker Academic, a division of Baker Publishing Group. Used by permission of the publisher. Excerpts from *The Weakness of God*, by John Caputo, © 2006 (John Caputo). Reprinted with permission of Indiana University Press. Excerpts from *On Religion*, by John Caputo, © 2001 (John Caputo), Routledge. Reproduced by permission of Taylor & Francis Books UK. Excerpts from *God, the Gift, and Postmodernism*, ed. by John Caputo and Michael Scanlon, © 1999, reprinted with permission of Indiana University Press. Special thanks to the Journal for Cultural and Religious Theory for the reuse of source material from: "The Return of Anti-Religion," by John Caputo, first published in Volume 11, Issue 2; "Jacques Derrida (1930-2004)," by John Caputo, first published in Volume 6, Issue 1; and "Weak Theology," by Jeffrey Robbins, first published in Volume 5, Issue 2.

For Jack Caputo

μακαριοι το ασθενες

Contents

Acknowledgments

I AM THANKFUL FOR the many people who supported this project from the start. I express my gratitude to the community of Brentwood Christian Church and to my friends and colleagues who graciously offered their feedback at various points along the way: Charlie Bahn, Micki Pulleyking, Jill Michel, Jeff Robbins, Chris Rodkey, Colleen Carroll, Peter Browning, Emily Bowen, George Latimer, Mary Bolan, Ross Lockhart, Chad Mattingly, Tara Thompson, Jon Bormann, David Hockensmith, Greg Turner, Alex Ruth, Darryl Schafer, and Mark and Janet Given. I would also like to thank my parents, Ann and Terry, for their unwavering support and constant love. I am inspired by the towering witness of Mike and Donna McGinnis and Charlie and Bette Wilcox. In some small way I hope my life reflects the generosity and kindness that has marked theirs.

The editorial acumen of Jana Riess in the early stages of this manuscript was exceedingly helpful. Special thanks to my co-conspirators, Matthew Gallion and Katharine Sarah Moody, for reading more drafts of this manuscript than any human being should ever have to do and still being willing to provide invaluable feedback.

I am forever in the debt of the Association of Chicago Theological Schools' preaching program. In addition to my friends and colleagues who offered encouragement, laughter, and wisdom in our three-year journey together, I would like to thank my teachers: Thomas Long, Frank Thomas, Scott Haldeman, Charles Rice, and Craig Satterlee, dean of the program. The leadership of Susan Thistlethwaite and Alice Hunt during my time at Chicago Theological Seminary was impeccable. I am especially grateful for the wise counsel of Rich Kirchherr and Dow Edgerton, whose insights and suggestions were instrumental in the formation of this book. I also remain thankful for my teachers at Phillips Theological Seminary. Their influence and vision have stayed with me over the years, and I would not be who I am without them.

The superb scholarship of Jack Caputo is exceeded only by his generosity of spirit. By helping me find my homiletical voice, he gave me a gift that he did not have. Truth be told, he has given lots of us on the fringes of the church multiple gifts that he did not have. Words are not enough to express my gratitude for his support and encouragement.

It is an honor to collaborate with Wipf and Stock Publishers. They caught the vision of this book early on, and I am grateful for the opportunity they provided to share possibilities for preaching that are very close to my heart. Special thanks to Christian Amondson, Charlie Collier, Ian Creeger, and Jacob Martin for all of their help along the way.

As always, my family has been by my side during each stage of the writing process. Thank you for not changing the locks. My love to each of you: Amanda, Elijah Cole, Samuel Micah, and Lily Grace.

Introduction

How is it possible that a figure such as Derrida who says of himself that he
rightly passes for an atheist should be read as a religious thinker? For Caputo,
at least, therein lies the great paradox and value of postmodern philosophy.
Not that Derrida himself would claim to be either a postmodern or religious
thinker, but by reading Derrida through the lens of postmodernism it is shown
how even (or perhaps especially) someone like him can help to create the open
space by which a tradition can live up to its promise.

—Jeffrey Robbins[1]

EVEN THOUGH THE POSTMODERN return of religion—particularly as
represented by philosophers like Jacques Derrida, John Caputo, and
Slavoj Žižek—is perhaps the most formative school of thought shaping
the future of twenty-first-century theology, it's only fair to wonder how
preaching might find inspiration from the work of theorists who "rightly
pass for atheists."[2]

Haven't we been taught that Derrida, for example, is the devil in disguise, the author of unholy anarchy, the central driving force behind deconstruction's *destruction* of all our cherished values and practices? Isn't

1. Caputo and Vattimo, *After the Death of God*, 18.

2. The postmodern return of religion is a shorthand way of referring to a significant
shift in philosophy that gained attention in the second half of the twentieth century, in
which several highly influential continental philosophers began interacting with religious figures and categories in order to develop their respective theories. I will say much
more about this throughout the course of the book, but for now I want to offer this quick
point of reference for those who are new to the phrase. For the nuances of the way that
Derrida and Caputo invoke the language of atheism, see esp. Caputo, *Prayers and Tears
of Jacques Derrida*, xvii–xxvi, 331–39. Also note that Žižek's approach is significantly
different than Derrida and Caputo's, which is a subject I explore in ch. 12.

1

the promotion of postmodern deconstruction—a phrase that still sends a shiver down the spine of many a homiletician—the first step down the path of a reckless relativism in which Christian proclamation is viewed as problematic at best and impossible at worst? And given the postmodern emphasis on the contingency of all truth claims, how can preachers even begin to make meaningful statements in relationship to faith, belief, and ethics, not to mention God, Jesus Christ, and the Holy Spirit? Don't these categories, in the process of being *deconstructed* and *deabsolutized*, go by the wayside? Aren't they lost in the midst of confusing language games that are the contemporary equivalent of the Tower of Babel, the proverbial location where meaning and communication break down?

Such is the common caricature.[3]

What this book aims to demonstrate, however, is that the postmodern return of religion—contrary to popular misconceptions—actually opens up possibilities for preaching in fresh, engaging ways. Moreover, it does so in a way that is particularly beneficial for contemporary listeners who, in the aftermath of the Enlightenment, often find it difficult to maintain belief in God and rarely find conventional images of God appealing (including standard images that describe God as some sort of supernatural Supreme Being, as well as more "liberal" images of God as a universal/metaphysical Presence running in and through all things). By taking this point of departure, the homiletic I pursue has two interrelated purposes: (1) it highlights several of the deeply affirmative theological themes located within the postmodern return of religion, and (2) it shows preachers how to draw on these themes in order to develop sermons that highly resonate with postmodern listeners who, as we often say in the congregation where I pastor, *believe in God some of the time, or none of the time, or all of the time.*

In order to help readers of this book understand why I am inviting them to embark on this journey with me, allow me to quickly state that a practical (pastoral) concern related to this second purpose is constantly on my mind throughout these pages (and I suspect it has crossed several of your minds as well, especially those of you who preach or teach in

---

3. While this caricature is more prevalent in evangelical circles (for a representative example, see David Allen's "A Tale of Two Roads"), my primary interests are related to the dominant streams of thought among mainline/progressive homileticians who've frequently disregarded or domesticated the theological and philosophical implications of postmodernism. See esp. ch. 6.

Protestant liberal churches or divinity schools). While it is true that I wish to offer a bit of a homiletic *apologia* for Derrida and company—and I freely admit that I am a huge fan of postmodern theorists like Caputo, Catherine Keller, and Peter Rollins, who serve as guides throughout much of this book[4]—my central motivation for writing is tied to concerns raised by a variety of contemporary homileticians, who rightly argue that far too many sermons in mainline/progressive contexts are consistently relegated to grand ethical exhortations that are far more *anthropological* in focus than theological.[5] For a variety of reasons that I describe in part one of this book, progressives who live in the aftermath of the Enlightenment find it difficult to believe in the activity and agency of God, at least insofar as it is beyond human manufacture, and this in turn leads progressive preachers to consistently replace the activity and agency of God in their sermons with the activity and agency of human beings (I refer to this dynamic throughout the book as the "modern homiletical crisis").[6] While many progressives are drawn to social justice, compassion, mutuality, and so on, a significant number of progressives have difficulty—sometimes explicitly and other times implicitly—believing that God exerts some sort of external activity and agency that is beyond the actions of human beings. This can be summarized in a quote I recently saw on the sign of a progressive church: "Let us listen to our prayers. It is we who will make them real." Many participants in progressive com-

4. In the hopes of receiving Caputo's *nihil obstat* and *imprimatur*, for which I promise him a fancy robe and mitre in return, I like to describe the approach developed in this book as a "homiletic of the event," which plays off of Caputo's "theology of the event." See Caputo, *Weakness of God*.

5. Throughout this book, I use the words *mainline* and *progressive* synonymously and often throw the phrase "post-Enlightenment Christians" into the mix in order to make the same reference. Generally, though not exclusively, I refer to mainliners/progressives/post-Enlightenment Christians as the inheritors of the Protestant liberal tradition that in large part was shaped by the Enlightenment. My primary homiletical concerns are related more to theological dynamics than structural ones, though inevitably these dynamics overlap, and I deal with them accordingly. I also recognize that an increasing number of those involved in the somewhat nebulous "emergent" conversation identify with progressive theology as well, though the approaches to preaching in emergent circles are often quite different than mainline approaches—at least structurally, if not theologically. For the latter concerns, see esp. Rogers, "Emerging Church Preaching."

6. It's important to note that the modern homiletical crisis I describe is far more prevalent in Eurocentric mainline pulpits than in other contexts, and it is irresponsible to think that any given congregation is made up of people who all view the world the same way. See esp. Allen, *Preaching and the Other*, 36–37.

munities of faith tend to believe that continuing the mission of Jesus is important, and so is working for justice—but what about God? Is God necessary for this work? Or is the name of God just a product of a bygone era? If "God only becomes real through our actions," as progressives are prone to say—if human beings are the ones responsible for making their prayers come true—then what role does discourse about God's activity and agency have in progressive sermons, if any at all? Is it even possible for progressives to authentically preach about the activity and agency of God in a post-Enlightenment setting with any viable degree of credibility, without preachers having to provide an unspoken but mutually agreed upon "wink, wink" to the congregation?

Nietzsche called attention to the pervasive apotheosis that became particularly prominent during the Enlightenment (the idea that human beings replaced God to the degree that God was rendered obsolete),[7] and nowhere is this dynamic seen more starkly than in standard progressive sermons, which, when carefully analyzed, generally consist of little more than a grand ethical exhortation that (to borrow the words of William Willimon) "unintentionally (but blasphemously) puts us in the place of God in Scripture, stresses people's misdeeds more than God's deeds, and talks about what we should do rather than what God is doing."[8] Karl Barth might have diagnosed this problem a century ago, but progressives still haven't overcome it all these years later, and we aren't showing many signs of doing so anytime soon.

Mike Graves describes the modern homiletical crisis this way: "In so much of our preaching, we have lost sight of where to aim our telescopes . . . *We settle for sermons focused almost exclusively on human behavior*, and as a result the center of our solar system becomes us . . . This tendency toward moralizing at the expense of the gospel's good news has repeatedly taken the church down a dead-end road, theologically and homiletically."[9]

As Graves indicates, the consequences of the modern homiletical crisis are far from benign, hence the practical concerns that represent the primary reason I have written this book. Not only is it theologically

7. See Carl Raschke's reading of Nietzsche and the apotheosis of modernity in his *Next Reformation*, 35–48.

8. Willimon, *Preaching and Leading Worship*, 71–72.

9. Graves, "God of Grace and God of Glory," 110–11. Emphasis mine. While Graves describes the modern homiletical crisis, he does not use the phrase "modern homiletical crisis."

problematic for the actions of God to be relegated only to the actions of human beings, but, from a pastoral perspective, it also leads listeners to frequently experience quiet and unspoken feelings of despair. When progressive preachers primarily focus on what human beings must do in order to actualize God's agency in the world and the role that God plays in this process is largely missing, preachers and listeners alike experience a tiring drain. While progressives feel an important need to do their part in ushering in God's reign, they also recognize their limitations as human beings. Instead of sermons being sites of celebration and hope (in which listeners are lost in wonder, love, and praise), they frequently reinforce deep-seated feelings of despair. To borrow imagery from the prophet Isaiah, listeners can feel so faint and weary that they quietly fall exhausted—and they aren't all that convinced that waiting on the Lord to renew their strength is even an option. *Not when it is all up to them.* Simply put, to paraphrase Thomas Long, the predominant streams at work in progressive preaching condemn listeners to failure and despair because they heap problems on listeners that are beyond their capacity to solve.[10]

The purpose of this book is not simply to get a word in edgewise so that Derrida and company will have their reputations restored in the various preaching journals, though that would be fine by me. I am, more importantly, trying to offer a remedy to a homiletical crisis that continues to plague all too many congregations, especially those from progressive contexts similar to my own, and I contend that the postmodern return of religion provides wonderful opportunities for accomplishing this task. As such, this book should not simply be viewed as an exposition of postmodernism that seeks to be in dialogue with the fashionable spirit of the times, nor as a comprehensive survey of theology and homiletics from a postmodern perspective. Rather, I am appropriating the postmodern return of religion for a specific homiletical task: to help those of us living in the wake of the Enlightenment to credibly preach *after* God (or at least after Nietzsche's proclamation of the death of God) in ways that don't reduce sermons to grand ethical exhortations in which God becomes, as Frederick Buechner once put it, "the most missed of all missing persons."[11]

The theological themes at work in the postmodern return of religion help preachers develop sermons that (to use language I will unpack

10. Long, "Imagine There's No Heaven."

11. See Long, *Preaching from Memory to Hope,* 38.

throughout the course of this book) highlight what Caputo refers to as the unconditional call that is harbored in the name of God, the event that stirs restlessly in the name of God, the promise sheltered in the name of God that provokes, solicits, and inspires us—*all in ways that, quite importantly, aren't dependent upon supernatural and/or metaphysical images of God that progressives, in the aftermath of the Enlightenment, have difficulty believing in.* The postmodern return of religion doesn't just help progressive preachers shift the emphasis in their sermons from the activity and agency of human beings toward the activity that is stirring restlessly in the name of God (from the *anthropological* to the *theological*), but, perhaps more significantly, it also helps progressives recapture a sense of celebration in their preaching (one of the first things to go when sermons are reduced to grand ethical exhortations) so that their sermons might be full of hopes and sighs and dreams and tears too deep for words, so that listeners might properly be *lost* in wonder, love, and praise.[12] This approach remains intellectually honest and at the same time restores theological grammar in ways that are not bound to the constraints of progressive Protestant liberalism and the subsequent disappearance (death?) of God in far too many mainline pulpits.

While the homiletic I pursue carries significant implications for those from a wide variety of Christian traditions, it is especially helpful for progressives who aren't sure what to make of God in a postmodern era, who sometimes experience God language as being far too intertwined with superstitious beliefs, and who maybe even wonder if God language is necessary at all. It is for those who, to recall the words of Mark Twain, often struggle to identify as Christian because they feel like they have to believe "twelve unbelievable things before breakfast." It is for those who, as one of my congregants once described, "don't do the supernatural well," which often includes those who feel like they are on the fringes of the church and maybe even of Christianity and religion altogether. It is for those who want to find a credible way out of the modern homiletical crisis and would like their sermons to inspire far less compassion fatigue and much more wonder, love, and praise—yet in a way that doesn't rely on images of God that progressives, for good reason, tend to resist. Such a homiletic, we will see, counts many atheists as friends, as odd as that

12. Here I find Frank Thomas's approach to preaching indispensible. See Thomas, *They Like to Never Quit Praisin' God.*

might sound to those being introduced to the postmodern return of religion for the first time.[13]

* * *

Even though there are a good number of theologians (and, consequently, homileticians) who wish to keep postmodern theology at arm's length,[14] I am hardly traveling this road alone. For nearly twenty years, in large part due to the influence of Caputo's groundbreaking *The Prayers and Tears of Jacques Derrida*,[15] followed by Žižek's seemingly endless flow of books focused on, among other things, the subversive kernel of Christianity, theologians and philosophers alike have radically reevaluated the import of postmodernism, especially in relationship to categories of religion and faith. As Caputo and others have passionately argued, the postmodern return of religion, despite popular misconceptions, is actually out to celebrate the unconditional and the undeconstructible—what Christians might call the "Holy"—not to destroy it. Following Derrida's death in 2004, Caputo wrote an obituary accessible to the general public that not only summarized Derrida's legacy, but also sought to set the record straight regarding the affirmative role that deconstruction plays in our lives and culture:

> What everyone has more or less picked up about deconstruction, even if they have never read a word of it, is its destabilizing effect on our favorite texts and institutions. Derrida exposes a certain coefficient of uncertainty in all of them, which causes all of us, right and left, religious and non-religious, male and female,

13. Here we also see some of the promising possibilities stirring in the return to Paul among figures such as Žižek and Alain Badiou, which Peter Rollins draws on in his most recent works. This is a turn that is not simply about following in the way of Jesus (i.e., as a "Red Letter Christian"), but rather as an undergoing of the transformative event expressed in Christological language of crucifixion and resurrection. In addition to Rollins' *Insurrection*, see Caputo, *St. Paul among the Philosophers*.

14. Postmodern theology is to be distinguished from postmodern culture, for reasons that I describe below.

15. As Marko Zlomistić and Neal DeRoo comment: "While Mark C. Taylor was instrumental in bringing Derrida into conversation with theology as far back as the 1980s, it was not until the publication of *Prayers and Tears* in 1997 that people came to understand how central religious themes were to all of Derrida's thought. If Taylor pioneered bringing Derrida into theology, it could be said that Caputo pioneered bringing theology into Derrida (although he adeptly shows that it was, in fact, Derrida who originally brought theology into Derrida)." See Zlomistić and DeRoo, *Cross and Khôra*, 1.

considerable discomfort. That was the side of deconstruction
that grabbed all the headlines and made it in the 1970s a kind of
academic *succès de scandale*. Without reading very closely, it all
looked like a joyous nihilism. But what his critics missed (and
here not reading him makes a difference!), and what never made
it into the headlines, is that the destabilizing agency in his work
is not a reckless relativism or an acidic scepticism but rather an
affirmation, a love of what in later years he would call the "undeconstructible." The undeconstructible is the subject matter of
pure and unconditional affirmation—*"viens, oui, oui"* (come, yes,
yes)—something unimaginable and inconceivable by the current
standards of imagining and conceiving. The undeconstructible is
the stuff of a desire beyond desire, of a desire to affirm that goes
beyond a desire to possess . . . His critics had never heard of this
because it was not reported in *Time Magazine*, but they did not
hesitate to denounce what they had not read.[16]

In *Preaching to Postmoderns*, Robert Kysar and Joseph Webb devote a
chapter to Derrida that catches the affirmation at the heart of deconstruction: "Deconstruction itself has gotten a bad name," they write, "largely
because of scholars for whom the best synonym for deconstruction is
'destruction.'" They observe that, strangely, "this has become the popular
view of deconstruction."[17] They then incorporate Derrida's own imagery
in order to clear up several of these misunderstandings: "Deconstruction
is endlessly 'inventive,'" they affirm, "because it alone 'opens up a pas-
sageway' into a new way of seeing and thinking . . . Deconstruction itself
is an 'affirmation' of something, an event, an 'advent,' an 'invention,'" all
for the sake of a new future that cannot be designated in advance.[18] As
Anna Carter Florence succinctly states in her wonderful book *Preaching
as Testimony*: "Postmodern practices are not for the purpose of demoli-
tion. They are for the purpose of encounter."[19]

16. Caputo, "Jacques Derrida (1930–2004)."
17. Kysar and Webb, *Preaching to Postmoderns*, 151.
18. See ibid., 154–55.
19. Florence, *Preaching as Testimony*, xv. John McClure's words are apropos:
"Sometimes criticized as parasitic, nihilistic, or relativistic in nature, deconstruction is
essentially an ethical practice, insisted Derrida. Although some have attempted to elevate
deconstruction to a worldview, Derrida saw it as a critique and as therapeutic in nature,
not meant to replace constructive ontological reflection, but to keep ontological constructions open, honest, and changeable in the face of human suffering." See McClure,
"Deconstruction," 147.

Several years ago, when a panel of prolific philosophers and theologians gathered at Villanova University in order to engage in conversation with Derrida about the religious themes that accompanied so many of his later works, Derrida felt as though he didn't quite belong. In a 1997 journal entry related to his appearance at Villanova's inaugural "Religion and Postmodernism" conference, Derrida said that these two things, *religion* and *postmodernism*, felt very strange to him. Then he added, introspectively and memorably, that "my atheism gets on in the churches, all the churches, do you understand that?"[20] This is quite a surprising phenomenon to be sure, one that made Derrida wonder why he kept getting invited to speak at religious conferences, particularly because he didn't view himself as a trained theologian or biblical scholar. The conveners of these conferences, which included Caputo, told him not to worry, for they did not "expect him to do theology, just his own work, and to leave it to [them] to reinscribe his texts within the context of the great questions of theology and philosophical theology."[21] They then added a word of both caution and encouragement that those of us interested in appropriating Derrida's work for the sake of homiletics will also want to keep in mind: "This is a delicate operation, to be sure, one that must resist co-opting Derrida's work for religion, distorting his insights, or above all confining the energy of deconstructive analysis within the limits of a determinate faith. *But it also cries out to be done.* For what else can one do with a philosopher who writes about the gift and forgiveness, hospitality and friendship, justice and the messianic, with someone who has radicalized these notions in such a way that anyone with an ear for these matters, with half an ear, can hear the biblical resonance, even if that is not something that Derrida himself is conscious of or consciously monitors?"[22]

20. See Caputo, Dooley, and Scanlon, *Questioning God,* 1.

21. Ibid., 1–2.

22. Ibid., 2. Emphasis mine. Caputo more recently highlighted this tension by saying "My hypothesis in [*The Prayers and Tears of Jacques Derrida*] is that the key to understanding deconstruction is also the key to understanding religion, viz., that *both* are brewed from a devilish mix of faith and atheism, radical doubt and faith . . . That makes for a delicate and scandalous blend, an exquisite commingling that requires a trained palate. It is easily misunderstood—as the violence with which Derrida is denounced *both* as a nihilist and a negative theologian testifies. It allows deconstruction to seem to the faithful now like an enemy, now like an ally, even as its secular critics will say that it consorts with religious fanaticism." See Caputo, "Return of Anti-Religion," 9.

My wager in this book is that if progressive preachers are willing to give an ear, even half an ear, to the affirming religious themes stirring in the work of the postmodern return of religion (including the work of Derrida and Caputo, but also of Žižek, Keller, Rollins, Richard Kearney, Jean-Luc Marion, as well as many others), then we will find fresh ways to develop sermons that highly resonate with postmodern listeners— especially listeners who struggle to imagine God in terms of "being" or "presence," or don't believe in God at all, which I tend to think includes some of us all of the time and all of us some of the time, if we have permission to admit it. In a postmodern era, religion *sans* religion is compelling, contagious, and inviting, which is all the more reason to reflect on its implications for preaching.[23] As we shall see, it is possible to be "deeply and abidingly 'religious' with or without theology, with or without religions. Religion may be found with or without religion."[24]

* * *

Before proceeding to the main body of this work, allow me to offer four brief disclaimers: First, for those of you who are familiar with the postmodern return of religion and are already keeping score, it should be clear by now that the homiletic I pursue highly values Caputo's appropriations of Derrida. At the same time, I recognize that the postmodern return of religion is hardly monolithic. Just as the era of "modernism" contained a variety of perspectives that were often at odds with one another, so too does the era of "postmodernism." Žižek, for example, offers an alternative reading of the postmodern turn that significantly diverges from Derrida and Caputo (Žižek wouldn't want to be associated with the promotion of Derridean-influenced deconstruction and its subsequent interest on

23. Close readers will note that the theological postmodernism at work in the homiletic I develop is obviously connected more to a Caputo-Derridean deconstructive hybrid than to the kinds of radical theology exemplified in the thought of theorists like Thomas Altizer (and to a degree Žižek), though I have great appreciation for their work, and there are certain affinities that we do indeed share. My primary reservation with Altizer and his brand of death-of-God theology is expressed in a comment Caputo made in response to Gianni Vattimo, which is particularly relevant for a project that is trying to serve as a remedy to the modern homiletical crisis described in this book: "Deconstruction would always worry about a divine kenosis that resulted in filling up someone's pocket with the transferred goods of divinity." See Caputo and Vattimo, *After the Death of God*, 80.

24. Caputo, *On Religion*, 3.

the "wholly other").[25] Theorists like Marion and Keller offer their own variations of the postmodern turn as well. While I prefer hitching a ride with Caputo and Derrida (and Kearney and Keller) more than with Žižek, I don't think the respective schools of postmodernism are as mutually exclusive as some might think, including Žižek himself, and I tend to draw on each of them in various ways that will become clear throughout the course of this book.[26] In order to provide a range of postmodern preaching possibilities, I've provided sample lectionary-based sermons in part two that are informed by not only Derrida and Caputo but also by Kearney, Marion, Rollins, and Žižek. While there are other theorists to draw from (there always are), the ones who consistently appear in this book represent several of the most formative thinkers associated with the postmodern return of religion.

Second, although I resist the modern homiletical crisis's tendency to reduce sermons to little more than grand ethical exhortations, please know I am not undermining the importance of acting ethically in the world and doing one's part to usher in the reign of God. Not for a second. I simply contend that preaching should consist of both *call* and *response*, and when the (theological) provocation of the call is consistently absent from progressive preaching, it leads not only to a loss of wonder, love, and praise, but also to a debilitating sense of compassion fatigue felt by listeners and preachers alike. From a rhetorical perspective, I contend that this compassion fatigue actually *diminishes* ethical engagement, and it subtly and unintentionally has the potential to serve as a symbolic gesture that actually keeps radical transformation at bay. But make no mistake about

25. For a nice introduction to Žižek, see Depoortere's *Christ in Postmodern Philosophy*, 92–143. I also recognize that even as I draw on Caputo's reading of Derrida, his is not the only reading of Derrida. For a counter to Caputo, see Hägglund's "The Radical Evil of Deconstruction."

26. Moreover, it should be noted that there is no such thing as "religion" in the singular, as any introduction to religion course will quickly note. As Caputo writes at the beginning of his book *On Religion*: "Any book entitled *On Religion* must begin by breaking the bad news to the reader that its subject matter does not exist. 'Religion,' in the singular, as just one thing, is nowhere to be found; it is too maddeningly polyvalent and too uncontainably diverse for us to fit it all under one roof. There are Western religions, Eastern religions, ancient religions, modern religions, monotheistic, polytheistic, and even slightly atheistic religions; too many to count, too many to master, too many languages to learn. I am not complaining or making excuses. Indeed the uncontainable diversity of 'religion' is itself a great religious truth and a marker of the uncontainability of what religion is all about." See Caputo, *On Religion*, 1.

it: a homiletic of the event is a big fan of—as St. Augustine put it—"doing the truth," or "making the truth happen" (*facere veritatem*). But it does so by celebrating the *provocation* of the call that, in Derridean terms, is connected to a longing—a hoping and sighing and dreaming—for the advent of the "wholly other," for what eye has not seen and ear has not heard, for which all our hearts are restless, *inquietum est cor nostrum*, believer and atheist alike. But rest assured that in a deconstruction, like Moses standing in front of the burning bush or Mary being visited by the archangel Gabriel, the *call* demands a *response*. Which may or may not be cause for comfort.

Third, it is widely recognized that the cultural emphasis on items such as plurality, diversity, mutuality, ambiguity, inclusivity, and so on are directly related to postmodernism, and as a result there are several homiletical studies available that focus on preaching within the ethos of postmodern *culture*. I find great value in these studies, and I think they are essential for the preaching task. However, for the purposes at hand, I am more interested in the ways that postmodern theory shapes the *theological* content of progressive sermons.[27] The homiletic I am interested in pursuing, particularly as a remedy to the modern homiletical crisis, is connected to the difficulty that post-Enlightenment Christians have when it comes to believing in supernatural and/or metaphysical images of God, which includes the difficulty of believing in God's activity and agency, so it is necessary for such a homiletic to be concerned with theological questions that consider, to adopt a question put forth by Jean-Luc Nancy, "what comes after the God of metaphysics?"[28] A homiletic of the event is an attempt to preach *after* God, which, given the varied nuances at work in the word *after*, is part of the reason that both Friedrich Nietzsche and St. Augustine make frequent appearances in this book. What might it mean to preach not only *after* the death of metaphysics but also in pursuit (*after*) the unconditional claim that is visited on our lives, in the wake of what Caputo calls the event harbored in the name of God, for which

27. For a nice introduction to the differences between postmodern culture and post-modern theology, see Raschke's *Next Reformation,* 11–15. As Raschke observes, "the postmodernist revolution in philosophy—as opposed to the general usage of the term 'postmodernism' in contemporary culture—has tendered an environment where the Christian gospel can at last be disentangled from the centuries-long, modernist gnarl of scientism, rationalism, secularism, humanism, and skepticism."

28. Caputo, Dooley, and Scanlon, *Questioning God,* 2.

our Augustinian hearts are forever restless? Theological questions such as these are at the heart of a homiletic of the event.

Fourth, several of the most influential postmodern theorists prefer not using the term *postmodern* at all. Derrida once said he "is not sure what [postmodern] means and [he] is not sure if it is useful to understand what is going on today,"[29] so instead of understanding himself as a postmodern, he preferred describing himself as a person of the Enlightenment, "albeit of a *new* Enlightenment, one that is enlightened about the Enlightenment and resists letting the spirit of the Enlightenment freeze over into dogma . . . Derrida seeks an Enlightenment 'of our time' . . . in which the 'certainties and axioms' of the *old* Enlightenment require reconsideration, translation, and transformation."[30]

In the same way, I do not wish to pass over the Enlightenment—rather, I seek to go through it. The postmodern turn does not frown upon reason and intellectualism—they simply are not viewed as idols to be worshiped. Caputo once quipped that in the midst of all these "posts" (postmodern, postsecular, poststructural, postliberal, etc.), he doesn't want to be post-intellectual! Nor do I. To appropriate Caputo's words, the "post" in postmodern should "not be understood to mean 'over and done with' but rather *after having passed through* modernity, so that there is no danger of the emergence of an irrational relativistic left, on the one hand, or of a lapsing back into a conservative pre-modernism masquerading under the guise of post-modern, on the other."[31]

In addition, Caputo and others often emphasize the problems associated with breaking history down into simple periodizations like premodern, modern, and postmodern. There is simply too much overlap

29. Caputo, "Apostles of the Impossible," 182.

30. See Caputo and Scanlon, *God, the Gift, and Postmodernism*, 2. *Pace* Allen, *Preaching and the Other*, 21–22. Preeminent postmodern homiletician David Lose points out that the "post" in postmodernism is usually understood in one of two distinct ways: "For some, 'post-' implies a complete 'leaving behind' of what it modifies. Postmodernity therefore represents an absolute rejection of the modern period, stressing the discontinuity between the ages and roundly denouncing the goals of modernity. Others, however, use the milder form of 'post-' to imply 'following after,' and for this reason view the advent of the postmodern in less disjunctive terms, stressing the inherent relationship between the two epochs and sometimes describing postmodernity as the final stage, or inevitable evolution, of modernity." See Lose, *Confessing Jesus Christ*, 8. Given these options, the theorists I converse with in this book generally fall into the latter camp.

31. Caputo, *On Religion*, 60–61. Caputo is here describing "postsecular" in the same way I describe postmodern.

and diversity of thought among and between these periods that it is irresponsible to say they can so easily be delineated. No clean break exists between the modern and the postmodern, and some of the most informative voices on these pages are from a variety of time periods (folks like Augustine, Luther, Kierkegaard, and Barth, just to name a few). Throughout this book it is wise to heed the advice of homiletician Ronald Allen: "The designations premodern, modern, and postmodern are not to label people and put them in boxes but are to help get a sense of patterns of thought, feeling, and behavior."[32]

Even though I prefer the term *postsecular* to postmodern, and I recognize that continental philosophers are already in the process of considering what comes after the postsecular and the postmodern,[33] I do fall back on the designation postmodern more times than not simply because it is the most readily available term—especially in the field of homiletics—that "points to the difference between our time and that era of confidence in reason's mighty progress in history that we name modernity."[34]

* * *

The structure of this book is similar to a plot-driven sermon in the sense that it moves from conflict in the early chapters and works toward resolution in the later chapters. I begin by highlighting the roots of the modern homiletical crisis and the problems associated with it (chapters 1–3), and then I introduce readers to the affirmative trajectories of the postmodern return of religion, which help serve as a remedy to the modern homiletical crisis (chapters 4–6). The second part of the book offers sample lectionary-based sermons and commentary based on several prominent themes located within the postmodern return of religion (chapters 7–12). I recognize that some readers may not be familiar with the postmodern return of religion, so I describe it with nonspecialists in mind. While the concepts I describe can be complex in their own right, I don't want this book to be lost in academic minutiae, but to be accessible for those who, like myself, preach on a regular basis in a local congregation. This is why I draw heavily from the likes of Caputo and Rollins, for both have done a remarkable job of communicating in-depth theory in accessible ways

---

32. Allen, *Preaching and the Other*, 8.

33. See Smith and Whistler, *After the Postsecular and the Postmodern*.

34. See Caputo and Scanlon, *God, the Gift, and Postmodernism*, 11.

with an eye toward the church.[35] Readers interested in more technical discussions will want to pay particular attention to the footnotes.[36]

One last comment before we begin: If it is *not* difficult for you to find ways to persuasively preach about the activity and agency of God in a post-Enlightenment context (especially to listeners who are sometimes unsure what to make of the word *God*, or are often suspect of supernatural theological language), then this book may not be of much interest to you. But if you do sometimes struggle to find meaningful ways to preach about the activity stirring in the name of God in a post-Enlightenment era, and if you (and perhaps your listeners as well) aren't sure what to make of supernatural images of God and are perhaps looking for homiletical alternatives that can be authentically engaged, then I hope you will keep on reading. This book isn't for theologically *certain* preachers, nor for those who have all of the answers. Instead, it is written for preachers and congregations who are living the questions, who are on a journey, who aren't sure what to make of God, who may not even believe in God, and who think that might even be okay. Which in progressive circles may include just as many preachers as congregants.

35. For instance, Caputo's *On Religion* and *What Would Jesus Deconstruct?* are written for general audiences, while most of his other works, including *The Prayers and Tears of Jacques Derrida* and *The Weakness of God*, are written with an academic audience in mind. The book you are now reading belongs in the former category in terms of audience and scope, particularly because I want preachers on the ground to find it helpful. See Zlomislić and DeRoo, *Cross and Khôra*, 324.

36. For those interested in technical theory, I cannot commend enough McClure's magisterial *Other-wise Preaching*. McClure is a first-rate scholar who provides an in-depth engagement with postmodern theory that remains unparalleled in homiletical circles. While my book incorporates similar theory, I offer introductory remarks accessible for nonspecialists that are designed as a direct response to what I am calling the modern homiletical crisis, which in turn leads me to focus especially on the theological implications stirring in a Caputo-Derridean deconstructive hybrid (whereas McClure's work is primarily driven by an ethical appropriation of the deconstructive thought of Emmanuel Levinas). I have found McClure's *Other-wise Preaching* and Florence's *Preaching as Testimony* to be invaluable in the formulation of this book. While I haven't had the opportunity to personally collaborate with either of them, I am incredibly grateful for their scholarship. Another good resource for those interested in technical theory is David Lose's *Confessing Jesus Christ*, though he and I share somewhat different readings of deconstruction, as will become clear in ch. 6.

PART I

The Modern Homiletical Crisis
and the Postmodern Return of Religion

1

The Domestication of Transcendence[1]

Has it not become colder? Is not night continually closing in on us? Do we not need to light lanterns in the morning? Do we hear nothing as yet of the noise of the gravediggers who are burying God? Do we smell nothing as yet of the divine decomposition? Gods, too, decompose. God is dead. God remains dead. And we have killed him.

—Friedrich Nietzsche[2]

God is not humanity said loudly.

—Karl Barth[3]

I'LL NEVER FORGET THE palpable silence I once felt while sitting in a room full of preachers. We had gathered for a continuing education class on preaching, and our instructor was telling us that we could only preach what we'd personally experienced. It was necessary, he said, to locate the ways that God had acted in our own personal lives before we could even begin to proclaim the ways that God might act in the lives of others.

---

1 I'm grateful to the late William Placher for introducing me to the phrase "the domestication of transcendence," which I borrowed from his book by the same name.

2. Nietzsche, *Gay Science*, 181.

3. As paraphrased by Graves, "God of Grace and Glory," 113. The exact quote from Barth reads, "One can not speak of God simply by speaking of man in a loud voice." See Barth, *Word of God and the Word of Man*, 195.

After sharing this advice, our instructor lifted his eyes from his lecture notes, looked up at us, and asked what seemed to be, at least on the surface, a very simple and direct question: "Can you share a few examples of the times that God has acted in your own personal lives?" Given the fact that his question was directed at a room full of preachers, it should have been an easy one to answer. After all, we attempt to speak of God on a weekly basis. Yet none of us—*none of us*—could offer concrete examples of the ways in which God's agency had been exerted in our personal lives.

Since no one ventured a response, our instructor rephrased his question, this time with much more urgency and curiosity in his voice: "Surely you can tell me about some of your experiences with God, can't you?" Another pregnant pause followed, until finally a couple of courageous hands went into the air. One pastor shared about a time she needed financial assistance to help her get through a rough period in life, and her friends from church stepped up to the plate. "I felt God's love through their actions," she reflected. Another pastor told us about the time he was recovering from unexpected surgery in the hospital and some of his friends came by to extend the love of Christ to him: "I felt God's presence through their lives," he said.

No doubt about it, the incarnated love of Christ embodied in each of these stories is reason for celebration. Without such love, I hesitate to think about where I'd be in life. But I must also confess that, as the pastors around me continued to share about the times God had personally touched their lives, I couldn't help wondering why the activity of God, *in every single example*, was restricted to the actions of human beings. Shouldn't the activity of God be beyond human manufacture?

While I didn't brave a response to the instructor's question, it did make me start thinking about tendencies in my own preaching. Things quickly got more personal—not to mention more uncomfortable—than I would have liked. Why did so many of my own sermons focus more on the activity of human beings than on the activity of God? Why did the vast majority of my own sermons end with finite moral exhortations such as "Let us" or "May we" as opposed to more infinite proclamations such as "God has" or "God will"? Why was the focus of most of my sermons on following the example of Jesus—on what *we* must do? Why was Jesus always the moral exemplar par excellence—in line with Martin Luther King Jr. and Mohandas Gandhi—but never the *saving* Christ? Of course God's action is a mystery, but shouldn't Christian proclamation be more about God than ourselves? Or is God nothing other than humanity said loudly? I feared that my own sermons had become proclamations of veiled humanism, for they were rooted much more in human behavior than in the activity of God.

I also started to wonder if those who heard my sermons on a regular basis got the impression that God can only exert agency through our actions, which of course carries with it the quite clear implication that, when this is the case, God's activity in the world must be manufactured by human beings. Like several other preachers at the continuing education event that day, my discourse about God is all too often relegated to either (1) the compelling ethical vision of Jesus, or (2) the ways we experience God's love through the ethical actions of others.

I'm certainly not alone. When it gets down to it, an alarming number of sermons delivered in mainline congregations place hope on the ethical agency of human beings much more than on the activity of God. Consider the standard admonition that, in varying form, accompanies no small number of progressive sermons: "And now, let us think about the ways we might partner with God in the building of the kingdom." This is an important statement that should be taken with utmost seriousness— our partnering with God in the work of the kingdom should be at the forefront of our faith. But, realistically speaking, how many progressive Christians who hear and heed such affirmations actually expect God to exert agency in this process? When we get past such rhetorical veneer, don't we usually figure that, in the end, the building of the kingdom is up to us much more than it's up to God?

For a simple example, consider the way that progressive sermons on Jesus' miraculous feeding of the multitude often unfold. We are told that the disciples and the gathered crowd are tired and hungry, and there isn't enough food to go around. The fish and loaves are brought to Jesus, and he wondrously multiplies them to the degree that there is not only enough for everybody, but there is plenty left over. It is an act that defies both common sense and (as many understand them today) "natural" laws. However, after describing Jesus' miracle (and reminding listeners that there are lots of "true stories in the Bible that never happened," which is something I heartily agree with), the progressive preacher usually moves to the primary emphasis of the sermon, which goes something like this: *If we will do our part to share what we have (especially as privileged first-world Christians), then there will be enough food and drink to go around for all the world's hungry people.* This is an ethic that I am certainly a fan of, and it is one that I wish to follow. But I wonder why the primary focus of the sermon almost always minimizes the activity of God and replaces it with the activity of human beings.[4]

I am hardly the first person to voice these concerns. Contemporary homileticians consistently point out that on the heels of the Enlightenment, in which the role of religion was largely reduced to ethical categories, the activity and agency of God in Protestant liberal pulpits is often replaced by the activity and agency of human beings. In many cases—and here my sermons can be viewed as Exhibit A—the soteriological import and transcendence of God are given lip service at best and are ignored at worst. Since Protestant liberalism as a whole has yet to overcome the problems posed by the Enlightenment—particularly modernism's suspicions concerning supernatural conceptions of God—preachers aren't sure how to speak of God's activity in ways that might be considered transcendent, which is to say in ways that might be rendered as "other." Jewish philosopher Emmanuel Levinas once said that the history of Western philosophy can be viewed as a destruction of transcendence,[5] and nowhere is the destruction of transcendence more evident than in the inability of progressive Christians to speak of God's activity in ways that are beyond human manufacture.

Paul Scott Wilson states that contemporary preachers frequently "omit from their sermons significant discussion of God and *focus instead on human action*," and from this "the gospel message becomes dos and don'ts that have an *anthropocentric* flavor."[6] Pablo Jiménez notes the way mainline Protestant preaching "has perfected the sermon that barely mentions God, stressing either the psychological dimensions of pastoral care or the social responsibility of the church."[7] When Susan Hedahl reflects on most of the sermons she hears as a professor of homiletics, she wonders why the presence of Jesus Christ is so often absent: "One hears much about mission: what people must do, figures to imitate (e.g., Mother Theresa), local soup kitchens in which to participate. The prob-

---

4. It is no wonder that progressives tend to like Thomas Jefferson's Bible so much. After all, he cut out all of the supernatural "miraculous" parts and kept the ethical teachings of Jesus.

5. Levinas, *Of God Who Comes to Mind*, 56.

6. See Wilson, "Preaching as a Theological Venture," 148, 155. Emphasis mine.

7. Jiménez, "Response to David Buttrick," 119.

lem is that often these approaches tend to be standalones. Where is the accompanying reflection on Jesus Christ, who is to inspire and elicit the listeners' actions in response to the Gospel? Often there seem to be few connections made between the sermon's proposals and the Lord who is to inspire them."[8]

Thomas Long makes this point most strongly when he describes the way that mainline sermons are consistently rooted in a *"functional atheism"* in which the "God who intrudes upon the closed system of the present tense is the most missed of all missing persons."[9] Oddly enough, he observes, even though preachers are charged with speaking clearly and boldly about what "the God we know in Jesus Christ through the Holy Spirit has done, is doing, and will do among us,"

> this is the language that seems most missing from much current preaching. Yes, there is plenty of God-talk and religious chatter in the pulpit today, but what seems absent is the vibrant sense of the living divine reality . . . Perhaps this is an overly harsh judgment, but listen to sermons being preached these days in the broad mainline churches, and see if they do not often have the hollow sound of an old oak whose living center has died and rotted away. Yes, yes, there are sincere words about God and the "power of our faith," that sort of thing, but frequently it all seems to come as an act of nostalgia, with a cool detachment from the possibility that the sermon itself might be caught up in the event of revelation, and accompanied by the tacit admission that, really, when we get down to it, *whatever good there is in life is the product of our own industry and intention*, that when all is said and done, this world is all we have and we are the only ones in here.[10]

Long doesn't think this "lack of attention to the presence of God" is due to a willful neglect or lack of faith on the part of most preachers, but rather is the result of a sort of cultural accommodation in which pulpit talk is viewed as a domesticated habit of speech. Our culture, he says, uses religious language "as holy sounding talk with all the edges filed away, so that it refers not to the wild, undomesticated presence of the living God, but only to us, to our sincere hearts, spiritual intentions, and our desire to

8. Hedahl, "Jesus Christ in the Sermon—Presence or Absence?"

9. The "functional atheism" reference is from an Association of Chicago Theological Schools DMin Parables class lecture (26 June 2008). The quote is from Long, "Imagine There's No Heaven."

10. Long, *Preaching from Memory to Hope*, 34. Emphasis mine.

do good things in life. *In other words, there is plenty of morality and good counsel, but no desert bush bursting into flame.*"[11]

Hearing mainline sermons with a near-exclusive focus on "morality and good counsel" is almost like having to listen to John Tesh's *Intelligence for Your Life* radio program without reprieve. To adopt imagery from the venerable Fred Craddock: When the good news of the gospel disappears from our sermons, "in its place comes just constant exhortation, constant 'we ought to do this, there are so many problems, the trouble with us is,'" which leads preachers to "then fill the air with ought and must and should until the church just becomes a pile of dark cinder blocks where a few good people meet every week to make each other miserable."[12]

An extended treatment of this point represents much of the subject matter of Paul Scott Wilson's important book *Setting Words on Fire: Putting God at the Center of the Sermon.* Here he reflects on sermons he has heard as a teacher of preaching, as well as published sermons:

> Something was often missing [from the sermons]. Students preached from the Bible. They did good exegesis of their texts, applied the texts to today, treated significant doctrines that linked with tradition, employed vivid images and metaphors, told fine stories, established important tensions within the sermon, addressed ethical, social justice and pastoral issues, and revealed something of themselves as people, but something was often absent.
>
> Perhaps I simply assumed that when the Bible was in the sermon, God was the subject. It slowly dawned on me that people were the main focus, and the reason many sermons had no power was that God was largely absent. . . . Sometimes the Bible does not mention God, and all too easily we turn biblical texts into human-centered, moralistic instructions that usually are not their intended purpose.
>
> . . . Published sermons today generally focus on human action and make important claims about what believers are to do by way of loving God and neighbor. However, more often than not they fail to focus on God in significant ways. . . . What [we] get may be a kind of drive-by gospel; God seemingly wheels by the church and waves in the general direction of the open doors.[13]

11. Ibid., 34. Emphasis mine.
12. Craddock, *Tell It,* ch. 4 of DVD.
13. See Wilson, *Setting Words on Fire,* xii, 1–3.

To see the modern homiletical crisis in perhaps its most obvious form, consider contemporary approaches to Christian funerals—or, to be more precise, quasi-Christian approaches to memorial services.[14] Karl Barth famously argued that theology should not be confused with anthropology, but when I attend a memorial service in a mainline church I am hard-pressed to think that anything but anthropology is on display.

While the reflections in this book aren't focused on funerals or the afterlife, the easiest way to point out the degree to which Christians struggle to speak of God's activity and agency in post-Enlightenment contexts is by taking a look at modern approaches to funeral sermons. The point of the following paragraphs isn't to argue for or against the existence of an afterlife (for the record, I am much more concerned with life before death), but to simply point out the extent to which anthropological language has replaced theological language in modern sermons.

So what does a minister say in the face of death? Ministers certainly shouldn't get away with superficial platitudes or shallow theology (nothing makes us squirm more than when the minister says our loved one was called home "because the furniture in heaven needed to be rearranged," which is something I actually heard at a funeral not long ago), but what else is there to say besides anthropological observations that end up being said on most occasions: "We experienced God's love through Margaret" or "We take comfort being held in God's arms through the hugs of family members and friends"?

While writing this chapter, I went to a funeral at a mainline church where the pastor shared a story about his seven-year-old daughter being afraid during a midnight thunderstorm. Being a good dad, he went into his daughter's room and assured her that God was with her and everything would be okay. However, a few minutes later, his daughter was still crying. He went back to her room in order to check on her again. She said, "Daddy, I know you told me that God is here with me. *But I need somebody with skin to hold onto.*"

As you might expect, the pastor used this story to say that in the storms of life it may be hard to know that God is with us, so we too need "somebody with skin" to hold onto. He concluded his sermon with a telling remark: "Sometimes it's hard to believe that God is with us, but it is through our friends and family members—*those who have skin*—that we experience the presence of Jesus." While I agree with this sentiment, I am not convinced that it needs any kind of theological language—whether it be about God or Jesus—in order for it to convey the meaning the preacher intended. Could he not have made the exact same point by saying "We experience comfort and support through the presence of our loved ones in times of great need"?

I suppose it is possible to make claims about the resurrection and, hence, God's cosmic restoration of all things, but, when it gets down to it, does such rhetoric really stand a chance of resonating with progressives living in post-Enlightenment contexts? As John Shelby Spong rightly observes: "clergy quickly learn that the traditional pious assertions of the past do not engage many of those in attendance at funeral services," and it becomes "painfully obvious that pious clichés do not penetrate genuine grief. Indeed they sound exactly like what they are, religious narcotics designed to dull pain."[15] For reasons such as these, William Willimon states that in a post-Enlightenment world, the "most interesting (and, for Christians, most disturbing) modification in views of eternity is the *disappearance* of God."[16]

It is true that one of the central Christian beliefs referenced most often at an average Christian funeral is the concept of resurrection, and appropriately so. But as Barth presciently stated in one of his most famous sermons, modern listeners don't know what to make of the resurrection, at least insofar as the resurrection is dependent upon the action of an external agent and not ourselves: "[We allow the resurrection] to be proclaimed to us, but that the victory in no sense grows or issues from us, that it is God's victory, and that this victory is contrary to our wishes, and comes as a result of our impotent helplessness—this is what we do not care to hear at all." This leads Barth to conclude that modern Christians turn the meaning of resurrection into "*something human* . . . And then, in our preaching on Easter day, we say something about the rejuvenation of nature, or the romantic reappearing of the blossoms, or the revival of the frozen torpid meadows. We interpret the message that Jesus is Victor, not in its literal sense, but we interpret it as a symbol or a human idea."[17] (It's

15. Spong, *Eternal Life*, 5–6.

16. Willimon, "What's Next," 29. Emphasis mine.

17. See Barth, "Jesus Is Victor," 74–81. Emphasis mine. About two hours after I wrote this paragraph at a local coffeehouse, one of the members of my church started to tell me about a conversation he had just had with a friend in which they were talking about the

no secret that most progressives find the first ending of Mark far more palatable than the more elaborate resurrection narratives that developed later in the tradition.) From Barth's perspective, the standard liberal interpretations of the resurrection wouldn't be all that different from the conventional New Age approach reflected in the words of Deepak Chopra offered as an endorsement on the back cover of Spong's recent book, *Eternal Life: A New Vision*: "The only way [fear of death] can be conquered is through knowledge and experience of your eternal being. [It is necessary] to *find this part of yourself* and be liberated."[18] In post-Enlightenment contexts, it seems, everything is up to us. Language about the activity and agency of God—especially in the face of death—is a mere formality, a nostalgic nicety, but nothing that references anything beyond our own best efforts.

Logically speaking, of course, it only stands to reason that if progressives rarely celebrate God's activity and agency in ways that are beyond human manufacture on any occasion, not just on funeral occasions, then we really shouldn't expect them to be able to smoothly and suddenly switch gears when it does come time for a funeral. Think about it this way: If a congregant attends worship on Easter Sunday only to hear about a metaphoric resurrection that isn't to be taken literally (e.g., "God didn't *really* raise Jesus from the dead, but we are inspired by his life, and that is how he continues to live on in us"), and then attends a funeral for her beloved three weeks later in which the preacher assures the family that their beloved will rise with Jesus on the last day, how in the world will she hear conventional proclamations about the resurrection in the funeral sermon in ways that don't produce a major disconnect, especially when hearing the popular passage from 1 Corinthians 15 that basically says if Jesus wasn't raised from the dead then we are of all people the most to be pitied? God didn't actually raise up Jesus, but God will raise up my beloved? To heaven? At the second coming? *Really?* Put another way: "It is somewhat hollow to be silent on the large eschatological themes, and then suddenly to start speaking eschatologically at the graveside."[19]

For progressive preachers, about the only option is to give lip service to notions such as the resurrection (usually in a Call to Worship or

---

way they no longer believe in a literal resurrection, but that "Christians being the hands and feet of Jesus makes the resurrection real."

18. Emphasis mine.

19. Long, *Preaching from Memory to Hope*, 129.

Scripture reading), and then move on with more anthropological procla-mations about the beloved's life, as well as our memories of the beloved that continue to live on long after they are gone. *Such an approach doesn't lack meaning, it's just not particularly theological.* This is why I end so many of my own funeral sermons with a quote from St. John of Chrysostom, even though I fully recognize it is laced with anthropological language and has no need of God whatsoever in order for it to be meaningful: "She whom we love and lose is no longer where she was. She is now wherever we are."

When we take all of this into consideration, is it any wonder that pop culture references to funerals in a post-Enlightenment setting never take the minister's words about God seriously? Whether it be through ignor-ing traditional religious language altogether—as in the film *Love Actually* (in which the funeral scene consists of reflections from family members about their beloved's life, followed by a video tribute featuring pictures of the deceased set to music by the beloved's favorite band, the Bay City Rollers)—or in belittling the words of the minister, as seen in the film *Gran Torino* (in which the presiding priest is accused by the bereaved widower of being an overeducated virgin who holds the hands of super-stitious old ladies and makes promises he can't keep), ministers' attempts to speak of God's activity and agency in the face of death, with very few exceptions, are trivialized at best and mocked at worst.[20]

TRANSCENDING TRANSCENDENCE

I can only imagine how my friends who know me well are reading these paragraphs. It sounds as if, God help me, I would like to reclaim a sense of religious magic and superstition and literalism and a high Christology and all manner of things I have sworn off! No, please no,

20. As a bit of respite, the wisdom of Thomas Long is worth noting: Funeral sermons should not be "short on gospel and long on eulogy, full of rhapsodies about the life of the deceased at the expense of descriptions of the life of God. [This] is a caution worth heeding, of course, not to preach the noble adventures of the dear departed deceased instead of the gospel of the eternally present Christ. *On the other hand,* we do not know about any God who can be described apart from the stories of the people with whom this God chooses to get involved. Properly told, God stories are always human stories, and human stories are always permeated by the wonder of God. Good funeral sermons will be enriched by honest memories of the one who has died. The idea here is not to tell stories that act as showcases for the virtues of the deceased but as examples of how this life was a prism, refracting the grace of God." See Long, "Funeral," 389. Emphasis mine.

please *know*—that is not the case. Lest my progressive sisters and brothers ask for my credentials, let me assure you that I am in large part still a Jesus Seminar kind of guy (kind of, that is), with framed posters of the venerable saints Crossan and Borg hanging on my office wall, right next to my "Living the Questions" diplomas. In as much as being a progressive Christian means trying to find a way to be Christian in a post-Enlightenment context, despite the problems embedded in the very word *progressive* (isn't one of the lessons of modernism the realization that we didn't quite progress as much as we thought we would?), I am on board, signed up, ready for the journey.

All I am trying to do at this point is show just how difficult it is for progressives to speak about the activity and agency of God in post-Enlightenment contexts, at least in ways that are beyond (anthropological) human manufacture, which in turn raises serious questions surrounding the theological integrity of so many progressive sermons, including many of my own. I am the chief of sinners.

To be fair, this is not the case with each and every progressive sermon. Hardly. It is rather a generalization representative of a prominent tendency that several mainline homileticians notice on a frequent basis, especially within the more progressive streams of Christianity (these are the streams where I usually swim). Unlike several of the homileticians who point out the problems inherent in the modern homiletical crisis, however, I don't wish to go back to what I view as the same (onto-)theological wells in order to draw up a remedy, especially when I consider such wells to be a significant source of the problem in the first place. Instead, I contend that if we wish to employ persuasive and compelling theological rhetoric in our sermons, then we have to *shift* the very ways we imagine (and talk) about God, especially in terms of God's transcendence, activity, and agency. If the task of postmodern theology is the overcoming of metaphysics, so too is the task of postmodern homiletics.

So rest assured that I am not setting up this problem in order to say, "Okay, progressive preachers, go reclaim a literal resurrection and an omnipotent God and a magical reading of miracles, and all will be made well in your sermons!" (What progressive listener should let us get away with that, and why should we want to anyway?) And even more importantly, I am not denigrating the wonderful human responses of love that are displayed in the examples above: In relation to the feeding of the multitude, it is of course a good thing for us to share what we have; in relation to the minister saying that in times of crisis we sometimes need "somebody with skin to hold onto," I concur wholeheartedly. I quite like this story, and there is a good chance I will adapt it for use sometime down the road in one of my own funeral sermons. My point is that progressives rarely speak of God's agency in a post-Enlightenment setting without having recourse to the agency of human beings, which leads to sermons that basically consist of either (1) a grand ethical exhortation, as in the example about the feeding of the multitude, or (2) a reliance on human beings to take on the role of God (in God's absence, one wonders?), as in the example about needing somebody with skin to hold onto. Most striking of all is that we can, most of the time, make the very same points in our sermons—or convey the same meaning—without having to refer to God at all.

In this book, I make no apologies about wanting to help progressives recapture a sense of transcendence in their sermons, including a sense of the activity stirring in the name of God, and thus provide a remedy to a modern homiletical crisis in which God becomes the most missed of all missing persons. However, it's important for me to point out that when I highlight problems associated with the modern homiletical crisis and in turn encourage progressive preachers to develop sermons that celebrate a sense of transcendence—of the activity stirring in the name of God that is beyond human manufacture—I have no intention of setting up the same old song and dance that primarily consists of recovering a sense of "otherness" that imagines God as some sort of supernatural Supreme Being that intervenes whenever He (it usually is a He) deems fit. Let me be emphatically clear that I consider such a perspective to be an essentially magical way of viewing the world, and I have no taste for it. The last thing I want to do is reimagine transcendence with these ideas in mind—for funeral occasions or any other occasion. The homiletic I pursue in these pages is a materialist homiletic for a materialist Christianity.

While the modern homiletical crisis is connected to the modern domestication of transcendence, I want to be very clear in stating that the remedy I present does not seek to reclaim a sense of God's "otherness" in the ways one might expect. Most of the time—especially in religious circles—transcendence is used as a club that, in the end, only serves to reinforce dominant streams of supernatural theology that are primarily interested in maintaining idols of Absolute Might, Domination, and Authority. The idea of a transcendent God, summarily and generally speaking, is often viewed as a type of Supreme Being that is in love with grand displays of power and can divinely intervene on a whim. Such an image of God seems to me to have much more to do with magic and superstition than anything else, and I don't want anything to do with it. I contend that such idols, rather than conveying the purported sense of transcendence, further solidify a God made in our own image, for they baptize the traits most valued by humanity and then place them onto God. I must warn the reader that the track I take—though it highlights transcendence and leaves room for the activity of the "wholly other"—is unabashedly tied to theological approaches that don't turn on power but on weakness, on what John Caputo calls "the weak force of God," which, on his reading, just might be the only thing strong enough to save us.[21] Homiletically and otherwise.

My wish in this book is to help progressive preachers loosen their tongues so that their preaching might be full of passionate sighs too deep for words, full of prayers and tears that hope and sigh and dream and weep for the unexpected advent of the "wholly other," *but not in ways that are tied to some sort of supernatural Supreme Being or Presence that progressives—including myself—tend to resist.*

Through theorists like Derrida and Caputo, the postmodern turn to religion provides an opportunity to recast the way we imagine God's transcendence in a post-metaphysical context, which in turn allows us to appropriate religious language in a way that resonates with believers and atheists alike. Soon I will begin describing their approach to religion, but before getting too far ahead of ourselves I first want to describe four major pastoral problems the modern homiletical crisis consistently per-petuates, and why the postmodern return of religion can be helpful in our attempts to move past them. While in the next chapter I will briefly refer to a handful of themes that are prominent in Derrida and Caputo's thought, readers might wish to note that I will more fully introduce their approach to religion in chapter 4.

21. See esp. Caputo, *Weakness of God*, 36.

2

Why the Modern Homiletical Crisis Is a (Pastoral) Problem

How else can one write but of those things which one doesn't know, or knows badly? It is precisely here that we imagine having something to say. We write only at the frontiers of our knowledge, at the border which separates our knowledge from our ignorance and transforms the one into the other.

—Gilles Deleuze[1]

Progressive preaching tells people to gird up their loins and to use the resources at hand to make the world into God's kingdom, and such preaching necessarily condemns people to failure and despair.

—Thomas Long[2]

EVEN IF THE CENTRAL argument of the previous chapter is affirmed—that the domestication of transcendence at the root of the modern homiletical crisis leads to sermons in which the activity of God is relegated to human manufacture—it's still possible to say that it's not a big deal for anthropological language to take the place of theological language in sermons, and that the domestication of transcendence in progressive preaching isn't cause for concern. After all, if the same shift is seen in the culmination of liberal theology, as I describe in chapter 3, it only makes sense for

1. Deleuze, *Difference and Repetition*, xxi.
2. Long, "Imagine There's No Heaven."

progressive sermons to follow suit. Yet at the same time, from a pastoral perspective (I am a pastor, not a philosopher or homiletician), sermons that consistently replace the activity and agency of God with the activity and agency of human beings can lead to a handful of concerns that demand our attention. I will name four of them.

1. *Compassion Fatigue.*

The ideals of progressive preaching are tied to the modern period's emphasis on the ability of human beings to morally progress and thus usher in the kingdom of God. As Kay Northcutt reminds us, the Enlightenment taught us that with enough human effort every problem can be fixed (she says this dynamic came to the fore in Harry Emerson Fosdick's highly influential "solution-based" homiletic). We are conditioned to believe that if we try hard enough, then we can solve the world's problems. Yet "when it comes to intractable tragic suffering and war, poverty and violence—that which is beyond problem solving and which by its nature is insoluble," listeners who are conditioned to believe that with enough human effort they can fix the world's problems are repeatedly condemned to the kind of "failure and despair" that Thomas Long lays at the feet of progressive preaching, for progressive preaching heaps problems on listeners that are beyond their capacity to solve, especially when progressive preachers find it difficult to celebrate the role God might play in the mending and repairing of the world.[3]

Listeners who live in the post-World Wars, post-Holocaust, post-Hiroshima, post-Enlightenment world recognize the naïveté of the modern period's belief in inevitable human progress, yet as *progressives* our theological capacities for imagining God are still usually wedded to modern liberal theologies that are grounded in such things—even though we know better. This is part of the reason post-Enlightenment progressives often

3. For the Northcutt quotes, see *Kindling Desire for God*, 50. Long contrasts progressive preaching with eschatological preaching: "Progress preaching tells people to gird up their loins and to use the resources at hand to make the world into a better place, and such preaching necessarily condemns people to failure and despair. Eschatological preaching promises a 'new heaven and a new earth' and invites people to participate in a coming future that, while it is not dependent upon their success, is open to the labors of their hands." See Long, *Preaching from Memory to Hope*, 125. I agree with Long's critique, but I offer a different remedy to the problem by drawing on Derrida's structure of the messianic, which doesn't contain the same theology as Long but still keeps the future open in a very affirming—yet risky—way.

find it easier to preach Lenten sermons than Easter sermons. During Holy Week of last year, one of my friends posted his upcoming Easter sermon to his blog, and a reader responded in the comment section by stating the reason why he was glad to be preaching Good Friday that year instead of Easter: "Those who come to a Good Friday service are prepared to hear death but I don't suspect that many attending Easter Sunday are actually expecting to hear life."[4] His honest, candid reflections are similar to others I have heard progressive preachers make on several occasions. As I read his comment, I wondered just how many progressives would agree with what he wrote. Is it true that those in progressive circles are prepared to hear *death*, but don't expect to hear *life*? Just how representative is this comment? It reminds me of the famous quote by the philosopher Martin Heidegger, who, recognizing the despair felt in the wake of the break-down of Enlightenment ideals, once lamented, "Only a God can save us."[5] Postmoderns who also live in the wake of the modern meltdown are well aware of the fragility and limitations that mark our condition. While progressives recognize the problems of "sin," systemic and otherwise, we are generally, when it gets down to it, left to our own devices when it comes time for salvation. Therefore, instead of sermons being sources of celebration and hope, they frequently reinforce deep-seated (and often unspoken) feelings of despair. We do Lent well, but Easter not so much. I'm reminded of a line from a Jewish chaplain at Princeton University. After hearing about the emphasis that Christian students were placing on important service projects—tutoring kids after school, working in a soup kitchen for the homeless, protesting social injustice—he voiced a few of his concerns: "You're saying that they are involved in good social causes, and they are. But what I was thinking is that the one thing they lack is a vision of salvation. . . . If you don't have some vision of what God is doing to repair the whole creation, you can't get up every day and work in a soup kitchen. It finally beats you down."[6]

---

4. He went on to say, "I don't know how I would preach an Easter Sunday service at this point." See Rodkey, "Easter Sunday Sermon: 'Too Good to Be True!'" Emphasis mine.

5. Heidegger, *Der Spiegel* interview, 11. For the contextual nuances of this quote, see Caputo, *Mystical Element in Heidegger's Thought*, 253ff. It's worth comparing Heidegger's statement to the trope Thomas Long develops surrounding the film *No Country for Old Men*, especially the comment made by the character Ed Tom Bell related to the second coming of Christ (*Preaching from Memory to Hope*, 121).

6. Long, *Preaching from Memory to Hope*, 123–24.

One of the struggles progressives face is that they don't expect God to ride in on a white horse and save the day, nor do they necessarily expect God to intervene or exert agency in order to bring about necessary change. On the one hand, this can lead to a greater sense of responsibility by human beings,[7] but on the other hand, it can feel debilitating because we are continually reminded that the problems are incredibly immense and beyond our capacity to solve. Progressives who don't expect God to exert some sort of interventionist agency that will (magically) repair all of creation—if that is how salvation is understood—are in dire need of developing and imagining fresh ways of speaking words of life into what can at times be a very brutal, cold world, especially to those who recognize the frailty and limitations that mark the human condition. How can progressives imagine salvation and/or eschatology in partial, vulnerable, meaningful, this-temporal-world kinds of ways that don't lead listeners to the brink of despair, all the while being aware of what Caputo calls our weak and mortal flesh? We need fresh ways to imagine the activity harbored in the name of God—fresh ways that keep the future from closing in on us, fresh ways that keep the future open, fresh ways that celebrate newness of life—not draining ways that reinforce an exhausting sense of compassion fatigue that diminishes possibilities for transformation more than inspiring them.

In an engaging Lenten sermon preached by the late Peter Gomes, former minister of The Memorial Church at Harvard, we are not only introduced to the difficulties modern listeners have opening themselves to the kind of salvation that is beyond their best efforts but also to the challenges progressive preachers face in their attempts to provide viable alternatives to the modern homiletical crisis. In his interpretation of the story about the rich young ruler (Matt 19:25–26), Gomes first leads listeners to the conventional conclusion that remains the norm in most progressive circles: The rich young ruler, in his quest to gain eternal life, is unable to let go of his possessions, which leads him to go away sad, for he was a man of great wealth. "Thus, we say, this is a story of greed, materialism, and misplaced values." We know what we should do, but we are unwilling to do it. "Here, of course, would be the neat little moral: You must lose in order to gain . . . You must give in order to get." Yet just when we think Gomes is going to leave listeners with an ethical admonition,

7. Žižek is right on this point. See ch. 12.

he turns the tables on his progressive listeners and draws his sermon to a close with the following reversal:

> [I]f this young man of ability, promise, and achievement, who had everything going for him including modesty and spiritual ambition, if this young man cannot be saved, in the words of this text, "Who then can possibly be saved?" "Humanly speaking," Jesus says, "it is impossible." In rational, human, sociological, sensible, psychological, physiological, philosophical terms, nobody is going to do as Jesus directed, and therefore, because nobody is going to do it, nobody is going to be saved. . . .
>
> Thank God salvation is God's business and not ours. Unitarians at the turn of [the twentieth] century had as one article of their reformed and liberal creed "Salvation by character." . . . [B]ut few could depend upon their character for salvation, then or now. . . . "Humanly speaking, it is impossible, but with God anything is possible." Anything, including, perhaps, the salvation of the rich young man himself. . . . Anything, including perhaps your salvation and mine, despite our virtue, despite our wisdom, despite our riches, despite our knowledge, despite our fears. God saves us in spite of ourselves because of himself. *If God can make the universe out of nothing, think of what he can do with you and with me.* "Humanly speaking, it is impossible, but with God anything is possible . . ." Even this.[8]

In this sermon, Gomes is upfront about the struggles and difficulties we face in our attempts to do the right thing. He acknowledges that even our best efforts come up short. But instead of falling for the trap of the modern homiletical crisis by further reinforcing feelings of "failure and despair" that subtly lurk in far too many progressive sermons, he moves the sermon to its proper focus: the activity stirring in the name of God.

However, some significant problems remain, at least from a progressive perspective. Just as this sermon serves as a good example of the importance of not reducing sermons to grand ethical exhortations, it is also a good example of the way that theological imagery can easily trip up progressive listeners. When taking into consideration the final lines of the sermon, progressive listeners who are suspect of supernatural images of God are going to have significant difficulty hearing God's power to effect salvation connected to God's ability to "make the universe out of nothing." While some may hear this poetically, most hear it as a

---

8. See Gomes, *Sermons*, 55–61. Emphasis mine.

reference to an interventionist supreme being type of God. Such a statement may very well resonate with those who don't have much trouble believing in a supernatural God who created everything out of nothing before the dawn of time, but it produces a disconnect for a significant number of progressive listeners who aren't quite sure what to make of God in a postmodern era and are suspect of supernatural images of God, either on a conscious or an unconscious level. This puts progressive preachers in a quandary: On the one hand, preachers must be careful not to reduce sermons to grand ethical exhortations, especially when taking into consideration our fragility and limitations as human beings. But on the other hand, progressive preachers must find a way to incorporate theological imagery in sermons that celebrates the activity stirring in the name of God, yet not in terms that evoke a supernatural (ontotheological[9]) divine interventionist agent/entity.

In addition, given the violence of the twentieth century (what was supposed to be *The Christian Century*, at least as the popular Protestant liberal magazine envisioned) and utter lack of moral progress that went with it, preachers are responsible for incorporating responsible images of the activity of the divine that don't trivialize or disgrace the reality of those who have suffered, but rather preserve and honor their memory.[10] If we choose to draw on theological language and imagery in an attempt to speak "Easter words in a Lenten world," it's important to do so carefully, with integrity and authenticity. Too much pulpit talk that speaks of the activity and agency of God—especially in Bible-thumping circles—is insulting to those who are suffering or who have suffered, yet the liberal myth of inevitable human progress and goodness sentimentalizes evil and fails to offer a viable alternative. When reflecting on the Holocaust, the Jewish theologian Irving Greenberg once wrote: "No statement theological or otherwise should be made that would not be credible in the presence

9. While the term "ontotheology" is used in a variety of ways (particularly by Kant and Heidegger), I generally use it as a shorthand way of referring to theology that conceives of God in terms of being, power, and causality (what Caputo often refers to as "strong theology"). By contrast, from the vantage point of a theology of the event, God (or the event harbored in the name of God) is not conceived of in terms of being. For Caputo and many others drawn to the postmodern return of religion, God is otherwise than being. See especially Caputo, *Weakness of God*, 40, as well as pages 76–77 of this book.

10. See Caputo, *Weakness of God*, 248.

of the burning children."[11] No quote is more important for preachers to heed, progressive or otherwise.

2. *Symbolic Gestures.*

It is widely recognized that during the era of modernity, ideas about religious truth were largely reduced to what could be proven in the same way that a scientist could prove whether or not soap floats. While God couldn't be put in a laboratory, it was believed that through the use of Reason (with a capital *R*) it was possible to prove whether or not God exists. As a result, the meaning of Christianity was boiled down to sets of propositions that one could cognitively regard as being true. Not only is this the inverse of Anselm's "faith seeking understanding," but it is also why to this day in most evangelical worship services in the United States participants are encouraged to become a Christian ("get saved") by cognitively believing certain sets of propositions—that Jesus is God's divine Son, for example, and that he rose from the dead. To become a Christian, one *cognitively* affirms certain beliefs to be true about God and Christianity.

Progressives rarely do the same thing in worship services, at least at first glance. Instead of having altar calls in which participants declare their cognitive belief in the validity of certain sets of doctrinal propositions, progressives have moments of commitment in which participants are charged with reaffirming their desire to be "the hands and feet of Christ in the world." However, progressives like myself must also admit that our approach to the truth of Christianity largely remains cognitively locked in our minds as well. Mainline sermons, for instance, frequently reference very worthwhile concerns such as caring for the environment, opposing slave labor, critiquing unbridled consumer capitalism, protesting war, fighting poverty, dismantling racism, and so on. On a purely cognitive level, we hear these sermons and cognitively "agree" with the message. We are not in favor of ravaging the environment or supporting things like slave labor, consumerism, poverty, and war. Of course we are not. We oppose these things, for very good reasons. *Yet the truth remains that even though we cognitively oppose these things, we live our lives precisely as if we did not oppose them.* In fact, we can hear a sermon decrying environmental degradation and just after all of us say "Amen," we empty the church parking lot in our gasoline-powered vehicles. Or we can hear

11. Greenberg, "Cloud of Smoke, Pillar of Fire," 23.

a sermon against consumerism, child labor, and poverty and talk about how "meaningful" and "powerful" the sermon was, then drive to the mall to purchase goods we don't need that were made in sweatshops (I remember preaching a sermon that referenced the problems of sweatshop labor and later that week I went to a major department store because they had a deal I just couldn't pass up. "The good that I want to do I do not do . . .").

This is all a way of saying that what we believe on a cognitive level (who we believe we are) is very often at odds with the way we actually function in the world (the truth of who we are). To make matters worse, sermons and liturgies often reinforce rather than disrupt this disconnect because they function as the release valve that allows us to think we believe all of the right things, even though the way we function tells us a very different story. No one is better at describing how this plays out in Christian circles than Peter Rollins. He illustrates this idea in numerous ways, but my favorite is his example of comic book hero Bruce Wayne. By day, Bruce Wayne is a wealthy businessman; by night he is Batman. Following in the footsteps of his father, Bruce Wayne is obsessed with eliminating crime on the streets of Gotham City. His father tried to do this by being a philanthropist, but as Batman, Bruce Wayne decides to use his wealth to start his own vigilante war on terror. What neither one of them realizes, however, is that the subjective crime they try to remedy on the streets is actually a direct manifestation of the objective crime that their industrial company perpetrates on a daily basis. One could even go so far as to say that

> it is the very philanthropic work of [Wayne's] Father and the crime-fighting of Wayne that actually provide the valve that allows them both to continue in their objective violence. What better way to feel good about yourself than volunteering at a local charity in the evenings (like his Father) or beating up on street criminals in the evenings (like Wayne). Such acts (like a prayer meeting, worship service or bible study) can recharge the batteries and make us feel like our true identity is pure and good, when in reality it simply takes away the guilt that would otherwise make it difficult for us to embrace our true (social) self who is expressed in the activities we engage in for the rest of the week. The philosophy here is exposed as "do something so that nothing really changes."[12]

12. Rollins, "Batman as the Ultimate Capitalist Superhero."

Consider standard ethical sermons in predominately Eurocentric congregations that preach against racism. We talk about the sins of racism, the evils of racism, and sometimes we even dare to bring up the problem of white privilege. And on a purely *cognitive* level, the congregation affirms the "truth" and "meaning" of the sermon (they might even decide to go to the annual Martin Luther King Jr. Day march). But after church (or after the march) the majority of the members of the congregation go home to their white neighborhoods and have dinner with their white friends, and the reality of their social existence (the truth of who they are) is confirmed all the more. And, even more problematic, the sermon or the march sometimes serves as the release valve that keeps privileged folk from challenging the power structures of society the other six days of the week (or 364 days of the year). When sermons and liturgies function as the release valve that further perpetuates the problems we claim to cognitively resist, they become nothing more than well-intentioned—but ultimately problematic—symbolic gestures.[13]

Given these dynamics, it's little wonder that Rollins is a Pauline kind of guy, for "who will rescue me from this body of death?" (Rom 7:24). For Rollins, the truth of Christianity is not about a series of ideas that we cognitively affirm (whether related to doctrine, as in the conservative churches, or ethical issues, as in the liberal churches), but rather the truth of Christianity is the truth-event that disrupts and transforms our social and material existence (the truth of who we are). From this perspective, the truth of Christianity is not about cognitively "believing" that unbridled consumer capitalism and sweatshop labor devastate the least

13. Compare this to United Methodist scholar Justo González, who argues that the guilt felt by privileged classes does not change the oppressive systems of this world inasmuch as it further perpetuates them. From this perspective, privileged classes regularly hear about the ways God calls them to be part of the change God wishes to enact in this world. The basic message is that change can come about if they are willing to partner with God in making it happen, but this leads privileged people to feel guilty about themselves because they know that the standard of living they enjoy is dependent on the way the system is currently set up, and they aren't sure they want to transform it (to have their social existence transformed). Therefore, as they continually hear about the dreams of God for this world, their guilt isn't assuaged, but rather intensified. But it is precisely by continuing to feel guilty about such matters that those from privileged classes are able to maintain their hold on power, for the guilt subtly makes them believe they are still the ones with the power to change things if they so desired. Instead of guilt leading to change, guilt further solidifies the place of privileged people within the power structures of society because it implies that they are still the ones holding the power. See González, "Hispanic Perspective," 92–93.

of these, or that racism is evil, but rather the truth of Christianity is the event that transforms our very being, so that we are no longer held captive to the systems we claim to deplore. Here we undergo a materialist *metanoia*, a change of heart that is beyond our best efforts. As such, materialist Christianity is the ultimate antidote to a functional nihilism that in both conservative and liberal form believes that one's true self is manifested in what one cognitively believes (who we think we are) as opposed to one's everyday social existence (the truth of who we are).[14]

From the perspective of preaching, I'm not saying that progressives should avoid ethical conversations from the pulpit altogether. But we do need to be honest about the trappings of symbolic gestures (including the possibility of the sermon serving as a symbolic gesture itself) and focus our sermons on the celebration of the truth-event that disrupts and transforms our material existence, that short-circuits the systems and structures that bind us, lest we think we have arrived by cognitively "believing" and "agreeing" on what the right ethical stance is to take as opposed to hoping and sighing and dreaming and weeping for a materialist *metanoia*.

3. *Idolic Talk.*

A third problem with the modern homiletical crisis is that it makes it far too easy to place God in one's back pocket. When Voltaire said, "God created us in his image, and we returned the favor," he echoed voices ranging from Moses to Barth to Derrida. If human beings are good at anything, it is making sure that the perspectives of God are consistent with their own. As is often noted, the first person Uncle Sam drafts into the army in times of war is God, and the same is true for virtually every nation or organization that inflicts violence against another.

Perhaps Søren Kierkegaard expressed this problem best when he identified the "religiousness A" approach to Christianity in which "human beings invent spiritual goals that encourage them to do what they were going to do anyway to satisfy their own self-centered desires . . . The

14. While encompassing a variety of nuances that will become apparent throughout this book, the phrase "materialist Christianity," generally speaking, refers to a version of non-dogmatic Christianity that is not dependent on the presence or existence of a supernatural Being or overarching metaphysical "reality" (and sometimes explicitly resists such ontotheological constructions), and that also serves as an ideological critique of theological systems that privilege belief over practice. For the best introduction to materialist Christianity available, see Rollins' *Insurrection*.

'God' they are thinking about always turns out to be a creature of their own imagination, designed to support their sense of their own importance or virtue."[15] As such, preachers have the responsibility of honoring the "wholly other" by not confusing their own finite perspectives for those of God. To once again invoke Caputo (who is a scholar of Kierkegaard as much as he is of Derrida):

> When we open our mouths, it is only we who are speaking, we poor existing individuals, as Kierkegaard liked to put it, and we would be ill advised to think that we are the Mouthpiece of Being or the Good or of the Almighty. But on my hypothesis, that is not bad news, because it tends to check the spread of people who confuse themselves with Being, or the Good, or the Almighty, who think that they have been sent into the world to tell the rest of us what God or Being or Nature (or Whatever) thinks, when in fact what we are hearing is nothing more than the views of Harry Gutentag, who is a decent enough chap if you get to know him but who tends to take himself a little too seriously.[16]

Sometimes our lack of emphasis on the "wholly other" leads us to baptize our own finite observations in the name of God all the more. Preachers must be responsible in regard to the content of our proclamations, which means we must be aware of the reality that we see through a glass darkly, and we shouldn't be too quick to confuse our own perspectives for the absolute God's-eye view of the world. To borrow the words of Merold Westphal, "we need to look closely to determine just where and to what degree God-talk becomes the arrogant humanism that puts God at our disposal."[17] One might also recall what historians have termed the "Protestant principle" as reflected in a Latin maxim of the sixteenth century: *finitus non capax infiniti* (the finite is incapable of [expressing] the infinite).[18] Which is not all that different from Thomas Aquinas's famous statement that "the highest human knowledge of God is to know that one does not know God."[19]

---

15. As described by William Placher in *Triune God*, 28.

16. Caputo, *On Religion*, 21–22.

17. Westphal, "Overcoming Onto-theology," 161.

18. See Raschke, *Next Reformation*, 25.

19. As quoted in Marion, "In the Name," 35. At the same time, it's important to point out that for Caputo and Derrida, distinguishing between finite and infinite understanding of truth in relationship to the event is not a matter of denying knowledge of God in

To make a brief point that I think progressives should consider every bit as much as their evangelical counterparts: Amy Sullivan—a contributing writer for *Time* and a graduate of Harvard Divinity School—was recently named by Religion News Service as one of the twelve most influential voices in helping Democrats reach people of faith. Even though she admittedly leans to the left politically and theologically, she is quick to point out the problematic ways that mainline denominations have mistaken, over the last three or four decades, "the appeal of liberal politics for the appeal of liberal theology." Instead of speaking theologically, mainline churches have replaced liberal theology with liberal politics. While the reverse is also true in evangelical contexts (she once attended a Baptist church where she was told that "a good Christian can't be a Democrat"), the problem of baptizing God in the name of whatever cause one wishes to champion happens far too often on both the left and the right.[20]

Just as, according to Barth, "the gospel does not exist as a truth among other truths but rather sets a question-mark against all truths," so too does deconstruction set a question mark against all of our assumptions about truth. Deconstruction is rigorous when it comes to competing claims about truth, for it exposes the truth that we never have access to Truth, and so all of our perspectives are necessarily partial. Scott Black Johnston, while commenting on the similarities between Barth and Derrida, says this is a "risky proposition, an approach to the truth that will seem threatening to many elements of the church . . . [but] it is consistent with the parabolic teachings of the New Testament Jesus. For time and time again, the Scriptures tell of Christ calling established structures and norms into question."[21]

---

order to magnify an even higher, incomprehensible Being or Presence or Substance, as in mystical (or negative) theology's *hyperousia*. Caputo is not, as he describes, "speaking of truth in the Platonic sense of the sunlight of the Good, of the absolute being underlying the sensible appearances, or in the Hegelian sense of its essential being and *Aufhebung*, or in the Heideggerian sense of its unconcealment. By the truth of the event, I mean what the event is capable of, the open-ended and unforeseeable future that the name harbors, its uncontainable possibilities, which may contain bad news." See Caputo, *Weakness of God*, 5. For a more detailed discussion of what is meant by "the truth of the event," see ch. 4.

20. For the quotes from Sullivan, see the "Faith and Citizenship" podcast.

21. For the comparison between Barth and Derrida, see Johnston's comments in Allen, Blaisdell, and Johnston, *Theology for Preaching*, 76. So far as I can tell, Johnston is the first homiletician on record to recognize the positive import of deconstruction for preaching.

At the same time, it's important for me to offer a caveat that will play a central role throughout this book: We must also recognize that simply because deconstruction exposes the "contingency of what we like to call the 'truth'" (i.e., our own finite perspectives) *does not mean that deconstruction lacks a passion for truth.* Far from it. For there is a complementary theory of truth at work in deconstruction that is driven by a passion for the undeconstructible, what Caputo often refers to as *the impossible,* which is connected to a longing for the "wholly other," all of which I introduce in chapter 4.

> On my reading, which will sound a little too pious to impious deconstructors and downright impious to good and pious Christians, deconstruction is a theory of *truth,* in which truth spells *trouble.* As does Jesus. That is what they have in common. The truth will make you free, but it does so by turning your life upside down. Up to now, deconstruction has gotten a lot of mileage out of taking sides with the "*un*-truth." That is a methodological irony, a strategy of "reversal," meant to expose the contingency of what we like to call the "Truth," with a capital T—deconstruction being a critique of long-robed totalizers of a capitalized Truth, of T-totallers of all kinds. I have no intention of sending that strategy into early retirement or claiming that it has outlived its usefulness. We will need that strategy as long as there is hypocrisy, as long as there are demagogues pounding on the table that they have the Truth, which means forever. . . . But I do want to supplement it with a complementary theory of truth. For while deconstructors have made important gains exposing the hypocrisy of temporal and contingent claims that portray themselves in the long robes of Eternal Verity, it is also necessary to point out that deconstruction is at the same time a hermeneutics of truth, of the truth of the event, which is not deconstructible. This is the truth that disturbs and that we tend to repress. When a deconstruction is done well, the truth or—what seems like the same thing—all hell will break out. What the truth does . . . what Jesus does, is deconstruct.[22]

As such, a homiletic of the event demands that we shift what we mean by "truth." This is difficult for nonspecialists to grasp, in large part because it represents a different way of approaching theology that few of us are accustomed to (this is also why I introduce this approach at length in chapters 4–6, especially with nonspecialists in mind). The truth

22. Caputo, *What Would Jesus Deconstruct?*, 30.

of the event should be distinguished from the kind of metaphysical truth that attempts to describe The Way Things Are Behind the Scenes. It is better understood as a poetic truth related to what we passionately long for, what we hope and sigh and dream and weep for, what holds us in its grasp, what groans to be born, what solicits us and overcomes us, even as we can never adequately describe what "it" is (from the point of view of deconstruction, the determinate meaning of what is stirring in the name of God always slips away, and necessarily so). While I go into much more detail about this approach in chapter 4, perhaps it is helpful to briefly clarify that in deconstruction the truth of the event is not understood as the truth of Being, or of the Being of beings, or of a Super Something or Someone orchestrating things behind the scenes, or of the Really Real, or of whatever Substance or Presence constitutes Ultimate Reality.[23] Rather than thinking about the truth of the event in terms of its metaphysical or ontological essence, it is better understood in terms of what it calls forth from us, what it demands of us. This is why Caputo likes to say that God doesn't exist, God *insists*. Put another way, the kingdom of God doesn't exist, it calls. It *insists*. The justice and forgiveness and hospitality stirring in the name of God, or in the name of the kingdom of God, is what solicits us, calls us, challenges us, provokes us. From this perspective, truth is not something Out There that we describe, nor is it some sort of definitive metaphysical or ontological principle or essence on the plane of being or existence. Rather, the truth of the event that is stirring in the name of God is the truth that calls upon us, that overcomes us, that provokes us, that solicits us, that demands to come true, that groans to be born (to exist). The truth of the event solicits and provokes us, and it becomes true in the madness of the moment in which the truth gets done (*facere veritatem*, as Augustine put it), for the truth of the event is finally not a concept but a deed (this is why a homiletic of the event consists of both call *and* response). We are called to respond, to make the truth happen, all the while recognizing that the solicitation and provocation of the call is not of our own manufacture and resists all our efforts of confining it to the best of our ready-made ideas and intentions.

Here we see that a homiletic of the event is not averse to ethics—far from it. A homiletic of the event celebrates the provocation of the call stirring in the name of God, a call and solicitation that overcomes us, that

23. I love Sallie McFague's felicitous phrase: "We are super, natural Christians." See her book *Super, Natural Christians*.

demands a response, that is not of our own doing, even though it very well may be our undoing. God doesn't *exist*, God *insists*. The call demands a response.

4. *Lost Wonder, Love, and Praise.*

The last pastoral problem tied to the modern homiletical crisis is the loss of wonder, love, and praise in progressive pulpits. If our sermons are focused more on our own activity than on the activity of God; if "there is plenty of morality and good counsel, but no desert bush bursting into flame"; if our sermons lack a pulsating hope or expectation or longing for the advent of the wholly other to break into our midst, it's almost as if we've traded in the fire of the God of Abraham, Isaac, and Jacob for a mess of pottage.[24]

Perhaps this is one of the primary reasons for the decline of mainline churches, and I say this not just in relation to sermons, but to worship in general. If we view the name of God as little more than a relic of the past; if we are inspired by the teachings of Jesus and wish to continue his mission but really aren't sure we need God language to do so; if God is nothing more than the best of our ideals and ethical intentions, then, really, why would worship on Sunday mornings (including our sermons) harbor any kind of anticipation or mystery or longing, especially when the word *God* is invoked by the preacher? When this is the case, wouldn't the popular comparison of old-line churches with museums (or, as Nietzsche described, tombs and sepulchers) be on target? This is why the tired arguments about style and such always fall short—it is not about preaching with or without notes, in or out of the pulpit, with or without multimedia.[25] It is rather about cultivating a communal sense of anticipation, mystery, and longing, which, in Derridean terms, is fueled by the hope of the "other" to be visited upon the same, with the same being restless for the advent of the *tout autre*, the "wholly other," and never content with what *is*. The "same," for Derrida, can be compared to the humdrum reality of daily existence, of what *is*, which is important, of course—it

24. Or, as we will see in ch. 3, what Blaise Pascal called "the god of the philosophers." One wonders how much a colleague of mine represents other progressive preachers when he says, "I mainly put God language into my sermons because as ministers we are supposed to, it's what people expect."

25. This is a point Fred Craddock recognized early on. His comments on the context of preaching in the 1960s are quite similar to "emergent" homiletical conversations today. See esp. Craddock, "Inductive Preaching Renewed," 42–43.

demands our best efforts, always and uncompromisingly. But it's not what makes our hearts beat. Our hearts beat for the same to be disturbed by the "other," to be disturbed by what eye has not seen and ear has not heard (1 Cor 2:9), to be disturbed by what we can't see coming, which makes us long for it—as well as look out for it—all the more. Our preaching on Sunday mornings could use a taste of what Caputo describes: "Into the sphere of the 'same' (the familiar, the customary, the business-as-usual of Sunday services) bursts the 'advent' or the 'event' of the 'other,' of the 'coming of the other.'"[26] When Caputo speaks about *the event harbored in the name of God*, which is a central motif of his that serves as the driving force behind the homiletic of the event I pursue in these pages (see especially chapters 4–6), he is calling attention to the coming of the other that disturbs the same, "which makes the same *tremble* and *reconfigure*," which of course may be cause for concern more than comfort.[27] To be sure, the kind of deconstruction at work in the thought of Caputo and Derrida is risky business, the riskiest of all business, for it is rarely content with business as usual—which is why it has so much in common with faith. There is certainly more safety in the modern domestication of transcendence, which is part of the reason the modern homiletical crisis represents, if not the wisdom of this world, then at least the wisdom that usually governs the churches, for it keeps the word of the Lord—which Jeremiah describes as a hammer that breaks a rock in pieces (Jer 23:29)— at a safe, comfortable distance. Hence the reason so much of our pulpit language about God lacks a venture into the unknown. While domesticated pulpit language doesn't necessarily lack value or importance, it often shields us from a more radical encounter with the "wholly other." The insights of Thomas Long are once again apropos. When describing the risk of preaching ("We preachers are either fools for Christ or just damned fools: two awesome and awe-ful possibilities"), he says we often construct a third, safer (wiser) option:

> Take a romp through the thousands of church Web sites on the Internet and sample a sermon here and a sermon there, and what one finds is actually going on in pulpits across the land—at least in pulpits in churches with means enough to maintain Web sites— is an abundance of sage advice. There is sermon wisdom about parenting and wisdom about managing one's money and wisdom

26. Caputo, *What Would Jesus Deconstruct?*, 26.

27. Ibid., emphasis mine.

about finding purpose in one's work and relationships and wisdom about engaging in the struggle for justice and wisdom about being more caring toward others and wisdom about accepting differences and being more inclusive and wisdom about the doctrinal truths of the faith and wisdom about the biblical texts for the day and wisdom about nurturing one's spiritual life.

We need wisdom, of course; wisdom is an important biblical motif, and some of this pulpit wisdom is sound and mostly Christian, I suppose. But true biblical wisdom is less about life skill and the management of problems than it is a seeking of the shape of faithful living that results from an encounter with the living God. Biblical wisdom is grounded not merely in common sense or in the brilliance of some sage, but in holy encounter.

. . . Much pulpit wisdom, however, seems to owe less to the paths of life that are trod in breathless wonder on our way back from worship and more to the well-trod lanes of conventional wisdom. . . . Sermons on "Five Ways to Keep Your Marriage Alive" or "Keys to a Successful Prayer Life" or even "Standing Up for Peace in a Warring World" may possess some ethical wisdom and some utilitarian helpfulness, but they often have the sickly sweet aroma of smoldering incense in a temple from which the deity has long since departed. They can easily have the sound of the lonely wisdom of Job's friends, who can quote the Psalms and the Proverbs but who have ceased to expect the whirlwind.[28]

Elsewhere Long turns to Annie Dillard's oft-quoted observation that if we truly understood what was going on in worship, we would wear crash helmets and ushers would lash us to the pews, "for the sleeping God may someday awake and take offense."[29]

As we will see throughout this book, especially as introduced in chapter 4, deconstruction turns not on what is (the "same," the "present," the "conventional"), but on what might be (the "other," "the dream of a different future," "what we can't make out"). We can't speak of such a future, and necessarily so. We can only celebrate and dream of its coming, its advent, its promise, *lost* in wonder, in love, and in praise.[30]

28. Long, *Preaching from Memory to Hope*, 37–38.

29. As quoted in Long, *Preaching from Memory to Hope*, 31.

30. I also recognize that the advent of the future also contains a threat, which I will describe in ch. 6. Caputo is very upfront about this: "The event is not an essence unfolding but a promise to be kept, a call or a solicitation to be responded to, a prayer to be answered, a hope to be fulfilled. The event is subject to all the contingencies of time and tide, of chance and circumstance, of history and power—in short, to all the forces of the

"Deconstruction," Caputo writes, "is a dream and a desire for something *tout autre*, of something that utterly shatters the present horizons of possibility, that confounds our expectations, that leaves us gasping for air, trying to catch our breath, the first words out of our mouth being, 'How did that happen? How is that possible?'" Deconstruction is a love of the impossible, "the incoming of the other, the coming of something we did not see coming, that takes us by surprise."[31]

From this perspective, a homiletic of the event—which is the name I give to a homiletic influenced by Caputo's theology of the event—can be viewed as an attempt to heed David Buttrick's call for preaching to be an act of invocation:

> Our glib age, crowded with too much information, has no patience with the unknowable. And often our pulpits have been as glib, eager to dish up answers, but unwilling to invoke mystery. But there's the job: "preaching as invocation." If all our sermons can do is to declare a past-tense God revealed in stories scribbled in an ancient Bible-book, we are in trouble. Not much mystery if you can point to God, G-o-d, on the page of a book. . . . Mystery happens when we stumble on something we do not have and cannot explain, something that drops us to our knees stammering.[32]

---

world that conspire to prevent the event, to contain its disruption, to hold in check its bottomless disseminative disturbance, to betray its promise." Thus, "an event can result in a disintegrating destabilization and a diminished recontextualization just as well as it can create an opening to the future." See Caputo, *Weakness of God*, 5. This concern is picked up by Richard Kearney in his essay "Desire of God," which also features a response from both Derrida and Caputo. See esp. Kearney, "Desire of God," 124–36.

31. Caputo and Scanlon, *God, the Gift, and Postmodernism*, 3.

32. Buttrick, "*Homiletic* Renewed," 114. Allow me to offer a caveat related to a point Buttrick raises in his essay: In contrast to his view that presence is only possible if there is a future which can be talked about, a homiletic of the event emphasizes a future that cannot be talked about, that is unforeseeable. In Derrida's words: "The future is that which—tomorrow, later, next century—will be. There is a future which is predictable, programmed, scheduled, foreseeable. But there is a future to come (*l'avenir*) which refers to someone who comes whose arrival is totally unexpected. For me, that is the real future. That which is totally unpredictable. The Other who comes without my being able to anticipate their arrival. So if there is a real future beyond this known future, it's *l'avenir* in that it's the coming of the Other when I am completely unable to foresee their arrival." Derrida, from the transcript to the documentary film *Derrida*, directed by Kirby Dick (online: kirbydick.com/derrida/DerridaTRANSCRIPT.doc). I will pick this up in ch. 4 while discussing the structure of the messianic in relationship to Derrida's thought.

William Willimon picks up on a similar theme while reflecting on St. Paul's conversion experience on the road to Damascus. By highlighting the difficulty of speech in the wake of a transformative event, he points out the need for our proclamations to be caught up (*lost*) in wonder, love, and praise: "Be well assured—though those who experience the Risen Christ and his aftermath have difficulty bringing what they have experienced to speech—they have experienced an earthshaking event. If an event can be truly said to be earthshaking, a dismantling and a re-creation, the advent of a whole new world, that event will be by its very nature difficult to describe." Not surprisingly, he goes on to comment on the reasons why mainliners seldom preach on the letters of Paul, which in my estimation is related to the modern homiletical crisis: "There is, in my experience, a kind of prejudice, within the liberal, mainline church, against the letters of Paul. *I expect that it is a prejudice that is derived from the liberal tendency to avoid theology in favor of anthropology, to reduce the miraculous to the merely moral . . .*"[33]

Here we begin to recognize that our inability to speak of God—our inability to speak in the wake of the transformative, earthshaking event harbored in the name of God—actually puts us on the right homiletical track. To modify the quote from Gilles Deleuze at the beginning of this chapter: "How else can one [preach] but of those things which one doesn't know, or knows badly? It is precisely here that we imagine having something to say." In a homiletic of the event, we join a long line of theologians past and present who tell us that we are charged to speak of what we can never speak of, a point that Augustine made a long time ago: "[W]hile nothing really worthy of God can be said about him, he has accepted the homage of human voices, and has wished us to rejoice in praising him with our words."[34] Or as Barth famously wrote: "As ministers we ought to speak of God. We are human, however, and so cannot speak of God. We ought therefore to recognize both our obligation and our inability and by that very recognition give God the glory."[35] Peter Rollins provides a slightly updated postmodern version: "We must avoid confusion between remaining silent and saying nothing. For while the former is passive the latter is active. By saying nothing we endeavour to speak of that which

33. Willimon, *Conversations with Barth on Preaching*, 219. Emphasis mine.

34. See Augustine, *Teaching Christianity*, 1.6.6. See also Smith, "Between Predication and Silence."

35. Barth, *Word of God and the Word of Man*, 186.

manifests in our world as a no-thing, as an absolute mystery which infuses our world with light and life. To undergo and then speak of that which is not a thing but which transforms our relationship with all things . . . this is a sacred and subversive vocation."[36] This is why theological speech ultimately gives way to praise, and why our sermons should do the same.

* * *

Now that we have named a handful of pastoral problems related to the modern homiletical crisis, the next chapter examines the theological matrix responsible for the predicament progressive preachers currently find themselves in. In order to get a handle on why the domestication of transcendence is so prominent in progressive pulpits—and why post-Enlightenment Christians have been conditioned to downplay the activity stirring in the name of God—we'll explore the roots of the modern homiletical crisis, particularly by paying attention to the trajectory of Nietzsche's infamous proclamation of the death of God. Not only does this help us better understand the milieu from which postmodernism emerged, but it also allows us to better frame postmodern alternatives for preaching that take shape in subsequent chapters.

36. See Rollins, *How (Not) to Speak of God*, xi–xv.

3

Why Nietzsche Matters

The modern occurred when the world decided to get along without Christianity, and though the world surely did not fully appreciate this at the time, it was also a decision to get along without God.

—William Willimon[1]

How did we do this? How could we drink up the sea? Who gave us the sponge to wipe away the entire horizon?

—Friedrich Nietzsche[2]

WHEN IT COMES TO current approaches to progressive theology—particularly approaches to Christianity that are primarily responsible for ushering in the modern homiletical crisis—nothing remains more influential on us today than modern forms of philosophy and theology. In this chapter, we'll explore the "trickle-down effect" that modern philosophy and theology continues to have on progressive Christianity, even in the so-called postmodern era, and thus begin to understand why the modern homiletical crisis remains so ubiquitous in contemporary pulpits. After taking a look at the influence of modern theology and philosophy, we'll better understand the import of the postmodern return of religion, which then allows us to reimagine and/or shift the ways we appropriate theological language in our sermons.

1. Willimon, *Conversations with Barth on Preaching*, 64.
2. Nietzsche, *Gay Science*, 181.

While it's rarely intentional, the reality remains that despite all of our "postmodern" talk, many mainline/progressive preachers consistently resist the more radical implications of postmodern theory. Often, we simply don't recognize the modern waters we are drowning in. It's like a story the Sufi mystics tell about some fish who were anxiously swimming around looking for water. The more they swam the more anxious they became. One day they met a wise fish and asked him, "Where is the sea?" The wise fish answered: "If you would stop swimming . . . you would discover that you are already in the sea."[3] Similar to these fish, progressive preachers in North America have swum around so long in the waters of modernism and its Enlightenment project that we don't recognize we are doing so, even though we are so very enamored with "postmodern" talk.

Slavoj Žižek tells a joke about a grown man who thinks he is a grain of corn and is thus afraid he will be eaten by chickens. Because of this obvious disorder, the man is taken under care. After several weeks of therapy, the man is finally convinced that he is not a grain of corn but rather a human being and, therefore, does not have to worry about being eaten by chickens. The man is told he can pack his bags and return home. But just a few minutes after walking out the door, the man frantically runs back into his therapist's office shouting, "There is a chicken outside and he might eat me!" The therapist replies, "But you know you are a human being and not a grain of corn." "Yes," replies the man, "I know I'm not a grain of corn and you know I'm not a grain of corn. But does the chicken know I'm not a grain of corn!?"[4]

As this joke illustrates, the rhetoric we employ (as well as the cognitive ideas we have about who we are) is often very different from the way that we function. When we talk about developing postmodern sermons, yet continue to construct them around modernist (theological) foundations that refuse to come to terms with the breakdown of metaphysics, the landscape of contemporary preaching, like the man who thinks he is a grain of corn, remains at a standstill.[5] Perhaps the greatest irony of

3. Northcutt, *Kindling Desire for God*, 50.

4. See Žižek, *Sublime Object of Ideology*, 35.

5. For the most part, progressive preachers have yet to come to grips with Nietzsche's infamous proclamation of the death of God, by which he implied the death of metaphysics. This is one of the primary reasons that the modern homiletical crisis remains trapped in modern theological foundations, no matter how much postmodern rhetoric we might employ. By contrast, the postmodern return of religion has been wrestling with the reli-

post-Enlightenment preaching in mainline contexts lies in the fact that most of the glowing homiletical rhetoric in relation to postmodernism consistently resists the radical implications of postmodern theory—especially those voiced by figures like Derrida—and thus ends up repeating the same mistakes of modernism time and again (particularly in terms of modernity's domestication of transcendence). The most puzzling aspect to this irony is that even though Derrida's brand of postmodernism is hardly dependent on guaranteeing the presence of some sort of supernatural Supreme Being or Presence—the kind of God that Christians in a post-Enlightenment era have difficulty believing in—it still turns on transcendence, on the activity and agency (the specter) of what Derrida calls the *tout autre* ("wholly other"), which is precisely what the modern homiletical crisis lacks the most.

When analyzed carefully, most of our rhetoric related to postmodernism serves more as a buzzword for doing ministry in and among Millennials and "hipsters" (or whoever the youngsters are at the time) than it has anything to do with substantive philosophical and theological claims, denoting more "cultural style than theoretical weight," and it is largely because we have shifted the emphasis of postmodernism toward cultural descriptors rather than philosophical and theological ones that modernism continues to haunt our environs in detrimental ways.[6] Peter Rollins aptly notes, "The current religious landscape is cluttered with various expressions of faith that claim to rethink Christianity at the dawn of a new cultural epoch. However such groups often accomplish little more than the repackaging and redistribution of faith as we currently understand it. A repackaging that involves flashing lights, video projectors and 'culturally sensitive' leaders who can talk about the latest mediocre pop sensation."[7]

From the perspective of homiletics, this can be seen in the distinction that the authors of *Theology for Preaching: Authority, Truth, and*

---

gious and theological implications of the breakdown of metaphysics for more than half a century. Surprisingly enough, as we will especially see below, Nietzsche's proclamation of the "death" of God actually opens up religion and theology in a number of affirming, compelling ways that Nietzsche himself, as a self-professed despiser of religion, didn't imagine.

6. Raschke, *Next Reformation*, 11, 15.

7. Rollins, "Lessons in Evandalism Tour." See also Caputo, "On Not Settling for an Abridged Edition of Postmodernism."

Knowledge of God in a Postmodern Ethos perceptively make between *folk* postmodernism and *philosophical/theological* postmodernism. Folk postmodernism reflects general outlooks that are voiced and embodied by those who aren't necessarily familiar with the formal literature and subtle categories of postmodernism advanced by theologians and philosophers. It is representative of the way a growing number of people view the world. It is very common in progressive circles and is certainly the kind of postmodernism most frequently referenced in conversations about the emerging church. Examples of folk postmodernism include the following: "Many people today are uneasy with reigning authorities and institutions. . . . Science is still respected, but it no longer speaks with an imperial voice. Few people assume that new technology is automatically positive. . . . A growing number of people recognize relativity in the scientific method. . . . Many people are aware (sometimes dimly) of relativities in human perception. . . . [There is] an increasing respect for [premodernity] and for the guidance it may offer us."[8]

Folk postmodernism represents the way most of us view postmodernism. Unfortunately, it also limits our view of postmodernism. For example, progressives generally agree that (1) all of us inhabit particular social locations when we preach, and (2) we should be mindful of perspectives that are different ("other") than our own. These are valuable considerations that move preaching forward in helpful directions, and they have my full support. But in spite of these important gains, which are largely related to folk postmodernism, most of the theological language used in progressive preaching remains deeply entrenched in modern theological assumptions. Because the influence of postmodernism on our sermons is usually reduced to folk postmodernism, and is rarely open to philosophical/theological postmodernism, it's almost as if we are content to have postmodern preaching without much of the postmodernism mixed in, which is perhaps one of the better examples out there of a kind of postmodernism that has, like artificial orange juice, lost its pulp.[9]

8. Allen, Blaisdell, and Johnston, *Theology for Preaching*, 21–22.

9. John McClure recognizes as much: "Preachers must decide who they are in relation to the cultural phenomenon of religious postmodernism and the critical power of post-Enlightenment nihilism . . . Preachers must rethink what it means to speak sacred words in a world that is experiencing the weakening of all of its metanarratives." According to McClure, one reason that other-wise homiletics has gone largely unrecognized and unorganized as a movement is that it hasn't been explicitly articulated in relation to its deeper philosophical underpinnings. See McClure, *Other-wise Preaching*, xi, 7.

In order to move postmodern preaching forward in fresh, inventive ways, it is helpful for progressives to critically engage the trickle-down effect that modernism still has on preaching today. This requires that we not only consider *cultural* dynamics associated with postmodernism (folk postmodernism), but *theological* dynamics as well (theological postmodernism). To accomplish this task, we will embark on a brief journey through the thought of a handful of theorists, including one of the most polarizing figures of the last few centuries: Friedrich Nietzsche (1844–1900). While Nietzsche is not the only prophet of postmodernism, he is certainly one of the most influential. Readers might be surprised to learn that his infamous proclamation of the "death" of God, which is often referenced by skeptics in order to celebrate the end of religion, actually opens up religion in several vital ways that progressive preachers would be wise to heed.[10]

INTRODUCING NIETZSCHE'S MADMAN

When my ten-year-old son saw the book *After the Death of God* sitting next to my computer, it was an odd feeling trying to explain to him why as a pastor I was reading it.[11] Little did he know that it is actually quite affirming in its language about God, but how do you explain postmodernism to a ten-year-old? (Much less to grown-ups!) Not long ago, our congregation helped sponsor a conference at a local university that featured Jeffrey Robbins and John Caputo, both of whom contributed to the aforementioned book, and it made for some of the best—and most thought-provoking—conversations we've had in quite some time. In fact, the impetus of many of these Wednesday evening conversations helped give shape to the book you are now reading.

There's no doubt that Nietzsche gets a bad rap in Christian circles, and it's no secret that Nietzsche himself was no fan of religion. Yet, like Derrida, he has become a central figure in the postmodern return of religion, and for good reason. Nietzsche is pivotal in the move from modernity to postmodernity, for in his own bold, subversive, and provocative

10. McClure and others would not simply say that the problem can be fixed by the preacher finding the "right" theological method and then telling listeners about it from the pulpit, and rightly so. I engage these matters in ch. 5.

11. Caputo and Vattimo, *After the Death of God.*

way, he exposed the secret of modernity, which is the key to understanding the modern homiletical crisis.

If Mark C. Taylor is right in telling us that "every interpretation of Nietzsche's proclamation of the death of God as a nihilistic rejection of religion is wrong,"[12] then how do we come to terms with what Nietzsche was up to? The first thing we must do is understand the philosophical and theological climate at the time of his infamous proclamation.

As is often pointed out, due in large part to the influence of major philosophers such as René Descartes (1596–1650), the modern period tried to develop indubitable "first truths" based on human reason that could serve as a solid foundation for universal knowledge. For Descartes, truth was equated with certainty. Indeed, his entire philosophical enterprise can be understood "as an effort to overcome the insecurity brought by uncertainty and to reach the security promised by certainty."[13] Contextually speaking, Descartes lived in a time in which Aristotelian science had become outdated and economic changes had disrupted the social order. When you add to this the horrific bloodshed that marked Europe during Descartes' lifetime (as well as before), it's not surprising that his quest for certainty and stability was appealing to intellectuals searching for alternatives to the perpetual violence and discord that was often done in the name of religion. As homiletician David Lose explains:

> The modern era was inaugurated in the years following the Peace of Westphalia (1648) that brought an end to the Thirty Years' War and marked the dawn of the period known as the Enlightenment. Worn out by religious wars that had ravaged Europe, increasingly skeptical of the sectarian dogmas and disputes driving those conflicts, and more aware of the fissures in the edifice of the post-Reformation church, the intellectuals of that generation assumed the humanistic mantle of their Renaissance forebears and sought the means by which to order society by rational, rather than religious, means.
>
> It is difficult to underestimate the nature of the change that occurred as the early modernists sought to erect a society guided, not by *superstitious* belief, but by a universally valid rationality.[14]

12. Taylor, *After God*, 180.

13. Taylor, *Erring*, 22.

14. Lose, *Confessing Jesus Christ*, 8–9. Emphasis mine. What is often lost on such conversations is that the same anxiety was felt in the modern period as well. As William Placher describes: "The modern appeal to reason, rigorously defined, can appear less

The modern quest for certainty took at least two overarching forms. While Descartes emphasized rationalism, John Locke (1632–1704) emphasized empiricism. Locke maintained that all of our rational ideas stem from our sensory experiences, and only a method of empirical observation and verification can establish a reliable foundation for knowledge.[15] Whether through a version of Descartes' rationalism or Locke's empiricism, the desire for certainty "sought to pierce through the superstition [that] had governed earlier stages."[16]

For influential philosophers of the Enlightenment, it quickly became clear that *superstitious religious beliefs* had to be bracketed off or discarded, for they got in the way of the quest for certainty, primarily because they couldn't be rationally *proven* or empirically *verified*. Because it was impossible to prove or verify biblical claims, the value of religion was dramatically reassessed. This led Locke to conclude that, in the words of Carl Raschke, "what makes Christianity reasonable and persuasive is not its account of God's miraculous and supernatural effects, but its ethical effect on each one of us. . . . Since revealed truth cannot be adjudicated by the fallible intellect, it must be either discarded as a serious prospect for thought and reflection, or left as an item of private conviction."[17] In other words, because revealed truth cannot be proven, the value of religion is therefore reduced to *ethics*. For Locke, supernaturalism gave way to ethics, for the reasonableness of Christianity is its ethical effect on human beings.

Enter Immanuel Kant (1724–1804), who, like his Enlightenment contemporaries, believed that reason held sway over all matters and had

---

a matter of confident optimism than a kind of desperation. In a world full of so much uncertainty, one would want to be able to argue compellingly for one's beliefs, including one's beliefs about God, and to be clear about the relation of one's own moral efforts to one's salvation." See Placher, *Domestication of Transcendence*, 5.

15. I guess this is the reason that John Locke's character on the television show *Lost* became a believer in the power of the island, for he *empirically observed* the way the strength in his legs was restored while on the island. However, given the historical philosopher's emphasis on science and empirical observation, I was never sure why his TV character is portrayed as the man of faith, in contrast to Jack Shepherd, the man of science.

16. Lose, *Confessing Jesus Christ*, 9–10.

17. Raschke, *Next Reformation*, 28. Raschke goes on to detail how Locke's empirical thought was appropriated as "commonsense realism," which then paved the way for the advent of fundamentalism in the early part of the twentieth century, along with the apologetics school of Christian thought that went with it.

the ability to make definitive judgments that could be deemed universally valid. Kant and Locke had many differences, particularly in relationship to what we might call phenomenology,[18] but for the task at hand it's necessary for me to emphasize that the two shared in common what each viewed as, rationally speaking, the only *possible* role of religion: its *ethical* value.

> In the aftermath of Kant much of popular Christianity in the Germany of the nineteenth century had reduced the gospel to the moral law. Kant himself had fostered this idea by effectively assimilating the transcendence of God to "transcendental" morality . . . *More than any other historical factor, Kant's moralizing of Christian revelation is behind what today we call theological liberalism.* . . . The Kantian heritage has been the progressive amalgamation of the Christian tradition into a Christian moral-view of the world. . . . Kant did away with the Reformation theme of personal trust in a personal God and replaced it with what he alternately dubbed "moral faith," "rational faith," or the "metaphysics of morals." Completing the Enlightenment project inaugurated by Descartes, Kant's critical philosophy rendered the transcendent God superfluous. The truth of God was the truth of reason. Religion must be circumscribed "within the limits of reason alone."[19]

So to state the obvious, during the period of the Enlightenment, reason became the primary means of gaining knowledge. This led both Locke and Kant, in their own respective ways, to place the primary value of religion not on claims about a supernatural being, but on *ethics*. But before we turn to what all of this means for the modern homiletical crisis, there is one more key figure we need to consider who is as influential, if not more so, than the ones we've named thus far: the philosopher G. W. F. Hegel (1770–1831).

At the risk of oversimplification, Hegel believed that God (or "Being" in the philosophical sense) was progressively unfolding in history as Absolute Spirit. For Hegel, concepts of truth (i.e., creation, God, the trinity, etc.) are not statically true, but are in the process of *becoming*

18. I am following Raschke, *Next Reformation*, 37–48. For Kant, "things are not merely as they appear to us; things are as we comprehend the factors and functions that enable them to appear in the first place." In other words, we perceive reality not simply as we naively see it, "but as a system of signs and sign-relations." What we experience cannot be automatically equivalent to what is.

19. Ibid., 44. Emphasis mine.

true.[20] History is progressing in a teleological way, which is to say toward a certain end or purpose. God (or Being) becomes incarnate in and through the thinking subject (human being). Thus, as history progressively unfolds, God becomes progressively incarnate in self-reflective humanity.[21] For Hegel, the fulcrum of history is seen in the incarnation of Christ. As Raschke summarizes: "The incarnation is simultaneously God becoming humanity, and humanity on its way to becoming God." Being is manifested as thought thinking itself. Human beings assume the role of God, and the more this process moves along, the more history progresses toward a positive end.

When we take into consideration the influence that Descartes, Locke, Kant, and Hegel (among others) had on the modern theological project, we can begin to understand the import of Nietzsche's infamous parable about the madman who announced the death of God. For Nietzsche, the announcement made by the madman was intended to dramatically show that the blood of the transcendent God was on the hands of the modern philosophical enterprise. While Nietzsche is rightly remembered as one of the central thinkers who showed us that all of our ideas about metaphysical truth are subject to interpretation, he also, just as importantly, showed us that the apotheosis of the human in the "progress" of the West is the fruition of God's "death."[22] Carl Raschke puts it this way:

> The absorption of Being into thought by nineteenth-century philosophy is the tactical key to extracting meaning from Nietzsche's infamous saying that "God is dead" . . . Nietzsche merely developed and promulgated such an outlandish proposition with his wild and provocative Dionysian style of writing. Nietzsche's intent all along was not to convince his readers that God did not exist, or that we shall all cease on naturalistic or atheistic grounds to believe in, and worship, God. Nietzsche regarded himself as a seer who was simply proclaiming a historical "fact" that philosophy itself had established: God is "dead," Nietzsche implied, because

---

20. It is no wonder that influential process theologians like to draw on Hegel. See especially Peter Hodgson's *Winds of the Spirit.* Caputo offers a nice introduction to Kant and Hegel during his online lecture "Radical Theology Part I." Huge props to Tripp Fuller for making several of Caputo's lectures available for free online at http://trippfuller.com/Caputo.

21. See Raschke, *Next Reformation,* 41.

22. Ibid., 89.

there is no longer any need to interpret God as anything apart
from our self-awareness.

   ... By acceding to the new metaphysical model of the divine
as immanent spirit, or as Being as thought thinking itself, we have
literally "killed" God. [In the words of Nietzsche's madman:] "All
of us are his murderers." ... Modern thought can be intimated as
Luciferian thought, insofar as it launches a kind of angelic rebellion against God as the infinite Other ... Nietzsche was not casting
an argument for nihilism. He was diagnosing what he viewed as
the monstrous secret of modernity—the concealed and ubiquitous
nihilism of the times, in consequence of modern civilization slay-
ing God.[23]

Notice the way nihilism works in Nietzsche's thought: Contrary to
popular opinion, nihilism is not the product of atheism, but rather of
apotheosis: human beings taking on the role of God and thus, by launch-
ing "*a kind of angelic rebellion against God as the infinite Other*," rendering
God obsolete.[24] "In present-day discussions," Raschke observes, "nihilism
is for the most part explicated as a kind of social and cultural malady
that is somehow carried and spread by freethinkers and various intel-
lectual extremists. It is often associated with sundry experiments in un-
reason, especially in the arts and in the realm of human behavior."[25] But
as Nietzsche writes, it is "an error to consider 'social distress' or 'physi-
ological degeneration' or, worse, corruption as the cause of nihilism. Ours
is the most decent and compassionate age. ... The radical repudiation of
value, meaning, and desirability [does not give birth to nihilism]. *Rather:
it is in one particular interpretation, the Christian-moral one, that nihilism
is rooted.*"[26] Nietzsche goes on to ask: "What does nihilism mean? That
the highest values devaluate themselves."

    According to Nietzsche, it is the Christian-moral worldview largely
propagated by Kant, coupled with Hegel's declaration that God becomes
fully immanent in humanity's thought/progression in history, that is

23. Ibid., 41–43.

24. Ibid., 43. Emphasis mine. To reiterate a point I made in the introduction: This is
why I concur with Caputo's critiques of Vattimo and, by extension, Altizer's death-of-
God theology: "Deconstruction would always worry about a divine kenosis that resulted
in filling up someone's pocket with the transferred goods of divinity." See Caputo's comments in Caputo and Vattimo, *After the Death of God*, 80.

25. Raschke, *Next Reformation*, 43.

26. Nietzsche, *Will to Power*, 7. Emphasis mine.

responsible for nihilism. In Raschke's words: "The triumph of a European 'Christian' civilization in the nineteenth century had reduced revelation to reason and faith to morality—the self-idolization of a dominant middle-class culture. . . . Western humanity had made an idol of God, and all idols, as the biblical prophets thundered, are dead matter, not the living God." Notice the reversal at work in Nietzsche's parable about the madman who makes the announcement that God is dead: it is the so-called believers taunting the madman in the marketplace who are the bona fide unbelievers. *For the highest values devaluate themselves.*[27]

When human beings take on the role of God, Nietzsche provocatively declared, God is rendered dead, for there is no reason to consider God as anything separate (*different*) from humanity's best intentions, ethical ideals, or subjective thoughts, however progressive they may or may not be. This is why Søren Kierkegaard, another venerable prophet of postmodernism, makes a similar point: "*The fundamental error of modern times lies in the fact that the yawning abyss of quality in the difference between God and man has been removed.*"[28] As Mark C. Taylor documents, the trajectory of Nietzsche's metaphorical proclamation of the death of God led the influential philosopher Martin Heidegger, yet another precursor of postmodernism, to speak of the ways in which human beings—no longer determined by an Other—become self-determining.

> What is decisive is that man himself expressly takes up this position as one constituted by himself, as he intentionally maintains that it is that taken up by himself, and that he makes it secure as the solid footing for a possible development of humanity. Now for the first time is there any such thing as a "position" of man. Man must depend upon himself . . . There begins that way of being human which means the realm of human capability as a domain given over to measuring and executing, for the purpose of gaining mastery over that which is as a whole.[29]

Of course, this is where the rubber begins to hit the road, especially in terms of the modern homiletical crisis. For no Western philosophers are more influential on liberal/progressive approaches to theology than

27. See Raschke, *Next Reformation*, 45.

28. Kierkegaard, *Journals*, 222. Emphasis mine.

29. Taylor, *After God*, 45. This will to mastery, for Heidegger, ultimately portends to nuclear holocaust. Taylor puts it this way: "In this absolute voluntarism, divine creativity becomes human destructiveness."

Kant and Hegel, the two primary targets of Nietzsche's critiques. As Taylor summarizes: "Theological liberalism is defined by a commitment to reconciling religious faith with reason as it is expressed in the natural and social sciences," which usually combines "a Kantian interpretation of morality with a Hegelian view of history."[30]

The influence of Kant's moralism and Hegel's progressive view of history is easily seen in the leading figures of the emergence of Protestant liberalism: academicians like Albrecht Ritschl and Adolf von Harnack, as well as stalwart pastors like Harry Emerson Fosdick and Walter Rauschenbusch. No longer bound to belief in a supernatural being as the primary component of Christianity, such figures emphasized the way ethical actions would lead to the progressive realization of the kingdom of God in history. Ritschl, for example, echoed both the Christian moralism of Kant and the optimistic view of history described by Hegel by emphasizing the ways in which, through fulfilling one's secular vocation through the love of neighbor, the kingdom of God is progressively realized.[31] Von Harnack followed suit by stating that the faithful are "active agents whose love contributes to the arrival of the earthly kingdom in which the universal brotherhood of man becomes a reality."[32] The same influences can be heard in Rauschenbusch, who viewed the goodness of human beings as capable of ushering in the kingdom: "Rather than the fallen realm of sin and corruption, history is the stage for humankind's gradual progress toward a just and equitable society in which greed and competition give way to benevolence and cooperation."[33] While reflecting on modern approaches to preaching in general and Fosdick's homiletic in particular, Kay Northcutt observes a reliance on "Liberal theology's naive belief in the foundational goodness of the human person,"[34] which is capable of fixing the world's problems. From this vantage point, "God or his activity is immanent in the world and human beings are good if not actually divine."[35]

30. Ibid., 188–89.

31. Ibid., 189.

32. Ibid., 190.

33. Ibid.

34. Northcutt, *Kindling Desire for God*, 42. As Northcutt asks, "when the human condition becomes a problem to be solved for which [modern] science and psychology offer the cure, is there any need for God?" See her *Kindling Desire for God*, 48.

35. Taylor, *After God*, 200.

While some modern theorists believed that religion would natu-
rally fade away as humanity "progressed," others thought that religion
could remain viable so long as it could be understood apart from its
more primitive associations with magic and superstition.[36] As Jeffrey
Robbins explains:

> Our increased technological proficiency and scientific knowl-
> edge were thought to translate into a decreased dependency on
> outdated religious beliefs in God and supernaturalism. Indeed,
> the most prominent Enlightenment philosopher of them all,
> Immanuel Kant, defined the very project of Enlightenment by this
> most fundamental of all modern assumptions when he wrote that
> Enlightenment is the release from all forms of self-incurred tute-
> lage. . . . According to Kant, the enlightened subject would be one
> who could think for himself, and one in whom religion might still
> play a part, but only in the private sphere of morality.[37]

As time went by, Protestant liberalism responded to the
Enlightenment through theological approaches such as Paul Tillich's
ground of being, Alfred North Whitehead's process philosophy, and
Thomas Altizer's death-of-God theology (among other options), but the
import of the Enlightenment held sway: The Wholly Other (infinite) col-
lapsed into the Wholly Same (finite), so much so that, in the words of
Mark C. Taylor, most of the liberal theological approaches in response
to the Enlightenment lead to a God that "becomes so immanent as to
disappear."[38] As such, Nietzsche's indictment of modern philosophy
proved true for modern theology as well—even approaches to theology
that developed well after his death. This is one of the primary reasons Karl
Barth viewed religion not as humanity's greatest accomplishment but its
most profound sin, for it encourages individuals to "forget the qualitative

36. Taylor notes that secularism is actually a religious phenomenon.

37. Caputo and Vattimo, *After the Death of God*, 12.

38. See Taylor, *After God*, 35. For those interested in Barth's concerns regarding this matter, which are related to his reading of Ludwig Feuerbach, see Willimon,
Conversations with Barth on Preaching, 12ff. "What Barth most liked in Feuerbach,"
Willimon explains, "was not his notorious idea that Christianity was a mere projection
of human religious yearnings, but rather Feuerbach's bald reduction of theology to nothing but anthropology, thus typifying the fate of most theology of the age. . . . Feuerbach
furthered a process that began in Kant. Feuerbach merely exposed theology's nasty little
secret: it had become more interested in humanity than God."

distinction between man and God."[39] Modern theology, Barth decided, "had been misguided ever since Schleiermacher turned his gaze from the heavens to the earth and proclaimed that God, man, and world are one. The belief that God is immanent in the universe and the kingdom of God emerges historically through human actions commits the sin of idolatry by confusing the Infinite with the finite."[40]

It's little wonder that preaching entered a period of intense scrutiny throughout the twentieth century (from which we are yet to recover). Emphasis was no longer placed on God as "other" (not to mention the activity and agency that God as other might exert), but rather on the ethical implications of the Christian message. By the 1960s, secularism was the norm, even among students of preaching. For many seminary students in the post-60s era, John McClure observes, "preaching was accepted as patently unreasonable in a world come of age. Activism, not wordplay, was the order of the day. It was as if activists trusted that through their immersion in secular reason and secular reality they would discover something of the God who had died there."[41] Seminary students in the 1960s, Fred Craddock recalls, were too busy painting signs for the protests in town to critically reflect on the task of preaching, and they didn't view it as a valuable or important form of ministry. He memorably describes his first days as a professor of preaching this way:

> I was aware in 1965 of the revolution of the '60s—a social revolution, a sexual revolution, a drug revolution—and the establishment of Berkeley, California, as the new capital of the New America. What I was not aware of was how deeply the revolution had made an attack on tradition and authority, which included the pulpit. Among my students, I heard a lot of things, none of them complimentary. It was only my first semester, my first attempt to teach preaching, and one of the first things said at the beginning of the course was, "Professor, I guess you know that preaching is for dorks, for the ones who can't do anything better." Students were anticipating ministries, but ministries that had no pulpits. Protests, social action, civic change—those were the orders of the day and that's the world into which I moved.
>
> . . . The students were in favor of changing the course in preaching from a requirement to an elective. Seminaries across the coun-

39. Taylor, *After God*, 194.

40. Ibid., 192.

41. McClure, *Other-wise Preaching*, 81–82.

try dropped preaching entirely from the catalog. Once in a while a school would, under pressure from a few of the dorks, have a retired pastor from the community come out on Friday afternoon and share a few toothless reminiscences of his ministry. And that was homiletics.[42]

Activism became the rule of the day in modern preaching largely because God was no longer identified as anything other than a projection of the best intentions and ideals of the human spirit, if anything at all, and religion was reduced to activism (an important part of religion no doubt, but not the only part of it). When one considers the import of Kant and Hegel on liberal theology, it's no coincidence that sermons that fall prey to the modern homiletical crisis (1) place primary emphasis on a Christianity that is boiled down to ethics (what human beings must do) and (2) lose sight of the infinite qualitative distinction between God (the wholly other) and human beings. When God is just a manifestation or extension of our best selves on our best days, when there is no infinite qualitative distinction between human beings and the "wholly other," then God is, for all practical purposes, *dead.*

With theorists like Kierkegaard, Heidegger, and Barth in mind, the philosopher Merold Westphal has argued that so long as there is an infinite, qualitative difference between God and ourselves, one can fall on one's knees in awe and wonder before God (lost in wonder, love, and praise). But when (as in the most dominant expressions of the modern homiletical crisis) God is relegated to the best of humanity's ideas, ideals, industry, and ethical intentions; when God must always be contained within human categories of reason; when God's actions are limited only to the actions and thoughts of human beings; when Christianity is reduced to moralism and the best intentions of the human spirit—in short, when that which we call God is no longer "other" but rather an expression of our best selves on our best days—then, as Nietzsche portends, we have placed God at our disposal, at the beck and call of human understanding. Westphal quips: "But there is no awe, or singing, or dancing before such a factotum. And if there is any clapping, it will have the form of polite applause: 'Please join me in welcoming the *Ultima Ratio.*'"[43]

---

42. Craddock, "Inductive Preaching Renewed," 41–43.
43. Westphal, "Overcoming Onto-theology," 153.

But that is only part of the story. In order to understand the modern homiletical crisis most fully, particularly the way it commonly plays out today, we have to pay attention to contemporary approaches to progressive theology that also find their roots in modern philosophy and theology—specifically in relationship to the modern breakdown of superstition and supernaturalism, which is even more influential on the modern homiletical crisis than what I've described so far. As progressives, I contend that we have no business preaching sermons that are not much more than grandiose proclamations of our best selves on our best days, unless of course we wish to beat God, and perhaps ourselves, to death.

THE DEATH OF GOD, PART II

When progressive Christians talk with those who are suspect of Christianity—or with those who can't figure out for the life of them how a seemingly thinking person can believe in God—progressives often draw on a quote that Harry Emerson Fosdick popularly used in his own conversations with atheists: "Tell me about the God you don't believe in." As Fosdick and others have repeatedly shown, the God that atheists go on to describe very rarely resembles the God that progressive Christians claim to believe in.[44]

Indeed, the idea of a supernatural God with magical powers, who sits somewhere in the heavens above like a (somewhat) benevolent Zeus, occasionally intervening in history to thwart a natural disaster or to make sure that only a handful of passengers are lucky enough to have their lives spared when the airplane goes down, is not, by and large, an operative image of God for progressives. For good reason, progressives have no interest in such a God. Most are repelled by such an image, and if it is representative of Christianity, they want nothing to do with it.

This is why the so-called new atheists drive progressives up the wall.[45] The God under attack by Richard Dawkins and company is never the God of progressive Christianity, and the new atheists consistently show either a blatant disregard or woeful ignorance of progressive approaches to Christianity. For instance, when Bill Maher (the host of HBO's television show *Real Time with Bill Maher*) ridicules Christians

44. For a good example of this, see Borg, *Speaking Christian,* 67–68.

45. New atheists include popular figures like Richard Dawkins, Sam Harris, Daniel Dennett, and the late Christopher Hitchens.

for believing that snakes can talk, or reduces miracle stories in the Bible to literal readings, it makes progressives want to pull their hair out and scream in frustration at their TVs: "C'mon, brother Bill! Tell me you know better! *Please*, tell me you know better!" And because progressives tend to *like* Maher so much, it makes us all the more frustrated. Rarely is a progressive like Cornel West on hand to hold Maher's rather banal understandings of Christianity to account, and it drives progressives crazy that Maher hardly ever invites progressive theologians or biblical scholars to be on his show (and that he didn't feature any of them in his otherwise entertaining film *Religulous*). This is similar, of course, to the lack of engagement—or utter ignorance—that the new atheists show as a whole toward non-fundamentalist (or non-tribal) approaches to Christianity.[46]

Like our Enlightenment predecessors, the new atheists view reason as the primary means of gaining knowledge, and if a proposition doesn't hold up to the standards of reason—which is to say, if a proposition can't be rationally proven or empirically verified—then it doesn't have any business playing a viable role in our lives. They go on to state that the main problem with religion—particularly religions of the West, including but not limited to Christianity—is that they posit belief in a supernatural God that can't hold up to rigorous investigation any more than believing in the Easter Bunny can, and thus any rational human being should discard belief in God altogether. Such beliefs, they maintain, are nothing but childish superstitions that lead to terrible ethical practices done in the name of religion.

And progressive Christians generally agree. In fact, it is difficult for progressives and new atheists to have a "debate" about Christianity. As Tillich surmised, those on both sides of the debate are often not even at odds with one another: "For many centuries the leading theologians and philosophers were almost equally divided between those who attacked and those who defended the arguments for the existence of God. Neither group prevailed over the other in a final way. This situation admits only one explanation: the one group did not attack what the other group

---

46. Moreover, it should be noted that the God under assault by the new atheists (and sometimes by progressives as well) should not be equated with the "God of classical theism," which unfortunately functions as a kind of catch-all phrase for our negative views related to supernatural theism. The Christian tradition is much more nuanced and refined. See esp. Placher, *Domestication of Transcendence*, 7ff. Chris Hedges' *I Don't Believe in Atheists* offers a nice response to the new atheists, as does Robbins and Rodkey's "Beating God to Death."

defended. They were not divided by a conflict over the same matter."[47] The words of Bishop John A. T. Robinson, an Anglican priest who was one of the most influential mainline voices of the twentieth century, resonate with progressives: "Indeed, many who are Christians find themselves on the same side as those who are not. . . . [N]ot infrequently, as I watch or listen to a broadcast discussion between a Christian and a humanist, I catch myself realizing that most of my sympathies are on the humanist's side."[48] In a much more recent example, Fred Plumer, Executive Director of the Center for Progressive Christianity, explicitly sings his praises to Richard Dawkins: "I love Richard Dawkins! I never met the man, but I still love him and I am glad that he continues to get the press he seems to generate. The funny thing is that I agree with much of what he says . . ."[49]

Progressives have no interest in defending the views of the straw man God that the new atheists set up, and the new atheists, for reasons that remain lost on me, don't regard other images of God as being worth having a thoughtful conversation about. At one point along the way, Sam Harris does acknowledge that he doesn't have any quarrels with Paul Tillich's "blameless parish of one," clearly oblivious of the fact that no one has been more influential than Tillich in the shaping of mainline Protestant theology over the last half-century.[50]

Meanwhile, progressive Christians on the pews often feel conflicted. They are curiously drawn to books by both John Shelby Spong and Richard Dawkins, by both Anne Lamott and Sam Harris. Many fit under the umbrella described by *New York Times* columnist David Brooks, for they are "quasi-religious people [who] read the Bible, but find large parts of it odd and irrelevant. They find themselves inextricably bound to their faith, but think some of the people who define it are nuts."[51]

Unlike their clergy counterparts, however, progressives on the pews usually haven't had a chance to learn about alternatives to the problematic images of God referenced by the new atheists. In large part, this is because either (1) they haven't had access to the kind of theological education a pastor gets at a standard mainline seminary, or (2) pastors have done

---

47. Tillich, *Systematic Theology*, 1:204.
48. Robinson, *Honest to God*, 8.
49. Plumer, "I Love Richard Dawkins!"
50. See Harris, *End of Faith*, 65.
51. Quoted in Robbins, "Religion for the Rest of Us."

an inadequate job communicating alternative theological possibilities to their congregants. While Thomas Long gives clergy the benefit of the doubt in regard to the latter,[52] he also acknowledges that perhaps part of the problem is that the clergy themselves are in the same position as their laypeople: "Clergy swim in the same cultural stream as everyone else, and many clergy too are unsure of the trustworthiness of the church's language about God, perplexed about what to make of the scriptures and the theological traditions of the church, and they hardly know where to turn for help."[53]

No one denies that the import of the Enlightenment has challenged Christians to rethink the way they approach categories of belief, and both progressives and new atheists readily agree that the superstitions associated with the premodern era have no place in a post-Enlightenment world. Given this context, Long notes that many thoughtful people today "wonder if being a person of faith is foolish in a scientific age. Out of loyalty to clear-headed, scientific thinking, they put away the 'childish things' of faith and walk away, albeit with a wistful backward glance."[54] We have been caught in the sweep of modernity, in which "religious belief was in various ways denounced as *unreal*, 'unmasked' as a fantastic, escapist, reactionary superstition, a fiction woven from our unconscious, our weakness, or our guilt, that hard-nosed Newtonians and all too positive positivists were trying to drive out of our heads."[55]

Peter Rollins points out how the modern context gave rise to Dietrich Bonhoeffer's radical rethinking of Christianity. Bonhoeffer was one of the first major theologians to take Nietzsche's critiques seriously. While in prison, he started to sketch the move toward a "religionless Christianity":

> Interestingly, Bonhoeffer does not attack religion as such. However he reflects that in the 20th century (though he sees it beginning in the 17th century) religion has become possible for less and

52. "Many clergy yearn for their parishioners to be well-informed, deeply committed disciples," Long writes, "but they simply do not know how [in their preaching and teaching] to convey the life-giving, freeing, passionate, white-water adventure that is to be found in the scriptures, creeds, traditions, theological explorations, and practices of the Christian community. So they leave these questing parishioners to follow their own noses." See Long, *Preaching from Memory to Hope*, 63.

53. Ibid.

54. Ibid., 33.

55. Caputo, *On Religion*, 91.

less people because it has been problematical. Not because it has changed but because human beings have entered into a different epoch (my words not his, he talks of "man come of age"). In this new historical situation a religious expression of Christianity places God at the edges of human life as the *Deus ex machina*. Why? Because religion, for Bonhoeffer, is the belief in a metaphysical absolute from which everything hangs (onto-theology), and as human knowledge increases the more things in our existence do not require this metaphysical explanation. Religion is now exposed as advocating a God of the gaps. In addition to this the God of religion is only for those who feel a need to ask the metaphysical question, "Why," and in a "world come of age," this question is asked by fewer and fewer (a Nietzschian point par excellence).

. . . His [*Letters and Papers from Prison*] are clearly marked by a serious reading of Nietzsche and can thus be seen as one of the early theological attempts to reflect on what faith looks like after "the death of God." In these letters he imagines a church radically transformed, one which rethinks, at a core (ontological) level, its purpose and expression.[56]

It should also be noted that the Enlightenment's rejection of superstition and supernaturalism is not the only reason that progressives have difficulty believing in a supernatural Supreme Being governing the cosmos. Just as problematic is the difficulty of reconciling a good God with the horrible atrocities of the twentieth century, which made a mockery of the confident optimism associated with the modern period. It's not surprising that by the time Walter Rauschenbusch's *Theology for the Social Gospel* was published in 1917, as a follow-up to his pre-World War I *Christianity and the Social Crisis* (1907), which first introduced readers to his idea of the Social Gospel, "the scheme for interpreting God, self, and world developed in Protestant liberalism seemed naive if not pernicious."[57] Part of what makes Bonhoeffer's letters from a Nazi prison so compelling is that he was directly responding to the moral crisis of the twentieth century, which his martyrdom at the hands of a "Christian" Germany directly exposed. "Bonhoeffer's words and observations," Jeffrey Robbins writes, "came to the world as a prophetic voice from the grave and became the link, on the one hand, to a world-weary faith in shock and horror at its own moral failure and impotence and, on the other hand, an emergent re-

56. Rollins, "Religion, Fundamentalism and Christianity."
57. Taylor, *After God*, 190.

ligious and cultural sensibility that was now forced to pick up the broken pieces and to imagine, if not craft, an alternative future in the wake of the death of God and after the collapse of Christendom."[58] The words of political philosophers Antonio Negri and Michael Hardt weigh heavily upon us, as they should: "Modern negativity is located not in any transcendent realm but in the hard reality before us: the fields of patriotic battles in the First and Second World Wars, from the killing fields at Verdun to the Nazi furnaces and the swift annihilation of thousands in Hiroshima and Nagasaki, the carpet bombing of Vietnam and Cambodia, the massacres from Setif and Soweto to Sabra and Shatila, and the list goes on and on. There is no Job who can sustain such suffering."[59]

Scholars such as Marcus Borg have tried to prepare a highway in the desert for Christians who don't want to throw the baby out with the bathwater, but the options described by Borg and other progressive writers sometimes reinforce the very problems at the roots of the modern homiletical crisis. While they certainly offer a much better alternative to images of God than the ones described by the new atheists, the alternatives presented still remain wedded to modern foundations that hinder progressive preaching from moving forward.[60]

In his books *Speaking Christian* and *The Heart of Christianity*, Borg describes two basic approaches to the divine that are found in Christian tradition, beginning in the Bible and coexisting in Christianity ever since.

---

58. Caputo and Vattimo, *After the Death of God*, 8.

59. Negri and Hardt, *Empire*, 46. Cf. Pablo Jiménez's comments in *Renewed Homiletic*: "Jean-François Lyotard, the French sociologist, defines postmodernity as an attitude of incredulity toward the master narratives or narrative archetypes that sustained the modern world. These master narratives legitimized the crimes of modernity, crimes such as the violent conquest of America, the genocide against indigenous peoples, slavery, the oppression of women, and racism, among many others. Such crimes ultimately decried the basic tenets of modernity. The rationalistic view of life, with its blind faith on progress, did not lead us to a better world. No, it led us to Auschwitz; it led us to a nuclear standoff; it led us to a polluted and decaying world. For these reasons, Lyotard affirms that Auschwitz is 'the crime that opens postmodernity.'" See "Response to David Buttrick," 117.

60. I write this with great trepidation, because Marcus Borg is such a hero of the faith for me, and always will be. He helped me imagine ways of understanding God that kept me in the ball game, and here I feel as if I've taken on the role of a minor leaguer trying to tell Hank Aaron what is wrong with his swing. Please note that while Thomas Long also critiques Borg in a chapter titled "Reading Marcus Borg Again for the First Time" (*Preaching from Memory to Hope*, 79–110), I am not offering the same critique, as will become clear.

The first is what he calls "supernatural theism," which imagines God as a personlike being who exists as a being beyond the universe, or another being in addition to the universe. "God is an exceedingly superlative personlike being, is indeed the supreme being."[61] This view holds that a long time ago, God created the world as something separate from God, which leads to the conclusion that God is "up in heaven" or "out there." This supernatural God occasionally intervenes in the world. From a Christian perspective, these interventions include supernatural things like virgin births and miracles. This is the kind of God rejected by the new atheists, and many progressives as well.

The second way of thinking about God, Borg writes, is panentheism (literally, "God in everything"). "Rather than imagining God as a personlike being 'out there,' this concept imagines God as the *encompassing Spirit* in whom everything that is, is. The universe is not separate from God, but *in* God."[62] Borg connects this approach to Tillich's language about God as "ultimate realty," "the ground of being," and "being-itself."[63]

While Borg is clear in stating that no concept of God is adequate— neither supernatural theism nor panentheism—he claims that the latter is certainly better: "More expansive and less constricting, it avoids the limitations that have made supernatural theism problematic or impossible for many."[64]

Indeed, a panentheistic way of describing God offers a persuasive alternative for progressives who struggle to imagine God as a type of supernatural being who resides somewhere beyond the universe and occasionally intervenes as necessary, and it's certainly the case that theological approaches based on Tillich's thought usually resonate with progressives who aren't necessarily comfortable holding on to supernatural, magical conceptions of the deity. Caputo has said that the permanent debt we owe to Tillich is the recognition that "to think clearly about religion, you have to clear your head of supernaturalism and magic,"[65] and the same holds true for theorists like Borg. Given the options of supernatural theism and panentheism, I'd go with panentheism every time.

61. Borg, *Heart of Christianity*, 65.

62. Ibid., 66.

63. Ibid., 69.

64. Borg, *Speaking Christian*, 74.

65. As quoted in Caputo and Vattimo, *After the Death of God*, 144.

Yet a handful of concerns remain, at least in terms of the modern homiletical crisis. Perhaps the best way to understand how this is the case is by taking a look at one of the best-selling mainline books of all time, Bishop John A. T. Robinson's *Honest to God*, published in 1963. In many ways, *Honest to God* can be seen as a precursor to the kinds of popular books on religion authored by figures like Marcus Borg and John Shelby Spong, as well as to popular progressive Christian curriculums like *Living the Questions*, for it is designed to help bridge the "growing gulf between the traditional orthodox supernaturalism in which our Faith has been framed and the categories which the 'lay' world (for want of a better term) finds meaningful today."[66]

With Tillich in mind, Robinson highlights the existential implications of Christian theology and argues that "assertions about God are in the last analysis assertions about Love—about the ultimate ground and meaning of personal relationships."[67] They "are acknowledgments of the transcendent, unconditional element in all our relationships, and supremely in our relationships with other persons. Theological statements are . . . affirmations about human existence—but they are affirmations about the ultimate ground and depth of that existence."[68] Robinson recognizes that he is walking a tightrope: "[W]e must agree that in a real sense Feuerbach was right in wanting to translate 'theology' into 'anthropology' . . . Yet it is also clear that we are here on very dangerous ground," for to say "that 'theology is nothing else than anthropology' means that 'the knowledge of God is nothing else than the knowledge of man.'"[69] Robinson repeatedly attempts to overcome this concern, yet when he continues to relegate God to the ultimacy of personal relationships, it becomes difficult to avoid substituting anthropological assertions for theological ones. He admits that his view is closely linked to the one held by Rudolf Bultmann, who once boasted to Karl Barth: "I *am* trying to substitute anthropology for theology, for I am interpreting theological affirmations as assertions about human life."[70]

---

66. Robinson, *Honest to God*, 8.

67. Ibid., 104.

68. Ibid., 52.

69. Ibid., 50.

70. Ibid.

As much as the alternative of panentheism articulated by Borg (and in large part based on the perspectives voiced by Tillich) is appealing to progressives, it subtly reinforces one of the primary causes of the modern homiletical crisis: the lack of an infinite qualitative distinction between human beings and God. To recall the words of Mark C. Taylor, Tillich's image of God repeats the mistakes of modernism by disappearing through immanence: If "God is Being or, in Tillich's terms, 'the power of Being,' then everything that exists is, in some way, united with the divine . . . God, in other words, is immanent in self and world."[71] Because difference is a negative concept for Tillich, the estrangement and alienation between God and human beings "can be overcome only through the recognition of a more primal unity that is always present beneath or behind every form of separation." From this perspective, unity with the divine is never really absent. Such an approach, Taylor concludes, "revises the biblical narrative by erasing its primal distinction between creator and creature."[72] When progressives are left to choose between the two conceptions of God summarized by Borg and other progressive writers, it makes it difficult to find a way past the modern homiletical crisis. On the one hand, the supernatural God of theism is a concept that progressives hardly wish to embrace, for it is a version of a cosmic Santa Claus that has much more to do with magic and superstition than anything else. On the other hand, a panentheistic approach runs the risk of the "wholly other" (infinite) collapsing into the "wholly same" (finite), thus repeating the apotheosis of modernism that is the source of Nietzsche's proclamation of the death of God.[73]

When progressive preachers dismiss the supernatural God of theism as irrelevant but maintain an image of God that is more congruent with panentheism, then it is only natural for progressive sermons to lack significant discussion of the activity and agency of God, for panentheism

71. Taylor, *After God*, 35.

72. Ibid., 36. It is perhaps here that Protestant liberalism comes full circle.

73. Notice the way that Plumer's reduction of progressive Christianity to ethics leads to a collapse of transcendence: "What did Jesus mean? We have no way of knowing, but I suspect he meant something very different than what we normally perceive. I believe it is far more likely that he told his followers that by living a certain way, by extending themselves on behalf of others, by loving generously, for example, they too could experience Alaha ('God' according to Neal Douglas-Klotz, an Aramaic scholar.) Douglas-Klotz suggests that his Alaha term would best be translated as *Sacred Unity, All-ness* or *Oneness*." Plumer, "I Love Richard Dawkins!"

does not view God in an interventionist way (this is why those in progressive circles often say that it is up to human beings to do the "godding" because "God only becomes real through our actions"), or to lack significant emphasis on God as "wholly other," for in panentheism God becomes so immanent as to disappear (there is no longer any qualitative distinction between human beings and God). Hence, images of God related to panentheism become just as irrelevant as those related to supernatural theism. When the supernatural God of theism is written off as superstitious and primitive (and therefore not to be taken seriously), and when the God of panentheism doesn't function as an "other," the two seemingly opposite approaches end up functioning as flip sides of the same coin, at least in terms of the activity and agency of God.

Here the prescient words with which John A. T. Robinson ends the preface to *Honest to God* serve as a nice transition: "What I have tried to say, in a tentative and exploratory way, may seem to be radical, and doubtless to many heretical. The one thing of which I am fairly sure is that, in retrospect, it will be seen to have erred in not being nearly radical enough."[74]

GOD WITHOUT BEING, BEING WITHOUT GOD

One of the primary reasons that progressives struggle to celebrate the activity harbored in the name of God is that—as the postmodern return of religion contends—our concepts of God are generally tied to problematic views of *being*. As we have seen, God is usually viewed as a grand supernatural Supreme Being *up there* (the conventional transcendent way of putting it), or God is viewed in more immanent and panentheistic ("God is *in* everything") terms that envision God as the "ground of all being" or "being-itself." Progressives find the former view un-believable and incredible, yet when they turn to the latter, God gets confused for everything that *is*, and God's transcendence (i.e., *difference*) is subsequently lost.

Peter Rollins describes how conditioned we are to think about God only in terms of being, and how difficult it is for us to imagine God otherwise: "This way of thinking about the source of faith is so embedded in our thinking that it often seems impossible for us to consider the possibility that the source and truth of faith is something other than the object of contemplation. It seems ridiculous for us to even postulate the

74. Robinson, *Honest to God*, 10.

possibility of this source's being made manifest as existing beyond the categories of something and nothing, of this source's manifesting itself as *some(no)thing.*"[75]

Yet that is precisely what several theorists who identify with the post-modern return to religion contend. Instead of imagining God in terms of Being, a more postmodern approach to God is *otherwise than Being.* This approach transcends conventional (ontotheological) understandings of God, because God, or, better, the event that is harbored in the name of God, is not to be understood on the plane of "presence" or "existence" or "substance" or "entity" or "being," whether transcendent or immanent.[76] It's not the kind of "thing" that can be proven to exist or not to exist, for it is not a thing at all—it is not on the realm of existence.[77] The event harbored in the name of God doesn't exist, it insists. If a homiletic of the event is viewed as a "communal proclamation of prayer and praise for the advent of the wholly other," based of course on the interpretation of texts within the context of worship, then it is only possible from a *spectral* perspective, which, as we will explore in the next chapter, is at the heart of deconstruction. Emphasizing spectrality is crucial because—as much as I appreciate Karl Barth's critiques of Protestant liberalism—I don't want to be confused for a type of liberal Barthian who tends to understand God as an outside agent that intervenes in the world. The transcendence at the heart of a homiletic of the event is a *weak* transcendence at best, precisely because it doesn't turn on an outside "agent" (or an agent of any kind, for that matter, whether "inside" or "outside" the cosmos, including the God of *hyperousia* as described in negative theology). When I speak of the "activity and agency" of God that is the focus of celebration in a homiletic of the event, it is in an effort to reconnect transcendence with an unapologetic materialism, not to posit an agent on the plane of being that intervenes in the daily affairs of life. This isn't to say that a homiletic

75. Rollins, *Fidelity of Betrayal*, 87.

76. See especially Caputo and Scanlon, *Transcendence and Beyond*.

77. As Caputo writes: "With Tillich, I displace the notion of God as a *summum ens* or an *ens omnipotens* who can intervene in the course of natural events, as supernaturalism; but I also displace the notion of God as the Being of beings, or ground of Being as ontologism, and I locate the properly deconstructive or postmodern element of radical theology in God, or rather the event that transpires in the name of God, taken as the claim made upon us unconditionally but without force, physical or metaphysical, ontical or ontological. That might be called 'a death of God' theology, but . . . I take that to be a misleading description." See Caputo and Vattimo, *After the Death of God*, 185–86.

of the event precludes belief in a God of being—whether or not such a God exists, Derrida says, deconstruction cannot say—but I do wish to emphasize that it turns on spectrality, not on presence or existence.[78] A spectral approach, Caputo emphasizes, represents not a loss but a gain, especially in a post-Enlightenment context:

> The abstention that constitutes the diminished state of my the-
> ology—God is neither a supreme being nor being itself, neither
> ontic nor ontological, neither the cause of beings nor the ground
> of being—represents not a loss but a gain. Blessed are the weak!
> By untying the name of God from the order of being, it releases
> the event, sets free the provocation of this name, which dissemi-
> nates in every direction, setting it free as a vocative force, as an
> evocative, provocative event, rather than confining its force to the
> strictures of naming a present entity. I approach God neither as a
> supreme entity whose existence could be proven or disproved or
> even said to hang in doubt, nor as the horizon of being itself or its
> ground, either of which would lodge God more deeply still in the
> onto-theological circuit that circles between being and beings . . .
> for God is not being or a being but a ghostly quasi-being, a very
> holy spirit.[79]

In the next chapter, I will unpack what is meant by ideas such as spectrality and the event (particularly through the lens of Caputo), and we will discover why a homiletic of the event resonates with those who, like Derrida, rightly pass for atheists—as well as with progressive Christians who are, on the one hand, uncomfortable associating conceptions of God with supernaturalism and magic and, on the other hand, find themselves struggling to articulate images of God as that which is "other."

78. See Caputo, *Prayers and Tears of Jacques Derrida*, 333ff.

79. Caputo, *Weakness of God*, 9.

4

Religulous?

Postmodern deconstruction is not the world-denying, radically skeptic, and antireligious movement that its detractors made it out to be. On the contrary, it can only be understood by recognizing its animating and fundamentally affirmative passion, its radical and unconditional Yes to the promise of life.

—Jeffrey Robbins[1]

[E]veryone became great in proportion to his expectancy. One became great by expecting the possible, another by expecting the eternal; but he who expected the impossible became the greatest of all.

—Søren Kierkegaard[2]

AT A TIME WHEN the most conventional images of God in modernity were regarded to be little more than a projection of humanity's highest impulses ("humanity said loudly," to paraphrase Barth); at a time when philosophers emphasized that all of us make interpretations from different vantage points (it's not possible to have access to the God's-eye view of things); at a time when metaphysics (unchanging universal truths that can be accessed by human beings) were proclaimed to be "dead" (in large part because of Nietzsche's recognition that there is no "truth," only interpretation); at a time when religion was castigated as the opiate of the masses,

1. Caputo and Vattimo, *After the Death of God*, 18–19.
2. Kierkegaard's pseudonym Johannes de Silentio, as quoted in Caputo, *Prayers and Tears of Jacques Derrida*, xvi.

or a crutch we would do well to get rid of; at a time when it seemed that God was no more than a relic of the past—in such a time as this, no one expected God to make a comeback. For all practical purposes, God was dead. *The City of God* had given way to *The Secular City*.

Which is precisely what makes the most surprising feature of contemporary religious thought the most ironic: What nobody saw coming, what caught everyone by surprise, is that the influence of Nietzsche's proclamation of the death of God, which was supposed to put the final nail in the coffin of the old God,[3] actually opened up religious faith in fresh, inventive ways. In the wake of Nietzsche's proclamation of the death of God, which included the death of metaphysics and most of the things that otherwise sensible people have long associated with religion, God came back again, *otherwise*: "Levinas's God of Infinity, Derrida's and Caputo's *tout autre* (wholly other), Marion's God without Being, Kearney's God who may be."[4]

In this chapter, we'll explore the unexpected: Quite simply, how in the world did God make a comeback in postmodernity, and how does God's resurgence matter for contemporary preachers? To be sure, the idea that God was "dead" and is now "alive" is not intended to put a linear (literal) timeline on the history of God (though the language of death and resurrection does have a nice ring to it); rather, it is to say that in the latter half of the twentieth century, several highly influential philosophers shifted the way they viewed the role of religion, as well as the way they used language about God, and those of us in the more established Christian traditions were presented with fresh ways of imagining and interpreting the activity of God—as well as engaging in Christian discourse—that were previously unavailable, and we've been trying to catch up ever since.[5] It

---

3. See esp. Caputo and Scanlon, *God, the Gift, and Postmodernism*, 4–5.

4. Manoussakis, *After God*, xv.

5. Most philosophers are quick to point out that they aren't doing anything altogether new, but are simply following in a long line of venerated (as well as a few not-so-venerated) theorists down through the ages. When Caputo describes his theology of the event, he acknowledges the bipolarity of the history of theology (its love affair with power in contrast to what he calls with St. Paul the weakness of God), but he also describes the way "the long history of 'theology' (which, however venerable a name, has like the rest of us to stay on guard against hubris) has been an ongoing work of deconstructing the name of God in order to release the event that stirs within that name." Related to this is the way Caputo and Derrida view a text or tradition as always in flux: "it keeps 'happening' (*arriver*) without ever quite 'arriving' at a final, fixed, and finished destination." As such, the

was assumed that the end of metaphysics would spell the end of religion, or at least any viable notion of God, and that is why theologians from established seminaries and divinity schools tried to figure out what kind of role, if any, theology and the church could play in the newfound secular city. But just as progressives were preparing their eulogies for the old God, just as they were striking up the *requiem aeternam dei*, the death of metaphysics unexpectedly left the door open—unhinged, if you will—for the "wholly other" to emerge once again. "For who are we to drink up the sea? Who gave us the sponge to wipe away the entire horizon?"

The trajectory we'll take in this chapter can be summarized by two questions Jeffrey Robbins poses coupled with a follow-up question of my own:

(1) "How do we get from the post-Christian, post-Holocaust, and largely secular death-of-God theologies of the 1960s to the postmodern return of religion?"

(2) "How is it that this question of the return of religion is transmitted not by theologians and/or religious leaders but by and through philosophers and cultural theorists who heretofore had little or no expressed interest in religious or theological questions?"[6]

(3) How does the postmodern return of religion influence the way that progressives understand homiletics—particularly in terms of finding a way beyond the modern homiletical crisis?

As we will see, Nietzsche's infamous proclamation of the death of God, paradoxically speaking, serves as a certain opening to God (*adieu*)—an opening that time and again lays bare our idols, pretensions, and conceptions of God, an opening that encourages us to preach *after* that which is beyond all of our names, categorizations, and conceptions, an opening that draws us to the wholly other, "for whose coming, like teary-eyed old Augustine, deconstruction always prays and weeps."[7]

Christian tradition (as if it is singular) is not so much something we "derive" but is rather an ongoing task that we do. This is in an effort to keep theology open, to allow a "certain drift or free play," which allows tradition "to be creative and reinvent itself so that it can be, as Augustine said of God, ever ancient and ever new." Likewise, a homiletic of the event doesn't jettison itself from tradition, but emerges in conversation with tradition. See Caputo, *What Would Jesus Deconstruct?*, 57–59.

6. See Robbins introduction to Caputo and Vattimo, *After the Death of God*, 12–13.

7. Caputo and Scanlon, *God, the Gift, and Postmodernism*, 5.

The main focus of this chapter is an introduction to prominent post-modern motifs like deconstruction, the event, and spectrality, which are central to a homiletic of the event. At the heart of each of these motifs, and at the same time at the heart of religion, is a love for the impossible.[8] For what is religion—what is deconstruction—if not a love for the advent of the impossible, the unconditional, the undeconstructible, where our hearts long to go with a desire beyond desire and a hope against hope?

In a homiletic of the event, we begin by the impossible, if we can begin at all.

BEGINNING BY THE IMPOSSIBLE

A love of the impossible seems a curious place to start, especially since post-Enlightenment listeners have been conditioned to think that Christianity is mostly about believing impossible things that don't make any sense, like the earth being only six thousand years old, or that a person can handle poisonous snakes without fear of being hurt. Such impossible things don't make much sense to post-Enlightenment listeners, as *The Daily Show* host Jon Stewart shows in his own version of Luke 10:19–21:

> And Jesus said "Behold, I give unto you power to tread on ser-pents and scorpions, and over all the power of the enemy: and nothing shall by any means hurt you." And Simon Peter was . . . curious, and cried "Lord! Does that mean we should pick up poi-sonous snakes in church, and shake them around?" So Jesus said, "Sure, go ahead," and his sarcasm was palpable. But when Jesus saw the disciples were writing his words down, he said "Wait—don't do that!"[9]

8. As we will soon see, Derrida's use of the phrase "the impossible" functions differ-ently than the way it is commonly used in everyday speech. For Derrida, the impossible points to what cannot be pointed to, to what we are unable to foresee in advance, to what takes us by surprise, like a thief in the night (cf. ch. 2, footnote 11). Derrida likes to think of God as the "becoming possible of the impossible," the experience (the "coming true") of what we could not imagine or foresee, "the coming of something we did not see com-ing, that takes us by surprise and tears up our horizon of expectation." This is also why, for Derrida, the least bad definition of deconstruction is an experience of the impossible. See esp. Caputo and Scanlon, *God, the Gift, and Postmodernism*, 3. In this chapter, we take up this idea through an analysis of democracy. Derrida's most famous example of this, which we take up in ch. 10, is his analysis of the gift.

9. Stewart, *Earth*, 152.

The first thing to clear up is that when deconstruction confesses a love of the impossible, it is to be understood differently than trying to hold together ideas that are logically incoherent, like how a square peg fits into a round hole or (to use my favorite example from a creation science museum in Tennessee) how dinosaurs with long sharp teeth were still vegetarians while living in the garden of Eden, which mostly amounts to nonsense. We can leave these questions to the after-midnight dorm room conversations at all the Christian colleges (or maybe the G.O.P. national conventions).

For Caputo and Derrida, religion is not about belief in The Way Things Are or What Being Is; rather, religion is viewed as a basic structure of human experience. Accordingly, religion is best thought not in terms of a description of metaphysical realities that constitute Eternal Truth, but rather in terms of a poetics, or a theo-poetics, that is astir with longing and hope and expectation. A love of the impossible is connected to a love of the unconditional, the undeconstructible, where our hearts long to go, even though we don't know the way, even though we may or may not believe in God.

There are certain words, Derrida and Caputo like to point out, that are pregnant with possibility, with hope, with affirmation—words like *justice* and *democracy*, *forgiveness* and *gift*, to name but a few of their favorite examples. These words have a performative function on our lives, particularly because *they contain what they cannot contain*. Derrida is known for saying things like "My friends, there are no friends" or "My fellow democrats, there are no democrats." Unfortunately, this often leads people to mistake Derrida for saying there is no such thing as friendship or democracy and that we should all resign ourselves in hopeless despair and give up on such categories altogether. But this is to miss the affirmation at the heart of his thought, and it represents so much of the bad press that Derrida has received over the years. Allow me to quote Caputo at length in this chapter, for he is better than anyone else at explaining deconstruction in a nutshell.[10] In order to get our bearings, we'll begin with

10. This is a play on words Caputo likes to draw on that focuses on the idea in deconstruction that words contain what they cannot contain, so it is impossible to explain deconstruction in a nutshell, or to contain its meaning in a nutshell, which is the point, in a nutshell. See Caputo's *Deconstruction in a Nutshell* for a fantastic introduction to deconstruction.

the example of democracy, but we'll soon turn our attention to theology's main subject, God, which is when things really get going.

> [Derrida] once wrote an essay that cited Montaigne: "Oh my fellow democrats, there are no democrats." The ever-righteous Right, which has a tin ear for Derrida, gets up in arms when Derrida says things like that, and it self-righteously proclaims, again from on high (I think they must carry portable folding pulpits with them), the difference between the Western democracies and, say, the Nazis or the old Soviet Union. But that is rather a flatfooted and unpoetic way to take what Derrida meant. Kierkegaard could very well have stood up in church some Sunday morning and said to his fellow Danes, "Oh my fellow Christians, there are no Christians," by which he was not remarking that the Danes had all recently become Hindus. Anyone who hears what is resonating in the word "democracy" (or "Christianity"), anyone with an ear for its poetics, for what it promises and recalls, knows that no existing democracy, nothing that dares call itself a democracy today, is up to what is called for in that name. When we call something by a name like "democracy," something is being called for, something is being recalled and promised, an event of democracy, that, as the Scriptures might put it, eye has not seen and ear has not heard. When we speak of something (say the United States) being "worthy of the name" (say, democracy), we are speaking of the event that name contains. The event that is going on *in* the name is the event of a *call*, of something calling and of something being called for *by* the name. . . . Let us say that the event belongs to the "vocative" order—the order of what is calling, what is called for, what is recalled, and who is called on—while names and things belong to the "existential" order, the order of what actually exists, of natural languages and real things.[11]

In following the example of democracy, which will help us get a feel for what is going on in deconstruction, the first thing to notice is that there is a difference between a name and the event that is contained in a name. In the above example, the *name* democracy can never live up to all that the *event* harbored in the name of democracy evokes, solicits, and calls forth. *The name contains an event that it cannot contain.* There is something stirring in the name democracy, something restless to be born in the name democracy, and the event that is stirring, the event that is restless to be born, exceeds any actually existing democracies: "Anyone

---

11. Caputo, *What Would Jesus Deconstruct?*, 59.

who hears what is resonating in the word 'democracy' (or 'Christianity'), anyone with an ear for its poetics, for what it promises and recalls, knows that no existing democracy, nothing that dares call itself a democracy today, is up to what is called for in that name. . . . The event that is going on *in* the name is the event of a *call*, of something calling and of something being called for *by* the name." While we confess up front that we cannot attain or adequately conceptualize all that is called for in the name of democracy, still yet the call of the event harbored in the name of democracy makes us long for its advent all the more. The event harbored in the name of democracy does not exist; rather, it *calls*. The event that is called for in the name of democracy always exceeds the actually existing democracies, as anyone who lives in the United States can well attest.

When Caputo unpacks what he means by the "event," which is obviously quite important for not only a theology of the event but also a homiletic of the event, he usually highlights at least five interrelated things:[12] First of all, an event "is not precisely what happens, which is what the word suggests in English, but something going on *in* what happens, something that is being expressed or realized or given shape in what happens; it is not something present, but something seeking to make itself felt in what is present." In the example of democracy, the event is not the actually existing democracies (like the United States), nor even democracy "in action" (when we go to the polls), but rather the event is what is stirring in the name of democracy, the event that longs to be born. While it would be nice to think that an actually existing democracy lives up to all that is evoked in the word *democracy,* we know that isn't the case. (For example, when we who live in the United States go to the polls, we know how compromised the system is; we know that many voices have been silenced; so even as we acknowledge that we are participating in a democracy, we know that the actually existing democracy we are participating in is a far cry from all that is evoked in the name of democracy). The event stirring in the name of democracy, even though it isn't present, even though it doesn't exist, still groans to be born, to make itself felt, to become true. And the intensity of its call increases in proportion to its lack of actualization: the more we recognize how much the actually existing democracies fall short of all that is evoked in the name of democ-

12. For the sake of simplicity, unless otherwise noted, I am drawing on Caputo's discussion in Caputo and Vattimo, *After the Death of God,* 47ff. A more technical discussion can be found in Caputo, *Weakness of God,* 2–7.

racy, the more we long for the event stirring in the name of democracy to come true—to be realized on the existential order of things (to exist). In Derridean terms, beginning by the impossible is an aporia—which means "no way to go"—because the event that a name harbors is always beyond what actually exists as well as what we can actually imagine or foresee; the actually existing democracies always fall short of what the word *democracy* harbors, yet that is precisely what makes us long for the event harbored in the name of democracy to come true all the more, and is what sets us in its tracks. We begin by the impossible.

Second, as mentioned above, we must distinguish between a name and the event that is astir or that transpires in a name. "The name is a kind of provisional formulation of an event, a relatively stable if evolving structure, while the event is ever restless, on the move, seeking new forms to assume, seeking to get expressed in still unexpressed ways." Events exceed the names in which they are housed, even as the event is conceived and born within the body of the name.[13] "Names are historical, contingent, provisional expressions in natural languages, while events are what names are trying to form or formulate." The word *democracy* doesn't have any foundational meaning attached to it in a metaphysical sense, as in what the idea of democracy really means if understood properly, in the way it corresponds to "reality," or in the sense of us expressing through language what is "out there." Instead, the name democracy houses what is trying to be expressed in the name, and it can transpire under many names, for names are contingent; they don't refer to something outside of themselves.[14] In this approach to deconstruction, the meaning of a name does not provide a one-to-one correspondence between name and event, or between name and "reality": "By a 'meaning' [Caputo does] not mean a semantic content but what a name is getting at; what it promises; what it calls up, sighs and longs for, stirs with, or tries to recall."[15] As such, the question before us in this example is not, What is democracy? but rather, What is happening in the name of democracy, what is being promised in the name of democracy? In deconstruction, what undergoes rigor-

13. Caputo, *Weakness of God*, 3.

14. To quote Caputo: "The name of an event is continually subject to a 'reduction' to the event it harbors, which displaces the name, replacing it with other names, deliteralizing the name, subordinating the grammar of the name to what I call the poetics of the event." See *Weakness of God*, 4.

15. Ibid., 6.

ous analysis and scrutiny is not the definition of a name or thing, of an underlying essence or reality, but rather what is going on in a name or thing, what is happening in a name or thing. The name is not what is most important; the name is contingent, and the event that is stirring in the name could go by other names as well. The name is deconstructible; the event stirring in the name is undeconstructible. So the question is, What is trying to get done in the name of democracy? What is being evoked, recalled, and promised in the name of democracy? Or, to extend our analysis, what is being evoked, recalled, and promised in the name of justice? In the name of forgiveness? In the name of hospitality? More important than the name (democracy) is the event that the name harbors, the event that longs to be born (what Derrida calls the "to come"). To speak technically for a moment,

> "Democracy" is or harbors an injunction that calls or solicits us beyond the stable limits of the present, beyond the bounds of the possible, so that when we hear the word "democracy" (or "justice" or "gift") we are not cognizing an essence but coming under the influence of an injunction, of a call, a solicitation. The "truth" of the unconditionals is not the truth of a concept or a proposition, nor the truth of the preconceptual or prepropositional unconcealment on which propositions rest, but the truth of the *facere veritatem*, the truth which happens in the event, the truth which gets made or done in the madness of the "moment," which is a "response" but not an instance of a concept. The "truth" of the "gift" belongs to the order of the injunction *give*, the "truth" of hospitality to the order of the injunction "come," the truth of "justice" is call for justice that disturbs every law, the truth of the impossible in general, of any movement, is "go, where you cannot go." So we should not ask what they *are* but what *happens*, what is being promised, what is going on in these names?[16]

Third, and this is especially important for a spectral homiletic, "an event is not a *thing* but something astir in a thing. Events get realized in things, take on actuality and presence there, but always in a way that is provisional and revisable." To recall Caputo's words from the example about democracy: "the event belongs to the 'vocative' order—the order of what is calling, what is called for, what is recalled, and who is called on—while names and things belong to the 'existential' order, the order of what

---

16. Caputo, "Return of Anti-Religion," 74–75.

actually exists, of natural languages and real things." The event is part of the "vocative" order: it doesn't exist, it calls. The event is *spectral* because it is not on the plane of existence. "An event refers neither to an actual being or entity nor to being itself, but to an impulse or aspiration simmering within both the names of entities and the name of being, something that groans to be born, something that cannot be constricted to either the ontic or ontological order at all."[17]

Fourth, whatever becomes part of the "existential" order, which is to say whatever becomes part of actually existing things (the democracy of the United States, for example), be it a thing (the United States) or a word (democracy), is always *deconstructible*. By contrast, events are not deconstructible. Whatever gets actually realized in existence (the democracy of the United States) is subject to deconstruction, whereas the event that is harbored in the name of democracy, what is calling forth in the name of democracy, what groans to be born in the name of democracy, what wishes to make itself felt, what is restless to come true, is not deconstructible. This is why, practically speaking, we are always in pursuit of a democracy in the United States even as we live in a democracy. We pursue what we already have, because we realize we don't have what we pursue. What actually exists, the democracy that we have, always falls short of what is called for in the name of democracy, which is precisely what puts us in pursuit of it all the more. "Words and things are deconstructible, but events, if there are any such things (*s'il y en a*), are not deconstructible."[18] Here I emphasize the affirmation at the heart of deconstruction, which is so often lost on its critics. Deconstruction doesn't deconstruct names and things in order to destroy them, but rather in order to open them up, to

17. Caputo, *Weakness of God*, 5. Caputo writes: "Rightly understood, the event overflows any entity; it does not rest easily within the confines of the name of an entity, but stirs restlessly, endlessly, like an invitation or a call, an invocation ('come') or a provocation, a solicitation or a promise, a praise or benediction . . . An event is not an ontico-ontological episode on the plane of being but a disturbance within the heart of being, within the names for being, that makes being restless." See Caputo ibid., 5–11.

18. The French qualifier *s'il y en a* frequently shows up in Derridean-influenced discourse. It basically translates to "if there is such a thing." This is because, in deconstruction, everything turns on what can't be made out or brought into existence or presence. "For if whatever exists is deconstructible," Caputo writes, "then the event, which is undeconstructible, lies just beyond the reach and across the borders of what exists, which is the special province of postmodern theology." The evocative force of "things" is spectral, not on the order of existence. So the "thing" only exists spectrally, hence the disclaimer. See Caputo's comments in Caputo and Vattimo, *After the Death of God*, 56.

give them a future, so that the event that names and things harbor can be affirmed all the more. This is risky to be sure, but to be content with what actually exists, to resign ourselves to the actually existing order of things, is to confine ourselves to the conventional limits of the possible, the mundane, the "been there, done that." Deconstruction keeps the future open and alive by keeping the present from closing in on us. This is an act of affirmation, not destruction. The emphasis in deconstruction is on the "to come," which is why it is a matter of prayers and tears. Deconstruction is a prayer for the experience of the impossible—for the event *to come* true, to be born into the world. It is a continual prayer, a continual invocation: may it be, may it be, amen, amen, *viens, viens, oui oui*. On this point Barth and Caputo agree: Advent is the season of the church.[19]

Fifth, in terms of temporality, "events, never being present, solicit us from afar, draw us on, draw us out into the future, calling us hither. Events are provocations and promises, and they have the structure of what Derrida calls the unforeseeable 'to come.'" In this sense, events have a (weak) transcendence.[20] Because one must always be careful when using the word *transcendence*, allow me to clarify: events are not predicated on belonging to the ontological order of things, they don't have an outside agent making them happen or bending them to suit the divine plan, they don't inhabit some other realm, they aren't the Really Real, they don't have an inner essence, they don't have substance or presence, they are not metaphysically or eternally "true," but, still yet, *phenomenologically* speaking, they happen. They call us and provoke us, visit us and disturb us, solicit us and haunt us, all in a very temporal, this worldly, material way. And the less they exist the more they insist, which is why I emphasize their spectral lure (as well as their messianic structure, which I will highlight momentarily).

19. So as not to confuse us too much, Caputo offers this definition of prayer: "Prayer is not a transaction or interaction with some hyperbeing in the sky, a communication with some ultrareality behind the scenes, the invocation or appeasement of a magical power of supernatural intervention from on high. Prayer has to do with hearing, heeding, and hearkening to a provocation that draw us out of ourselves." See ibid., 57. This is why a homiletic of the event can be understood as a proclamation of *prayer* and praise for the advent of the wholly other, for it is a communal, liturgical act of "hearing, heeding, and hearkening to a provocation that draws us out of ourselves," consisting of course of actual words and references that are irreducibly deconstructible. More about this in ch. 5.

20. For a more detailed introduction to weak transcendence, see Caputo, "Temporal Transcendence," 188–203.

At the same time, events also "call us back, recall us to all that has flowed by the irremissible past, which is why they form the basis of what Johannes Baptist Metz calls 'dangerous memories' of the injustice suffered by those long dead, or not so long, a revocation that constitutes another provocation. Events call and recall." The lure of the event is beyond our own doing, beyond our own manufacture: "Events happen to us; they overtake us and outstrip the reach of the subject or the ego. Although we are called upon to respond to events, an event is not our doing but is done to us (even as it might be our undoing). The event arises independently of me and comes over me, so that the event is also an *advent*. The event is visited upon me, presenting itself as something I must deal with, like it or not."[21] It is Moses in front of the burning bush, Isaiah in the temple, Mary being visited by Gabriel, Saul on the road to Damascus . . .

And this is precisely where things get interesting, especially for preachers. For what might happen when what we mean by the event shifts to the name of God? What might happen when we take into consideration a certain messianic structure of the event? Perhaps most importantly for the purposes at hand, what might happen if we understand preaching as a public, communal act of proclamation of prayer and praise for the advent of the "wholly other," a communal act of proclamation for the advent/event harbored in the name of God? It is here, I contend, that we step foot upon the terrain of postmodern homiletics.

> [T]hings take a *theological turn* in postmodernism when what we mean by the event shifts to God. Or, alternately, things take a *postmodern turn* in theology when the meditation upon *theos* or *theios*, God or the divine, is shifted to events, when the location of God or what is divine about God is shifted from what happens, from constituted words and things, to the plane of events. When events take on the specific look or sound or feel of the sacred, when the sparks we experience in words and things are sacred sparks, divine promptings, or holy intensities, then we have stepped upon the terrain of postmodern theology.
>
>   . . . We might even say, to put all this in a bold and simple stroke, that in postmodern theology what happens to us is God, which is why we call it postmodern *theo*logy. Or, to couch it in slightly more cautious terms, in postmodern theology what happens to us is the *event* that is harbored in the name of God, which is why we want to cultivate the resources in this name, to nurture

21. Caputo, *Weakness of God*, 4.

and shelter them, and to let us ourselves be nourished by their force, made warm by their glow, charged by their intensities.[22]

WHAT DO I LOVE WHEN I LOVE MY GOD?

A love for the impossible, we might say, is a love for God, or for the event harbored in the name of God. And a love for the event harbored in the name of God, for the impossible, has an ancient pedigree. One of the questions that Augustine asked in his *Confessions* is picked up in Derrida's own *circumfession*, in which Derrida fesses up to being cut by something wondrous, something he knows not what.

Most of us are familiar with the line from Augustine's *Confessions* about our hearts being restless until they rest in God. Augustine is in pursuit of God, getting no rest until he rests in God, for God is the name of what he loves and desires. Augustine is hungry for the event harbored in the name of God, he is in its tracks, in pursuit of what solicits him, in the grasp of what he cannot grasp. So it only makes sense that his love for God is met with the question that Derrida picks up: "What do I love when I love my God?" What is my heart in pursuit of, what am I *after*, what do I love? Is it love that I love when I love my God? Is it justice that I love when I love my God? I do not know. "What do I love when I love my God?" Is God love? Or is love God? I do not know. "What do I love when I love my God?"[23]

22. See Caputo and Vattimo, *After the Death of God*, 49–50.

23. See Derrida, "Circumfession," 122. For the original quote from Augustine, see his *Confessions*, 10.7. Derrida writes: "If I had to summarize what I am doing with St. Augustine in *Circumfession*, I would say this. On the one hand, I play with some analogies, that he came from Algeria [as did Derrida], that his mother died in Europe, the way my mother was dying in Nice when I was writing this, and so on. I am constantly playing, seriously playing, with this, and quoting sentences from the *Confessions* in Latin, all the while trying, through my love and admiration of St. Augustine—I have enormous and immense admiration for him—to ask questions about a number of axioms . . . So there is a love story and a deconstruction between us." See Caputo, *Deconstruction in a Nutshell*, 20–21. In *Augustine and Postmodernism*, Caputo and Michael J. Scanlon note the ways that several of the most notable postmodern thinkers have shown a great interest in Augustine: In *Circumfession*, Derrida "confesses the secret that he is a man of prayers and tears, that he is interested in Augustine because of his love for writers who weep. By the same token, the last work on which Lyotard was working . . . was his *The Confession of Augustine*. In 1995 Heidegger's 1921 lecture course 'Augustine and Neoplatonism' was published [and a year later so was] Hannah Arendt's doctoral dissertation on Augustine. . . . Paul Ricoeur, of course, had been interested in Augustine

It's important to point out that when Augustine confesses that he doesn't know what he loves when he loves his God, when his faith *lacks* certainty (which is what distinguishes faith from knowledge), it is not because he is "stricken by a great hole or lack or emptiness which he is seeking to fill up" but instead because he is "overflowing with love and is seeking to know where to direct his love."[24] One of the great lessons from Augustine's writings is that love drives our search to know what we love, not the other way around: "We usually think that we first have to get to know something or someone in order subsequently to get to love them,"[25] but Augustine demonstrates that being caught in the grips of what we love drives our search to know what we love all the more. So it is with the event harbored in the name of God. What is it that we pray and weep for, long and hope for, what is it that keeps us "hoping, sighing, and dreaming"? What is it that puts us on our knees, "lost in wonder, in love, and in praise"? "What do I love when I love my God?"

From a postmodern point of view, this question is irreducibly open-ended, and necessarily so.[26] To draw on a handful of words that evoke religious imagery, there is an uncontainability to words like justice, the gift, and hospitality that exceed all actually existing instantiations of justice, the gift, and hospitality; there is something harbored in the name of justice, the gift, and hospitality that is bottomless, that we can never get to the end of, that we love and desire with a desire beyond desire. And when it comes to the name of God, Derrida says, we run up against a limit concept.[27] In Caputo's words, "The name of God is a name that we learn at our mothers' breast, a word that's deeply embedded in our language . . . We seem never to get to the end of this word, never to finish probing this word and its work on us, what it's done to us. In that sense, this word contains a deeper provocation than anything else, and what it means al-

for years, and the *Confessions* played a central role in the writing of *On Narrative*." See Caputo and Scanlon, *Augustine and Postmodernism*, 3.

24. Caputo, *On Religion*, 25. Caputo later alludes to the idea that maybe instead of spending so much time fretting over stolen pears, Augustine should have directed his love to his unnamed common-law wife!

25. Ibid., 30.

26. As Caputo says of Derrida's famous French neologism *différance*: "*Différance* is altogether too meager and too poor a thing to settle the question of God, as if there were only one question instead of a *mise en abîme* of questions spreading out in every direction." Caputo, *Prayers and Tears of Jacques Derrida*, 13.

27. See Caputo, "Return of Anti-Religion," 37.

ways lies before us."[28] For Caputo (*pace* Tillich), we can never identify an ultimate concern, "for that identification would immediately turn the gold of ultimacy into the lead of something proximate, thereby locking the event inside a name and confining the unconditional to something conditioned."[29]

One of the reasons religion and deconstruction have so much in common is that they turn on the unconditional, the undeconstructible, the impossible. Deconstruction can be viewed as a repetition of the religious, not something we bring to the religious. There is so much resonating in the name of God, so much simmering, so much that is called forth, so much evoked, and none of our actually existing concepts and categories for understanding can contain all that is contained in the name of God ("If we comprehend it," Augustine says, "it is not God.") *The name of God contains what it cannot contain.* We are in pursuit of what the name contains, even as we can never catch up to what the name contains. This is not entirely unlike the wisdom that has been passed down throughout the centuries by a litany of saints: "Knowledge of the divine involves sensing God's incomprehensibility" (Saint Basil); "The highest human knowledge of God is to know that one does not know God" (Thomas Aquinas); "The good which we can neither picture nor define is a void, but it is a void fuller than all fullness" (Simone Weil).

Augustine's question is also our own: "What do we love when we say we love our God?" Is it love that we love? Is it justice that we love? We don't know what we love, even as we love it. Anytime we think we adequately conceptualize or grasp the object of our love (confine the event harbored in the name to the name itself), we domesticate it. To use traditional language, we make an idol out of an icon. The event harbored in the name of God, which is undeconstructible, always exceeds the actually existing name or thing, which is deconstructible. The event harbored in the name of God doesn't exist, it calls.

Unlike modernism, which views absolute knowledge and certainty as the good, Richard Kearney points out that postmodernism views the *desired* as the good "precisely because it cannot be possessed, because it is invisible, separate, distant, different, transcendent,"[30] because it longs

---

28. Caputo and Vattimo, *After the Death of God*, 146.

29. Caputo, *Weakness of God*, 340.

30. Kearney, "Desire of God," 116.

for what eye has not seen and ear has not heard. To the careful reader, deconstruction opens us to a certain eschatological longing for the wholly other, which always exceeds our grasp even as it draws us in its train.

THE STRUCTURE OF THE MESSIANIC

Religion is a covenant cut with the unconditional, the undeconstructible, the impossible, in which we dream of the impossible becoming possible, in which the experience of the impossible shatters our conventional horizons of possibility. We fess up to being cut by something wondrous, something we know not what, and our hearts are forever restless, *inquietum est cor nostrum*, forever in pursuit of what we love when we say we love our God. And we are driven to our knees praying and weeping like mad for the event harbored in the name of God to come true.

Perhaps it's helpful to recall that in modernity, very clear limits were drawn that imposed certain constraints upon our thinking. Kant described certain "conditions of possibility," which, "like border police, mark off the boundaries and patrol the limits of possible experience."[31] A mature, enlightened human being is a grown up who confines oneself to what is possible, who agrees "to drive within the yellow lines, to keep the rules that are programmed in advance to produce what is possible." Yet for Derrida and other postmodern thinkers, everything interesting turns on what we can't possibly make out, on what we can't possibly see in advance, in which the lines of demarcation are ruptured. And an experience of the impossible—according to Derrida—is the least bad definition of deconstruction. This is one of the many places that deconstruction steps foot on religious ground, and it is representative of the structure of the messianic that is central to Derrida's later works.[32]

We can unpack a love of the impossible and the structure of the messianic by saying that a basic component to both religion and life is a connection to the future. Caputo describes two different futures: the future present and the absolute future.[33] The future present consists of the

---

31. See Caputo and Scanlon, *God, the Gift, and Postmodernism*, 2.

32. Thomas Long rightly observes that even though contemporary theology is marked by a vibrant resurgence of eschatology, so far this "renewal of eschatological thinking and language has bypassed the American pulpit, which remains stuck in the funeral rites of the death of nineteenth-century thought forms." See Long, *Preaching from Memory to Hope*, 123.

33. For most of what follows, unless otherwise noted, see Caputo, *On Religion*, 7–17.

future that we can realistically expect. It is the relatively foreseeable future "for which we are planning, the future on which we are all hard at work, the future we are trying to provide for when we save for our retirement or when a corporate team sets up a long-term plan." It is an important future that needs to be taken seriously: "I have no intention of lightly dismissing this future," Caputo says. "Institutional long-term plans, retirement plans, life insurance policies, plans for the future education of our children, all such things are very serious, and it is foolish and irresponsible to proceed without them."

But there is a different future, "another thought of the future, a relation to another future, which is the future that is unforeseeable, that will take us by surprise, that will come like a thief in the night (1 Thess 5:2) and shatter the comfortable horizons of expectation that surround the present." This is what we can call the absolute future. In the absolute future, "we move, or we are moved, past the circle of the present and of the foreseeable future, past the manageable prospects of the present, beyond the sphere in which we have some mastery, beyond the domain of sensible possibilities that we can get our hands on, into a darker and more uncertain and unforeseeable region, into the domain of 'God knows what' (literally!)." For the future present, the foreseeable future, "we need a good mind, a decent computer, and horse sense, those three; for the absolute future, we need hope, faith, and love, these three."

In the future present, little is actually happening. We pretty much know what we are going to get from the start, because it is full of "reasonable expectations" and "cautious optimism." It is the domain over which we have mastery, or at least try to obtain mastery. It confirms what is, and pays attention to what is, but it doesn't expect much else. It's what Jean-François Lyotard would call merely a new move in an old and familiar game.[34] "There is no surprise, no discovery, no 'event,' and no advent of the other, or not much of one."

By contrast, Caputo says, the absolute future is full of unexpected turns and twists, requiring a faith that can move mountains and supplemented by a hope against hope, where one does not see what one was trying to do from the start: "It is not a matter of becoming who you already are but of becoming something new, a *metanoia*, a new creation, which eye has not seen nor ear heard nor the heart imagined, an openness to the

34. See Caputo and Scanlon, *God, the Gift, and Postmodernism*, 3.

coming of the other, which we don't already possess. . . . It comes by way of an unexpected turn of events, by shattering our horizon of expectation."[35] It constitutes experience as experience. In the absolute future, we come unhinged, our powers and our potencies are driven to their limits, we are overwhelmed, "exposed to something we cannot manage or foresee," we experience the limits, the impossibility, of our own possibilities, and we "sink to our knees in faith and hope and love, praying and weeping like mad."

> The religious sense of life awakens when we lose our bearings and let go, when we find ourselves brought up against something that exceeds our powers, that overpowers us and knocks us off our hinges, something impossible vis-à-vis our limited potencies. The religious sense of life kicks in when we are solicited by the voices of the impossible, provoked by an unforeseeable and absolute future. Here is a realm where things do not bend to our knowledge or our will and we are not calling the shots. We are out of our element. This is God's element, not ours, the element of the impossible, God's realm or "Kingdom," where God rules. Something, I know not what, some element in things exceeds our grasp and eludes our reach. Here things are astir with some element of chance beyond our best-laid plans.[36]

When our religion is content with the "same" and is not restless for "the other," when our religion is content with the foreseeable future and is not hungry for the absolute future, when our religion is content with the conventional constraints of possibility and does not dream of the impossible, of the unforeseeable event harbored in the name of God, then we have become, as Kierkegaard might say, nothing more than a mediocre fellow, stuck with our same boring selves. We have lost our salt, our passion. We become Fyodor Dostoevsky's Underground Man: "I never even managed to become anything: neither wicked nor good, neither a scoundrel nor an honest man, neither a hero nor an insect," the Underground Man wrote. "And now I am living out my life in my corner, taunting myself with the spiteful and utterly futile consolation that it is even impossible for an intelligent man seriously to become anything, and only fools become something."[37]

---

35. Caputo, *What Would Jesus Deconstruct?*, 52–53.
36. Caputo, *On Religion*, 12–14.
37. Dostoevsky, *Notes from the Underground*, 4.

Religion is for dreamers, perhaps even for fools, for those who long for the impossible, for those who are not content with the same, for those who yearn for the "wholly other" to break into our midst, for those who pray and weep like mad for the event harbored in the name of God to come true. When Bobby Kennedy used to say, "There are those who look at things the way they are and ask why . . . but I dream of things that never were and ask why not?" he was speaking with a religious heart.[38] By contrast, when the Latin poet Terence told us that since what we wish for is impossible and we would have more peace if we resign ourselves to the possible, he was telling us we should give up religion.[39]

Religion is for dreamers, for those who have made a covenant with the unconditional, the undeconstructible, the impossible; for those who fess up to being cut by something wondrous, something we know not what, whose hearts are forever restless, forever in pursuit of what we love when we say we love our God, whether we understand ourselves as religious or not, whether we use religious language or not, whether we believe in God or not.

There is a certain messianic structure to the unforeseeability of the future, when our conventional horizons of possibility are driven to their limit and we long for something new to be born. As the editors of *God, the Gift, and Postmodernism* describe, "*deconstruction is structured like a religion.* Like a *prayer* and tear for the coming of the wholly other (*tout autre*), for something impossible, like a messianic prayer in a messianic religion, *viens*, like a vast and sweeping *amen, viens, oui, oui.* Like a *faith* in the coming of something we cannot quite make out, a blind faith where knowledge fails and faith is all we have to go on, which even believes in ghosts or specters."[40]

When we pray and weep for the event harbored in the name of God to come true, it is like we are praying for the coming of the messiah, only with a slightly postmodern twist in which the messiah never quite shows up. Caputo develops what Derrida calls the "pure messianic form" (an

38. See *What Would Jesus Deconstruct?*, 38. This quote was popularized in Ted Kennedy's eulogy for Bobby.

39. Caputo, *On Religion*, 10.

40. Caputo and Scanlon, *God, the Gift, and Postmodernism*, 4. I am reminded of Barth's commentary on Romans 8:3 ("for in hope we were saved"): "Redemption is invisible, inaccessible, and impossible, for it meets us only in hope." Barth, *Epistle to the Romans*, 314.

idea Derrida borrowed not from Plato but from Judaism) by saying that deconstruction can be viewed as "a call for the coming of something un-foreseeable and unprogrammable, a call that is nourished by the expectation of something *to come*, structurally to come, for which we pray and weep, sigh and dream."

> Deconstruction is (like) a deep desire for a Messiah who never shows (up), a subtle spirit or elusive specter that would be extinguished by the harsh hands of presence and actuality. The very idea of a Messiah who is never to show and whom we accordingly desire all the more is the very paradigm of deconstruction. The structural impossibility of his being given . . . is just what makes this Messiah possible, just what nourishes our desire and keeps the future open. The impossibility is not the doom and gloom of deconstruction; it is not an end but a beginning, for *we begin by the impossible.* Indeed, the end would only come if the Messiah were to actually show up, for what would then be left to hope for? In what could we have faith? What could we desire?[41]

Deconstruction's emphasis on a messiah that never quite shows up is due in large part to its hesitancy to confine the event harbored in the name of God to the name of God itself (to confuse idols and icons). Deconstruction begins by a desire for the impossible, a desire for the event harbored in the name of God that can never be contained to any actually existing (present) name or thing, a desire for an absolute future that we cannot imagine or foresee. "The event harbored in the name of God is unconditional," Caputo writes, "because it is the promise of something that is never realized under the existing conditions in which things are actually found."[42] It is helpful to recall that deconstruction turns on aporias,

41. Caputo, "Apostles of the Impossible," 185–86. It remains unclear to me why McClure "found Derrida's work unhelpful in the task of initiating an ethical deconstruction of preaching because it is grounded more in the Western metaphysical tradition than in the Judeo-Christian tradition," as he writes in *Other-wise Preaching*, ix. It seems to me that Derrida's later writings (especially his ethico-political-religious ones) were profoundly influenced by Judaism, and some of his most interesting and provocative work involves intertextual conversations with St. Augustine. Greek metaphysical traditions first prompted Tertullian to ask, "What does Athens have to do with Jerusalem?" and the vast Derrida corpus (especially his work since 1980) continually begs the same question. Derrida operates with a passion for justice, which he casts in terms of the structure of the messianic, which has much more to do with prophetic Judaism than Greek metaphysics and neoplatonism.

42. See Caputo, *What Would Jesus Deconstruct?*, 58–60.

when there is "no way to go," which is why we begin by the impossible. The intensity of the event harbored in the name of God is amplified not by its total presence or givenness but by its lack. What is called forth in the name of God (or in the name of justice, hospitality, forgiveness, the gift, etc.) is magnified all the more in light of our recognition of how much actually existing things fall short of all that is called forth in the name of God. To reiterate, "The structural impossibility of [the Messiah's] being given . . . is just what makes this Messiah possible, just what nourishes our desire and keeps the future open. The impossibility is not the doom and gloom of deconstruction; it is not an end but a beginning, for *we begin by the impossible.*"

The structure of the messianic can also be expressed in the ambiguity that is found in the letters G-O-D-I-S-N-O-W-H-E-R-E. Placed together these can be read as either "GOD/IS/NO/WHERE" or "GOD/IS/NOW/HERE." When we sense the messiah's absence, we long for the coming of the messiah all the more. The less the event exists, the more it insists. As Peter Rollins comments, "One could say that these letters capture something about the view of God housed within so much of the Judeo-Christian tradition, a tradition that affirms a presence that is absent, dwelling deeply in the 'now here' and yet experienced or understood as 'nowhere.'" This is similar to the way a lover experiences the absence of the one he or she loves, in which the hunger is intensified by the absence (think of the structure of Augustine's restless heart in which lack is not in opposition of excess), or like when one is waiting for an important phone call and the silence of the phone not ringing is far louder than the sound of the phone ringing.[43] This can easily be seen in the history of the church: Even though we confess that the messiah showed up in Jesus Christ, we've been praying for the messiah to come again ever since. We are hungry for the event that is harbored in the name of God—for the event that is harbored in the name of the messiah—to come true, and the less we experience its actualization, the more we pray and weep for it. We desire what is not present, with the recognition that the very lack of presence is constitutive of the desire. We are nourished by our hunger. G-O-D-I-S-N-O-W-H-E-R-E.

Perhaps it's time for a disclaimer. Given all of the emphasis on the "to come" of deconstruction that is never satisfied with what actually exists,

---

43. Rollins, *Fidelity of Betrayal*, 119. I can't quite remember where I heard Pete share the analogy about the phone ringing.

that is in pursuit of the impossible, I don't want readers to think this is a matter of despondency and resignation, "as if we were just dreaming about something that will never be."[44]

> *The unfulfilled does not mean the loss of an ideal but the never finished production of the idea to come,* the on-going genesis of something coming. "Democracy" does not have a "meaning" but a history and we in are in the midst of producing that history. There is no more sadness at this unfulfilled promise than there is in musicians whose deepest joy is found in the realization that every time they go back to Mozart they realize all they have missed, that Mozart is always ahead of them, that there is no paradigmatic performance, only an endless joyous repetition. In French *répétition* can mean "rehearsal," repeating in order to get it right, but in a deconstructive rehearsal trying to get it right begins by understanding that the performance that gets it right, let us say the Messianic performance (or reading of "Hamlet," etc.), is structurally to come, and this because it never exists. It insists but it does not and never can exist. Its incompleteness is the condition of possibility of its joy, so that everything turns on keeping open the future—of music, of democracy, of the university, of God—optimally, jussively, imperatively.[45]

The vocative call of the event that is harbored in the name of God, what is promised in the name of God, is precisely what calls us to respond, to be transformed, to do the truth (*facere veritatem*). The aporia of the impossible (the hunger for a messiah that never quite shows up) is what gets things going. Here, the emphasis that progressives traditionally place on "making the love of God real" is exactly right, for we make the love of God real by responding to the event harbored in the name of God that solicits us, calls us, and provokes us. In deconstruction, the truth of the event is in its "becoming true," where the name of God is the name of a deed. But far from being solely anthropological in focus, the event overcomes us, visits us, and demands a response. "We must be responsible to events, responsive to them, welcome them, and show them hospitality when they show up uninvited at our door."[46] Deconstruction consists of both *call* and *response*. The event stands at the door and knocks.

---

44. Caputo, *What Would Jesus Deconstruct?*, 60.

45. Caputo, "The Return of Anti-Religion," 30.

46. Caputo, *What Would Jesus Deconstruct?*, 61.

The paradigmatic example of this can be seen in the conversion of Saul on the road to Damascus. Saul is going about his business, paying attention to the mundane, foreseeable future of conventional possibilities. He is knocked to the ground and blinded by the incoming of the wholly other, by what he could not imagine, by what was beyond anything he could possibly conceptualize, foresee, or manufacture on his own. And the incoming of the wholly other demanded his response. The event overcame him—and he was never the same again. He underwent a fundamental change of heart (*metanoia*). It was a transformational experience of the impossible, of the impossible becoming possible. And make no mistake about it: the advent of the messiah led Paul to pray and weep like mad for the messiah to come again.

In narratives such as these, we find "human experience writ large, the defining features of our life magnified in moving and unforgettable stories, in brilliant religious figures."[47] This is why religious narratives are filled with so many wondrous stories. They are

> stories of transforming change more stunning than anything Lewis Carroll dared imagine could happen to Alice—virgins becoming mothers, mountains moving on command, seas parting, the dead rising from the grave, and—most importantly, because this is what these stories are all about—sinners being forgiven and given a new heart, *metanoia*. To forgive is to lift the weight of the past and give someone a new lease on life, a new future, which is arguably the most basic thing Jesus had to say.
> The scriptures are filled with narratives in which the power of the present is broken and the full length and breadth of the real open like a flower, unfolding the power of the possible, the power of the impossible beyond the possible, of the hyper-real beyond the real.[48]

"God is still speaking," as our United Church of Christ friends like to put it—which is to say, the event stands at the door and keeps on knocking. We are called upon by the event harbored in the name of God, solicited by an unforeseeable future that we can't quite make out, by the specter of a messiah that never quite shows up, and by dangerous memories of wrongs that demand to be made right. We are called by the event to do the truth, *facere veritatem*.

47. Caputo, *On Religion*, 8.
48. Ibid., 15.

We are thus not only called forward and called back by the event, but we are also called on. Remember that in the theory of the event, "truth" means what is trying to come true, which points to our responsibility to make it actually come true . . . That is how things work in the vocative order, where memories can be dangerous and where our dreams for what is promised are also dangerous, as two of the most famous orations in American history confirm (Lincoln's and King's). They endanger the present order, challenging the pretense of the present form of things—the existential order—to pass itself off as the event itself, to actually *be* democracy or justice or truth or Christianity or whatever it pretends to "be," whatever it says it "is," whatever the "powers that be" are trying to get away with. This is why when Derrida once famously described deconstruction as a critique of the "metaphysics of presence," he took the side of the better angels of our nature, even though his detractors thought he was the devil himself.

. . . Derrida sometimes describes the event by saying that while the event is possible, it represents a very special kind of "perhaps." This is because it is a prayer not for what is straightforwardly possible but for "the possibility of *the* impossible" . . . What is "possible" in the straightforward sense is the foreseeable future, the future that we can reasonably anticipate and plan for . . . But by *the* impossible he means something that exceeds the horizon of foreseeability and expectation and is not a simple logical contradiction . . . He means the possibility of something more "unconditional," which . . . takes us by surprise [and] lies beyond our horizon of expectation. That is the future of the event, like the way hope is truly hope when it has been pushed up against the impossible and everything looks hopeless.[49]

To be sure, Dr. King didn't preach when he was certain that he would get to the promised land ("I may not get there with you . . ."). Desmond Tutu didn't proclaim God's dream for the people of South Africa when he was certain that the ruling party would undergo a change of heart. Sojourner Truth didn't wait for white men of privilege to view African-American women as equals before rhetorically declaring, "Ain't I a woman too?" Instead, they preached in the midst of uncertainty, when they didn't know if justice or forgiveness or reconciliation were even possible. Yet the promise evoked in the name of justice, in the name of forgiveness, in the name of reconciliation, *in the name of God* (what do I love when I love

49. Caputo, *What Would Jesus Deconstruct?*, 61–62.

my God?) is precisely what motivated their preaching. The less the event exists, the more it insists. Or in slightly more biblical terms: when the kingdom of God is absent, the kingdom of God comes calling. We begin by the impossible.

While the event harbored in the name of God sometimes comes true, other times the event is brutally snuffed out (which the crosses in our sanctuaries, if they aren't made of too much gold, are supposed to bear witness to). Yet even when the strong forces of the world ("the present," what "is") destroy the weak call of the event (the messianic "to come"), the event still calls us, still provokes us, still haunts us, still stirs us, becoming what Johannes Baptist Metz calls a dangerous memory and what John Caputo refers to as a very holy ghost.

Thomas Long tells a memorable story about Sojourner Truth and Frederick Douglass. While addressing a Boston audience about racism in America, Douglass became more and more agitated as he spoke, more and more despairing, conveying to his audience that there was no hope for justice outside of violence and bloodshed. After speaking, Douglass sat down, and the hall fell into a tense hush. Just then, Sojourner Truth, who had been sitting right there on the front row the whole time, stood up and asked, in her deep and commanding voice, a question heard all over the room: "Frederick, is God dead?"[50] Her answer, of course, was *no.* What Sojourner Truth evoked in that moment is what all the great preachers throughout history have evoked: hope is truly hope when it has been pushed up against the impossible, driven to its limits—when our desire for the messiah to arrive is amplified all the more in the wake of the messiah's absence. The messiah stands at the door and knocks.

All of which gets us back to where this chapter—indeed, this book—got started.

THE DEATH OF THE DEATH OF GOD

In modernity, the "secular" and the "sacred" were clearly demarcated, and neither was to infringe upon the other. There were people who believed in God, and there were people who did not believe in God. Religion, at least in the West, was primarily about accepting certain sets of propositions about God, Truth, Reality, and so forth (metaphysical Truths about the Way Things Are). Religion was about cognitive belief in God. God exists,

---

50. See Long, *Preaching from Memory to Hope,* 34–35.

or God doesn't exist. God is true, or God isn't true. If God exists, then religion is true. If God doesn't exist, then religion isn't true. One is either religious or, to borrow a word from Bill Maher's lexicon, *religulous.*

It was believed that human beings had the capability to determine God's existence (or lack thereof) based on the use of Reason with a capital R. Instead of religion starting with passion and experience ("What do I love when I say I love my God?"), the question of God during the era of modernity was profoundly recast: "Instead of beginning on our knees," Caputo writes, "we are all seated solemnly and with stern faces on the hard benches of the court of Reason as it is called into session. God is brought before the court, like a defendant with his hat in his hand, and required to give an account of himself, to show His ontological papers, if He expects to win the court's approval."[51]

This approach to religion is still the most popular one today. We tend to associate God in terms of existence and presence (Being), and we associate Truth in terms of Absolutes based on a Divine Order. Religion is about the Truth in an ontological or metaphysical sense. God is a Being or a Presence. God exists or God is untrue.

Yet from the perspective of a theology of the event, these either/or constructions (sacred/secular, theist/atheist, true/false) break down. In the postmodern return of religion, religious truth is not about verifying whether or not God exists, or whether or not there is a Divine Order that ordains Cosmic Rules. As I described in the previous section, a theology of the event does not turn on questions of God's existence, but is connected to the (eschatological) structure of the future, the "to come," which is something that—at the risk of sounding like an other-wise homiletical heretic—all of us share. Like art or politics, religion is a basic structure of human experience.[52]

From a postmodern point of view, events *happen*. Contingent though they are, they call and recall. They *evoke*. And contrary to what Bill Maher or Sam Harris might tell us, it matters not if one is a believer, an atheist, or an agnostic, for in a hermeneutic of the event, the event comes knocking, whether one believes in God some of the time, or none of the time, or all of the time. This is why Derrida's religion is always

---

51. Caputo, *On Religion*, 46.

52. This isn't to say that the event manifests itself universally in the same way to everybody, as if it had some sort of inner essence or telos, which I address in more detail in ch. 5.

a religion without religion. A theology of the event is not concerned with settling Who or What the Super Source or Ultimate Cause of the knocking is. Instead of thinking about religion in terms of what is metaphysically True, the postmodern return of religion is interested in what (phenomenologically) *happens*.

In slightly more sophisticated terms, a theology of the event suspends the question of Who or What is responsible for the event knocking at the door. "The question of the determinate identity of the one calling, the name of the being or power behind it, of its cause or source, or the entity or hyper-entity who calls, *s'il y en a*, lies beyond our ken or *Erkenntnis*—in that lies its 'transcendence'—and so the question of causal origin may be suitably saved for evening conversations at the hotel bar after a day of conferencing." The point is not Who or What is responsible for the call of the event, because a theology of the event doesn't turn on identifying the Source of the call, if there even is such a thing. "Is it *really* God who calls?" we wonder. "Or is it some hidden power in my own mind? Is it *really* the call of conscience, of some Socratic daimon, or of a Cosmic Spirit? How am I to say? Who has authorized me to preside over that debate?"[53] Josh McDowell perhaps? Or maybe Lee Strobel? And when we preoccupy ourselves with determining the "Truth" of the call only in terms of identifying its source (its Source), then Peter Rollins' tongue-in-cheek comments are right on target, especially for preachers: "Philosophy journals would have to become a stable diet for the preacher who would, in fear and trembling, be working out whether belief in Christianity is still rational. Journals dealing with biblical scholarship would become the norm in home groups, and psychological journals would need to be read as an integral part of our devotional meditations (helping us work out whether our religious experience was likely to have descended from heaven or whether it really welled up from the depth of our unconscious)."[54]

When we pursue the question by focusing our attention only on the Source of the call, as opposed to the call itself, we treat the call "like a strong force with a definite place on the plane of being or power, not a weak one that solicits [us] from afar." Plus, to pursue the question of the call by only trying to determine the Source is a way of changing the subject. Caputo compares this to the way someone who has been caught

53. Caputo, *Weakness of God*, 114.
54. Rollins, *Fidelity of Betrayal*, 94.

cheating might respond by asking, "How did you find that out?"—which is not the point, of course. The event comes knocking at our door, whether we are able to identify the Source or not. Events happen. That is the point.

> From a strictly methodological point of view, by *suspending* the question of the name or status of the caller in its ontical or onto-logical identity, we are sticking strictly to the formal or phenom-enological character of the call's being called and to what is being called for. As to the question of the "real" or entitative status of the caller, then, we practice a rigorous *epoche* or reduction. For after having pointed out its phenomenal indeterminacy, to persist in seeking out the identity of the caller. . . . is a way to wiggle out of the call. Events happen—don't change the subject.[55]

Whether we believe in God or not, whether we consider ourselves religious or not, whether we go to church on Sunday mornings or not, we are visited by events that provoke us and solicit us, that change us and transform us, that make our hearts beat for the unconditional, the unde-constructible, the impossible. Religious or not, we are caught in the grips of we know not what. "An event cuts across the distinctions among the various confessions, and even across the distinction between the confes-sional faiths and secular unbelief, in order to touch upon a more elemen-tal, if ambiguous quality of our lives, however this quality is given words or formulated, with or without what is conventionally called religion or theology."[56] This is why the postmodern return of religion, especially the streams associated with Derrida and Caputo, doesn't reside within the safe confines of atheism or theism but rather dwells in the desert of a/theism (it is religion *sans* religion). Deconstruction, being a phenomenology of experience, has to take a pass on settling the question of God's existence (or nonexistence): "There is nothing about a philosophy of experience that allows it to establish that there is nothing *beyond* experience. . . . As Derrida said to Kevin Hart when asked about 'supernatural' grace (as opposed to the grace of the event), 'deconstruction, as such, has nothing

---

55. Caputo, *Weakness of God*, 115. "By the possibility of the impossible," Caputo writes, "I do not mean the doer or the doing of some unbelievable deed, evidence of whose name, status, and origin I must produce for the prosecutor, but the weak force of an unconditional appeal. I am referring to the structure of an event of solicitation that stirs within—here—the Jewish and Christian scriptures, which on my hypothesis should be true of any religious tradition, any one of which, being sustained by an event, sustains a concrete form of life and is the subject matter of a possible hermeneutic explication."

56. Ibid., 4.

to say or to do . . . deconstruction has no lever on this. And it should not have any lever.' Deconstruction is entirely in the business of giving an account of *experience*."[57] From a deconstructive point of view, events happen—but it simply isn't possible to determine Who or What is beyond the experience, or whether there is some Reality we call God or not that is responsible for all of this. That is to change the subject.[58]

Approaching the Enlightenment idea of religious truth as if it consists in whether or not one can definitively prove the existence of God is (to borrow a line from Kierkegaard) of all things the most ridiculous. Likewise, to assume that the truth claims of Christianity can be affirmed or denied based on propositions like the accuracy of the Bible or the historicity of the resurrection—which the new atheists and fundamentalists agree upon—is to miss the boat entirely. Both are acceding to the

57. Caputo, "Return of Anti-Religion," 111. For more on this, see esp. 110–17.

58. For the record, neither Caputo nor Derrida believe in a metaphysical God. But about such things deconstruction cannot say a thing. As Caputo makes clear: "I am not arguing (and do not think) that there is a being called 'God' somewhere who does or fails to do impossible things. Nor do I argue or think that God is the Being of beings, or a hyper-Being beyond Being in the tradition of mystical theology, or the 'God without Being' of Jean-Luc Marion . . . Nor do I, God forbid, attribute any such views to Jacques Derrida, nor thank God did Derrida think I was doing any such thing. I am not theologizing philosophy but deconstructing Christianity, causing a scandal to the pious and a stumbling block to the theologians, re-imagining, reinventing 'God,' which is why my radical theology is considered radical atheism and a 'death of God' by my evangelical friends.

. . . In the view I strike, God is not an *ens realissimum* or perfect act (*actus purus*) but the name of an event in which we find ourselves at risk, exposed to what drives us to the limits, to what we desire with a desire beyond desire . . . 'God' is not the name of the perfect constellation and complete actualization of all possible perfection, but of a provocation, a perhaps, a solicitation, an unexpected visitation, an interruption, which calls us to the limits of joy and grief. God is figured not by the blinding sun of Platonism but by the stirring waters of the event, the face of the deep as Catherine Keller argues. God is not the hyperousiological I know not what of negative theology, but a call from I know not where. God is not an unlimited being but a name uttered in limit situations. God is not an ideal of being but the ordeal of an event astir within being, an impatience within the world that pushes the world beyond itself, beyond the horizons of foreseeability, making the world risky and restless with the promise/threat. God is not a pure act but a pure interruption, not pure perfection but pure provocation, not a being but an event, the name of an event whose name I do not know, the name of a secret, of the secret sources and resources of life. The name of God is the name of a stranger who seeks a room in our home, of a coming, an advent, which we are called upon to welcome. Such is the transcendence life permits, not the magical transcendence effected by a being almighty, but the transcendence of the 'might be' that stirs impatiently in the event, of the 'perhaps' that is restlessly astir in the provocation of God." See Caputo, "Return of Anti-Religion," 39.

Cartesian model of metaphysics, which even Descartes himself sometimes questioned.[59] When we approach religious truth as if it is something we can grasp based on our own thoughts and ideas, the game is over before it even starts.

From a postmodern perspective, the structure of religious truth—what we are calling the event harbored in the name of God, though it can go by other names as well[60]—is *beyond belief*. The truth of the event is not tied to whether or not a divine being we call God exists and whether we cognitively believe in Him (or Her). To quote Peter Rollins, "The truth affirmed by Christianity is not a description but an event, not a fact to be grasped but an incoming to be undergone."[61] To only understand religion as a pursuit of objective Truth that can be empirically verified based on the use of Reason is to hitch a ride with Greek metaphysics, not biblical narratives, which is one of the things Nietzsche's proclamation of the death of God (metaphysics) ironically exposed.

The structural significance of the postmodern return of religion, particularly as reflected in Derrida's work but missed by so many of his

59. At one point, Descartes wrote, "The idea of the infinite, if it is to be a true idea, cannot be grasped at all, since the impossibility of being grasped is contained in the formal definition of the infinite." Descartes, *Philosophical Writings of Descartes*, 2:253. This leads Rollins to comment: "Descartes was openly wondering whether his definition of God was in fact a definition at all or, in actual fact, a way of saying that God cannot be defined." Rollins, *Fidelity of Betrayal*, 107.

60. "By distinguishing between the name and the event," Caputo comments, "between the name of God and the event that transpires there, I have laid myself open to the possibility that this event, or stream of events, can twist free from this name and that we might then find ourselves out in the desert, in a khôral place of namelessness and the desire for new names. If we release the event that is harbored by the name of God, we might end up having to release that name itself, in the sense of letting it go, letting go of it. The event of solicitation that is issued in the name of God stands on its own, calls and solicits us on its own, whether or not someone named God is the author of that solicitation, in which case the death of the author, which would be here the death of God, is the condition of hearing this solicitation. In this desire for God, it is not God but the event that stirs within that name that is undeconstructible, and it would always be possible for that desire to take other forms, to find other formulations, now or in times to come. So my theology of the event is prepared to concede, if not exactly the death of God, at least the mortality or historical contingency of the name of God, the separability in principle of the event from the name, like a spirit leaving a lifeless body behind. For, however precious and prestigious it may be, the name of God remains a historical name and, as such, a contingent formation or unity of meaning." See Caputo and Vattimo, *After the Death of God*, 70.

61. Rollins, *Fidelity of Betrayal*, 113.

(homiletical) critics, demonstrates that beyond the "death of God" there remains the *desire for God*, which is the subject matter of the unconditional affirmation and call at the heart of deconstruction, for which we daily—believer and atheist alike—hope and sigh and dream and weep. This desire transcends categories of atheist/theist, secular/sacred, and so on. In the words of Jeffrey Robbins, "The love of God is a love without category or, better, a love that exceeds all categorizations—whether religious or secular, whether theist or atheist, and whether Christian, Muslim, Buddhist, Jewish, etc."[62] The death of God, as pronounced by the Enlightenment,

> is not the final word, and religion is more fundamentally about desire—even, or especially, when our old beliefs have been worn away or stripped apart, whether it is by the brutalities of modern life to which we have all become spectators, or more complexly still, *the pretense of self-sufficiency.* God is the (or, at least, one) name that we give to this desire, and religion is the (or, at least, one) means by which it takes its institutional form. But even when the name rings hollow and the form grows stale, it is the *event* of desire that stirs beneath that we still strive to articulate, that we still mean to affirm.[63]

This is why we can even imagine a cultured despiser of religion like Karl Marx operating from, dare I say it, a religious heart.[64] While Marx "fancied himself a cold-hearted scientist who was dispassionately exposing the futility of religious illusion in the name of revolutionary historical progress," can we not say that he still yet "had a bit of the wild-eyed Jewish prophet about him"? While working with what he and others viewed as cold economic laws, the "science" of political economy, all without God of course, could we not say that he was also doing all of this work because he longed for the messianic age, even as he was debunking religion?[65] "Marx was praying and weeping for an age in which the rich stop feeding off the poor and making their fortunes on the bent backs of the most defense-

62. Caputo and Vattimo, *After the Death of God*, 18.

63. Robbins, "Hermeneutics of the Kingdom of God." Emphasis mine.

64. For this take on Marx, see Caputo, *On Religion*, 16–17.

65. This is also why, I think, Caputo provides a more honest reading than Žižek. Every time Žižek invokes his love for the communism to come, is he not also doing so from a heart that longs for the (messianic) "to come"? Or is his communism already (absolutely) determined?

less people in our society."[66] Is this not in line with the Hebrew prophets, who longed for justice to "roll down like waters, and righteousness like an ever-flowing stream" (Amos 5:24)? Is this not the reason that Marx's atheism tends to play so well in liberation theology and in the churches of the poor? Is this not why, as Caputo describes, "the distinction between theism and atheism is a little more unstable than most people think, including most popes and bishops"? Is it even possible that the venerable Bill Maher—who devotes no small amount of time on his TV show to deriding religion for all of the ills it inflicts on society—launches his critiques of religion precisely in the name of religion, because he has a heart that beats for the event harbored in the name of justice, which can go by many names, including the event harbored in the name of God? Is he too not captivated by a religion without religion? Does he not long for an age of justice? Does not the event knock on his door too?

This world may very well be all that we have, and we may very well be the only ones in here, but still yet the event harbored in the name of God keeps on calling.[67] The messiah stands at the door and knocks. For reasons such as these, language about the death of God is ultimately misleading:

> To speak of the death of God in any final sense would be to speak of the death of "desire" or "the death of love" or "the death of affirmation" . . . [It] seems to me more productive and fruitful to think of God as the object of affirmation and desire. Then the question is not whether there is a God—no more so than there is a question about whether there is desire—but the question is the one that Derrida picks out of Augustine's *Confessions*: "What do I love when I love my God?" God is the name—an endlessly translatable name—of what we love and desire and of affirmation and for me the question is, what is that? What do I desire? So the "death of God" is not a notion for which I have found much use. . . . For, in the end, it is not the name of God that we affirm, but something—some event—that is being affirmed in our affirmation of the name of God.[68]

From a postmodern point of view, it is the event of desire that stirs within the name of God—the provocation that is harbored in the name of God—that postmodern preachers still strive to articulate, still try to

66. Caputo, *On Religion*, 17.

67. See esp. Caputo, *Weakness of God*, 37.

68. In Caputo and Vattimo, *After the Death of God*, 147.

affirm. And lest the event be confined only to our agency and manufacture, the event harbored in the name of God is not just the name of our passion, of everything we love and desire with a desire beyond desire, but "also the name of everything that desires us, everything that puts us in the accusative, that desires what is best in us and desires what is best from us."[69] According to Caputo, the anomaly of call and response "is figured in Derrida himself in the expression 'the decision of the other in me,' that is, that while it comes down to my action, my action is a reaction, a response, to a call, to something that overtakes me and calls for a response, that I act out the prompting of the other in me, the other who lays claim to me."[70]

By bracketing the question of the Source of the call, and by paying attention to the call itself (*an und für sich*), a homiletic of the event resonates not just with those who believe in God, but also with those who aren't sure what to make of God and don't necessarily think of themselves as religious, as well as with progressives who struggle to imagine God as "other." This isn't to say we can't have interesting conversations over coffee about whether God exists or not, or whether or not the resurrection historically "happened." I'm quite the fan of *Living the Questions* study groups, and I devote no small amount of time to helping people interpret the Bible from a postcritical perspective ("taking the Bible seriously but not literally," to recall Marcus Borg's apt expression). But it is to say that a homiletic of the event doesn't turn on the Source of the call but rather on the call itself. This may sound a little too heretical to my orthodox friends, and a little too pious for my devout atheist friends, but that is to change the subject and miss the point. Events happen. We can't weasel out of them, even though we might wish we could.

In Mark C. Taylor's words, it is "misleading to speak of a 'return of' or 'return to' religion. Religion does not return, because it never goes away; to the contrary, religion haunts society, self, and culture even—perhaps especially—when it seems to be absent."[71] Whether we understand ourselves as religious or not—whether we believe in God or not—we are in pursuit of the impossible, we are *after* God, we have been cut by something wondrous, we know not what. Our hearts are restless, believer and atheist alike. The event stands at the door and knocks.

69. Caputo, *Weakness of God*, 88.

70. Caputo, personal correspondence. See esp. Derrida, *Sovereignties in Question*, 160.

71. Taylor, *After God*, 132.

So how do we preach after God? How do we preach about what is beyond belief? How do we preach about the event harbored in the name of God? It is to these questions that we now turn.

5

Call and Response: A Homiletic of the Event

Certain words are astir with events, are swollen with the possibility of the impossible, are restless with elemental powers, with immemorial powers that make it impossible to forget, with promissory powers that make it impossible to be content with what is present and that long to be brought forth, yearning to be born. Words like "justice" and "democracy," "gift" and "forgiveness," "friendship" and "hospitality." The power of these words, or rather of the events that are astir in these words, is what "calls" us, solicits us, making our Augustinian hearts restless like a pregnant deconstructive mother eager to deliver. The power of that call, we might say, is the first yes, a solicitous yes, the yes that calls for confirmation. We in turn confirm, respond, answer. That is the second yes, *oui, oui.*

—John Caputo[1]

I am duty bound to warn the reader in advance not to expect too much. With all this talk of the stirring of the event, I do not mean to stir up expectations of power. [An event] is a more wispy and willowy thing, a whisper or a promise, a breath or a spirit, not a mundane force.

—John Caputo[2]

IF WE TAKE INTO consideration a theology of the event as described in the previous chapter and reflect on its implications for preaching—particularly

1. Caputo, "A Resonse to Olthuis," in Zlomistić and DeRoo, *Cross and Khôra*, 193.
2. Caputo, *Weakness of God*, 7.

in response to the modern homiletical crisis—what might a homiletic of the event look like in practice? How might it be differentiated from other approaches to preaching? And, perhaps most importantly, how might it resonate not only with those who believe in God, but especially with those who aren't quite sure what to make of God, or perhaps don't believe in God at all? In this chapter, I highlight several key characteristics of a postmodern homiletic of the event (the characteristics I describe should not be understood as exhaustive). I then turn to a handful of observations related to structure and style, especially in relationship to "other-wise" preaching, which a homiletic of the event values and, as I will describe, uses as a springboard of sorts.

CALL AND RESPONSE

If I was to try to describe a homiletic of the event in a nutshell, which is probably a dangerous thing to do, I would start by saying that it is not a proclamation of metaphysical Truth but rather a communal proclamation of prayer and praise for the advent of the wholly other—which is to say, for the event harbored in the name of God—in connection to the interpretation of texts within the context of worship. In response to the modern homiletical crisis, a homiletic of the event doesn't preach about God, but instead preaches *after* God.

Preaching after God can be understood in a variety of ways. At the very least, preaching after God heeds the implications of Nietzsche's proclamation of the death of God and offers viable possibilities for preaching in the aftermath of metaphysics, especially for progressives who, as one person from my congregation put it, "don't do the supernatural well." Instead of viewing the standard postmodern critique of metaphysics (which consists in recognizing our inability to ascertain and/or possess objective Truth) as a threat to homiletics, it is viewed as a gift to homiletics.

From another perspective, to preach after God is to be in pursuit of God, giving voice to a desire beyond desire, and a hope against hope, *for the event that is harbored in the name of God* (which is to be distinguished from a supernatural God of Being or Presence), consisting of proclamations of prayer and praise for the advent of the wholly other. It is a postmodern remix of Augustine's restless heart, which was always, relentlessly, with hopes and sighs too deep for words, with prayers and tears, *after* God—precisely because life is lived in the wake, in the aftermath, of the unconditional, unnamable, affirmative, infinite call that leaves us hoping, sighing and dreaming, holding on for dear life. A homiletic of the event is a circumfession of sorts, for we fess up to being cut by something wondrous, we know not what.[3] To preach after God is to preach after the impossible, for a homiletic of the event dreams of the impossible becoming possible, dreams of the truth being done, *facere veritatem.*

A homiletic of the event is also spectral, for it lends an ear "not to the noise of what is, a domain [left] to the more qualified, but to what silently calls . . . For the name of God is the name of an event neither inside nor outside, above or below, but up ahead, neither real nor unreal, but not yet real."[4] The event doesn't exist, it calls. And the less it exists, the more it insists. A homiletic of the event prays and weeps like mad for the coming of a messiah who never quite shows up.

As a communal proclamation of prayer and praise for the advent of the wholly other, sermons turn less on our best efforts as human beings and more on a hoping and sighing and dreaming and weeping for what we long for yet can't quite make out, for where our hearts long to go, for what we desire to be visited upon us with a desire beyond desire and a hope against hope, even though we cannot adequately conceptualize or name what it is, if such a thing even exists. A homiletic of the event envisions celebratory proclamations of prayer and praise for the advent of the wholly other that is beyond human manufacture, that is not of our own doing (though it may be our undoing), that keeps the future open, stirring with hope and possibility. Sermons are preached in restless pursuit of the event that is harbored in the name of God—the hope and desire that stirs *in the name of God*—which is an event that we can never catch up to, an event that we can't put words to yet at the same time can't resist, the event harbored in the name of God that leaves us hoping and sighing and dreaming and weeping, believer and atheist alike, holding on for dear life, caught up (raptured) in wonder, in love, and in praise.

From a postmodern perspective, the proverbial "hole in one's heart" isn't something that a metaphysical Presence or Being comes to fill, but rather is the metaphoric site describing the hunger that marks our lives as

3. When using the word *tears*, especially in regard to the prayers and tears of Jacques Derrida, Caputo embraces Mark C. Taylor's reading of tears as cries *and* cuts. See Taylor, *Tears.*

4. Caputo, *Weakness of God*, 123.

being forever restless, forever in pursuit, forever aching, forever desiring, forever *after* the unconditional and undeconstructible, what eye has not seen and ear has not heard (what a determinate religion might call God, and what I am referencing here as the event harbored in the name of God, which is irreducibly translatable), which is not unlike a messianic prayer in a messianic religion.

A homiletic of the event is *eschatological*. In contrast to the onto-theological God of metaphysics—in which the striving for fulfillment is based on a plenitude of presence and knowledge and certainty (and desire is construed as a *lack*)—an eschatological approach views the "desire of God as no mere deficiency or privation but its own reward—positivity, excess, gift, grace."[5] As the psalmist writes, "Those who seek the Lord lack no good thing" (Psalm 34). Why? Because, in the words of Richard Kearney, "such desire is not some gaping emptiness or negation . . . but an affirmative 'yes' to the summons of a superabundant, impassioned God." A homiletic of the event is eschatological in the sense that its hunger for God, its desire for God, suggests an "other" that is always "to come," what eye has not seen and ear has not heard. In Kearney's language, it can be understood as desire for the God who may be: "This desire be-yond desire I call *eschatological* to the extent that it alludes to an alterity that already summons me yet is not yet, that is already present yet always absent (Philippians 2:12), a *deus adventuras* who seeks me yet is still to come, unpredictably and unexpectedly, 'in the twinkling of an eye' (I Corinthians 15:52). 'Like a thief in the night' (I Thessalonians 5:2)."[6] Here we are reminded of the Psalms and canticles that speak of human desire for the Creator as "flesh fainting for God" (Psalm 63), or of an expect-ant bride yearning for her bridegroom. Augustine again comes to mind when he addresses God as impassioned lover: "You shed your fragrance about me; I drew breath and now I gasp for your sweet odour. I tasted you and now I hunger and thirst for you. You touched me and I am inflamed with love."[7] A homiletic of the event is forever *after* the God to come. As Caputo comments: "The name of God for Derrida is not the name of, and does not safeguard, the *excess or surplus of givenness* but the name of what

5. Kearney, "Desire of God," 114.
6. Ibid. See esp. Kearney, *God Who May Be*.
7. Augustine, *Confessions*, bk. 6.

is *never* given, the excess of what is always promised, hoped for, prayed and wept over."[8]

A homiletic of the event disturbs more than it orders, for, as Derrida once said, deconstruction is "produced in a space where the prophets are not far away."[9] Deconstruction was not sent into the world in order to confirm and ordain the present powers that be, but rather to open them up, to provoke them, to disturb them, which is not entirely unlike what Jesus did when he was said to be going about his Father's business. To subvert and provoke the ordered world (what John Dominic Crossan calls the "normalcy of civilization")[10] is not to deny truth and usher in reckless relativism, as deconstruction's detractors like to say, but rather is a response to the (eschatological) truth "to come," the truth that is harbored in the name of justice, in the name of love, in the name of God: "The 'present age' is not a fixed date in calendar time, like Paul's Rome or the Republican Right's America, but a floating structure of human existence . . . that permanently trembles under the stirring of the event." A homiletic of the event belongs not to the order of what is (the order of being, the order of the "present age," the order of the normalcy of civilization) but "to the order of the event of the call, not to presence but to provocation."[11] Here, to use traditional language, the preacher is called *by* the event to witness *to* the event that can't be witnessed to: to speak (*prophetes*) for justice, to call for justice, to warn about ignoring justice, all the while recognizing that the event harbored in the name is always beyond our grasp, which is why it is all the more provocative and praiseworthy, and all the more reason it should be the central focus of our sermons. It is precisely here, I think, that a homiletic of the event is most congruent

8. Caputo, "Apostles of the Impossible," 199. This perspective is in contrast with Jean-Luc Marion (see ch. 11).

9. In Kearney, *Debates in Continental Philosophy*, xx. Here we might also note where Derrida significantly differs from Augustine, especially in terms of the way Augustine defined peace as the tranquility of order that is the result of making peace with political power. See Caputo, *Weakness of God*, 30.

10. Here Crossan is significantly influenced by Walter Benjamin. See Crossan, *God and Empire*, 30.

11. This has affinity with McClure's other-wise preaching: "No matter what form it takes, other-wise commitment feels deeply the proximity of human others and the nearness of an impinging alternative reign of God in which things are indeed other-wise." McClure, *Other-wise Preaching*, 133–34.

with progressive preaching, especially given the progressive emphasis on social justice.[12]

A homiletic of the event is also the stuff of dangerous memories. In a certain sense, a homiletic of the event is a homiletic of the cross, of innocent suffering, in which the haunting memories of those who suffered still call to us now to right the wrongs of the past. We are not called to wipe away the tears of the past, but to preserve them, for these tears have a transforming power.[13] Caputo writes:

> In the Christian tradition, the force of the event that calls to us and overtakes us in the name of God arises crucially from the cross, where all the lines of force in Christianity intersect (cross). The life and death of Jesus are interwoven with defeat and death, and not simply death, but a humiliating public execution reserved for the worst criminals. God's mark is upon an executed man.
>
> . . . God is in attendance as the weak force of the call that cries out from Calvary and calls across the epochs, that cries out from every corpse created by every cruel and unjust power. The logos of the cross is a call to renounce violence, not to conceal and defer it and then, in a stunning act that takes the enemy by surprise, to lay them low with *real* power. . . .
>
> The effect of situating God on the side of vulnerability and unjust suffering is not, of course, to glorify suffering and misery, but to prophetically protest it, to give divine depth and meaning to resistance to unjust suffering, to attach the coefficient of divine resistance to unjust suffering, which is why suffering is the stuff of dangerous memories. The call, the cry, the plaint that rises up from the cross is a great divine "no" to injustice, an infinite lamentation over unjust suffering and innocent victims. . . . God's traditional top-down "transcendence" must be reconceived in such a way that all of its resources are deployed on behalf of lowliness and the despised. The effect of speaking of God's transcendence is not to support and top off presence with a hyper-presence, but to disturb presence with difference and to allow the lowliest to rise in divine splendor.[14]

A homiletic of the event is a homiletic of weakness, and I mean this in at least two ways: First, from a Christian perspective, the dangerous memory of the crucified Christ continues to speak, haunting us and

12. See esp. Caputo, *Weakness of God*, 30–31.

13. See ibid., 248.

14. Ibid., 42–45.

calling us and provoking us, and our preaching is done in the shadow of the cross. Here it's important to point out that the weakness of God—as an event that calls to us from the crucified one on the cross, as an event that emanates from below—does not represent a moment in time when Jesus temporarily kept his power in check in order to let his human nature suffer, so he could conform to the will of his Father for the divine plan of salvation, knowing all along that he could go to the divine power supply anytime he wanted to in order to smite the Romans who crucified him. That is what Caputo calls strong theology, and he has no taste for it. In contrast, Caputo writes, "Jesus was being crucified, not holding back; he was nailed there and being executed very much against his will and the will of God." The event harbored in the name of God is present at the crucifixion by virtue of its *weakness*: "the power of the powerlessness of Jesus, in and as the protest against the injustice that rises up from the cross, in and as the words of forgiveness, not a deferred power that will be visited upon one's enemies at a later time." In most of his recent works, Caputo is "trying to displace thinking about God as the highest being and best thing that is *there* by starting to think that God is the call that *provokes* what is there, the specter that haunts what is there, the spirit that breathes over what is there."[15] Here deconstruction is the repetition of the religious, the structure of the religious, not what destroys the religious. The crucified one on the cross is a specter that haunts, provokes, and solicits from below, calling down through the ages as an alternative to the normalcy of civilization, a challenge to the normalcy of civilization, a disturbance to the normalcy of civilization.[16]

Second, and closely related, a homiletic of the event is *weak* in the sense that the specter that disturbs what is, the (holy) ghost that haunts what is, doesn't exist. "It" is not on the plane of being. While strong theologies have strong powers that make strong guarantees, proclamations that are evocative of the event come laden with risk and lack a divine army to back them up. "I treat God," Caputo writes, "not as an eminent omnipotent onto-power capable of leveling tall buildings and reducing his enemies (no need for gender-neutral language here) to ashes, but as the weak force of a call. If pressed by the Lord Cardinal, His Eminence the Grand

15. Ibid., 42–54.

16. A homiletic that disturbs what is, that disturbs the normalcy of civilization, is best seen in feminist and African American approaches to preaching. See esp. Florence, *Preaching as Testimony*, 56.

Inquisitor, to say what then God 'is,' I would nervously defer because I prefer to say not that God 'is' but that God 'calls,' that God promises, not from beyond being but from below, without being or sovereignty."[17] The specter that provokes the world and disturbs the world—that makes *being* restless—is the weak force of a call, not a strong Presence where one's God is, as the vacation Bible school song describes, "so strong and so mighty that there's nothing my God cannot do." The weakness of God calls and solicits, but it doesn't have the power of an agency or entity working on its behalf. In a homiletic of the event, God's transcendent activity and agency is the activity and agency of a call, not the activity and agency of an entity that intervenes and makes things happen in the world. "Suppose we imagine God," Caputo says, "not as a prime mover unmoved, but as removed from the order of cosmic movements and cosmological explanations, removed from the onto-causal order altogether, from being, presence, power, and causality? Suppose we imagine God otherwise, not really having a seat in being at all, but below being and beings, simmering beneath the ontico-ontological difference, as the heart of a heartless world?"[18] Here, the name of God is not the name of what is the most real "thing" but rather what is most real *in* things.[19] While a homiletic of the event celebrates the event harbored in the name of God, the preacher bears witness to a call and provocation, not to an entity with causal pow-

17. Caputo, *Weakness of God*, 38.

18. Ibid., 36. "Another way to put all this," Caputo continues, "is to say that, in my vocabulary, the world is there, being is there, and there we are, there, in the world, being right there along with the world. By 'God,' on the other hand, I do not mean a being who is there, an entity trapped in being, even as a super-being *up there,* up above the world, who physically powers and causes it, who made it and occasionally intervenes upon its day-to-day activities to tweak things for the better in response to a steady stream of solicitations from down below (a hurricane averted here, an illness averted there, etc.). That I consider an essentially magical view of the world. I do not mean anything that is *there,* because what is *there* belongs to the order of being and power; to the strong force of the world, where you solve problems by raising money—or an army. I mean a call that solicits and disturbs what is there, an event that adds a level of signification and meaning, of provocation and solicitation to what is there, that makes it impossible for the world, for what is *there,* to settle solidly in place, to consolidate, to close in upon itself. By the name of 'God' I mean the event of this solicitation, an event of deconsolidation, an electrifying event-ing disturbance, the solvent or the weak force of this spectral spirit who haunts the world as its bad conscience, or who breathes lightly and prompts its most inspired moments, all the while readily conceding that there are other names than the name of God." *Weakness of God*, 39–40.

19. See Caputo and Vattimo, *After the Death of God*, 65.

ers on the plane of being. Which means that even as a homiletic of the event bears witness to the promise harbored in the name of God, there is no guarantee that the event, what is promised in the name, will come true. A homiletic of the event prays and hopes and dreams and weeps, but it doesn't offer guarantees. It is a homiletic of risk. Our preaching is done in the shadow of a cross that still speaks not because of its triumphalism but in virtue of a weak call that rises in protest as a disturbance to the normalcy of civilization, as the heart of a heartless world. A homiletic of the event has the audacity to proclaim with St. Paul that the weakness of the cross—in all its foolishness and absurdity—is stronger than the wisdom of the world.[20]

Yet we must not confuse the weak call of the event for a lack of passionate engagement. It is precisely in the face of uncertainty and risk that a homiletic of the event becomes all the more passionate, for we pray and weep and hope and dream precisely because we long for the transformative event "to come" true (*facere veritatem*), because we are not content with the present, because the disturbance that rises up from the cross, the weak call of God, demands that we speak of the event that we cannot speak of, that we bear witness to the dangerous memories that demand a response. The passion of faith, Kierkegaard once said, is directly proportionate to its objective uncertainty.[21]

By recalling Augustine's question from the *Confessions*, "What do I love when I love my God?" (Is it love that I love? Is it justice that I love? Is God love? Is love God? I do not know), a homiletic of the event doesn't give a definitive answer, but is always in pursuit of the question, is shaped by the question, is marked by the question, is haunted and provoked by the question. At a certain level, a homiletic of the event lives in the desert of undecideability, recognizing that when we invoke the name of "God" we are never sure what we are saying, we are never sure what is being evoked and provoked. We are walking by faith, not by sight, feeling our way like a blind person with a stick, not sure what we are running up against, if anything at all. Once again we must admit that this dwelling in

20. In relationship to the postmodern return of religion, Caputo says his weak theology of the event can accompany Derrida's "religion without religion" as a "theology without theology," or as a "weak theology" that accompanies Gianni Vattimo's "weak thought," or perhaps even as the "weak messianic theology" that accompanies Walter Benjamin's "weak messianic force." See Caputo, *Weakness of God*, 5–11.

21. See ibid., 11.

the desert doesn't come without risk, for we can never know for sure if the wholly other is a messiah or a monster, which is a conversation we'll pick up in the next chapter.

Even though the first chapter of this book began by describing the difficulty preachers have in speaking of God, a homiletic of the event is forced to admit that none of us is able to speak of God, and that is precisely what good Christian preaching should announce. Shouldn't everything interesting about a sermon turn on the *impossibility* of speaking about God? Shouldn't this be the subject of our celebration? Aren't Barth and Derrida right in saying in their own ways that it is *impossible* to speak of God, and doesn't our recognition of this, as Barth put it, give God the glory?[22] Doesn't our inability to speak of God make God all the more praiseworthy? Haven't the mystics shown us that the unspeakable is precisely the place where the most inspiring language begins?[23] Perhaps we should view our lack of knowledge not as a loss, but as a gain. In a homiletic of the event, this uncertainty, this lack of complete knowledge or comprehension, does not diminish the event that is harbored in the name of God, but keeps it safe and intensifies our passion for it, our reverence for it, precisely because "we would not be likely to praise the *tout autre* if we *did* have an adequate comprehension of it, just because anything of which we have an adequate comprehension will not be *tout autre*. Knowing that the *tout autre* is incomprehensible, that it is *impossible* to comprehend the wholly other, would seem to be for Derrida the condition of possibility for something eminently praiseworthy."[24] A homiletic of the event is not a demonstration of how to speak of God, but of how *not* to speak of God, which is a lesson we didn't need Jacques Derrida or Peter Rollins to teach us, for we learned it a long time ago through Moses' complaint with Aaron.[25]

Further, if the gospel is not a truth among other truths but sets a question mark against all truth, as Barth described, then a homiletic of the event cautions preachers to be careful of the idols we so easily construct. Instead of reducing preaching to propositional truth claims strictly

22. See Barth, *Word of God and the Word of Man*, 186; as well as Derrida, "How to Avoid Speaking" and Caputo, "Apostles of the Impossible," 191.

23. See Rollins, *How (Not) to Speak of God*, xiv.

24. Caputo, "Apostles of the Impossible," 191.

25. See esp. Rollins, *How (Not) to Speak of God*, which is influenced by Derrida's "How to Avoid Speaking."

in the service of Right Beliefs, or to grand ethical exhortations in which God as "other" is for all practical purposes *dead*, a proclamation of prayer and praise for the advent of the wholly other cultivates expectation and anticipation for what eye has not seen and ear has not heard, nor the human heart conceived. When we (homiletically) pray and weep for the wholly other, when we refuse to take the name of God in vain by signing God up for whatever causes we wish to champion, we don't diminish the name of God, we honor it. In terms of recognizing the contingency of our beliefs, and how we should maintain a certain epistemological humility in relationship to our own finite perspectives, Caputo describes the way this actually intensifies religious passion:

> We seek but do not find, not quite, not if we are honest, which does not discourage the religious heart but drives it on and heightens its passion, for this is one more encounter with the impossible. We may and we must have our opinions on [various subjects]; we must finally reach a judgment and take a stand about life, but my advice is to attach a coefficient of uncertainty to what we say, for even after we have taken a stand, we still do not know who we are. We do not Know The Secret (notice the caps!).
>
> Let there be no misunderstanding: I am not recommending a life of ignorance or of fence-sitting . . . Far from it . . . But I am saying that the condition of this [passion for the impossible] is non-knowing, that non-knowing is the inescapable element in which decisions are reached, which intensifies their passion. This non-knowing is not a simple garden-variety ignorance but rather more like what the mystics call a *docta ignorantia*, a learned or wise ignorance, that knows that we do not know and knows that this non-knowing is the inescapable horizon in which we must act, with all due decisiveness, with all the urgency that life demands.[26]

It is also possible for a homiletic of the event to preach after the event harbored in the name of God even without speaking of God; indeed, it is possible for the emphasis of our sermons to be on the solicitation and provocation harbored in the name of God even if the event transpires under new or different names. Here it becomes possible to preach after God without using the name of God (and if God is "the name above all names," we can even do this from a proper theological perspective). It is no accident that philosophical theologian Jean-Luc Marion utilizes a cross to mark out the name of God when he writes the word *God*, which

26. See Caputo, *On Religion*, 18–23.

is reminiscent of the Jewish refusal to pronounce the name of God or to even write it in a way that it can be pronounced (יהוה). It seems to me that so long as there is an emphasis on the event harbored in the name of God, its provocation and solicitation, then it is possible to preach after the event harbored in the name of God without using the word *God*. I attempt to do this every so often, as seen in ch. 7. Whether this runs counter to the modern homiletical crisis or not I will let you decide.

A homiletic of the event, I might add, is also pastoral. As I wrote this chapter, the small city of Joplin, Missouri, just about an hour west from where I live, was devastated by an EF5 tornado that ripped through it, killing nearly two hundred people and leveling virtually everything in its path, leaving much of the city in ruins. Around the same time, I received news that one of the most beloved, dedicated members of the church where I pastor was diagnosed with a severe form of cancer. As we are all too often reminded, life can be full of heartache and sadness and struggle, and it is in the midst of such struggle that pastors are called on to preach. Fortunately, nowadays there are not very many (if any) mainline pastors who say that such tragedies are the will of God. Such talk may take place in fundamentalist circles of the church, but not in progressive contexts. In times like these, pastors tend to say that such tragedies are not the will of God and that when heartache overcomes us, God is the first one to shed a tear. We are told that God is with us in our suffering and will help us through our suffering, that God, through Christ, identifies with our suffering. Which is all homiletically appropriate. Some progressive listeners may have difficulty with images of God that sound so personified (God as the first to shed a tear, or as one who consciously identifies with our suffering), but more times than not, these homiletical moves are usually experienced as quite meaningful, especially in a poetic sense. From the perspective of a homiletic of the event, it is also possible for preachers to incorporate language related to God as the *call* that solicits us to respond in the face of suffering, but of course not the cause of the suffering itself. For instance, in the wake of the Joplin tornado, dozens and dozens of people from my church contacted me as soon as they heard the news, wanting to know how they could help. They weren't sure what needed to be done, but they knew they had to do *something*. Thousands of people from the surrounding area—some who consider themselves religious and others who do not—are still involved in long-term recovery efforts. We may not have a Reason (capital *R*) to respond in the face of such suffering, but when we look into the face of the other (I am thinking of Levinas here) there is an infinite call upon our lives, and we cannot help responding. John McClure puts it this way: "Levinas makes it clear that fullness of life is found only in our openness to the absolute mystery of the other. In the neighbor's face (*visage*), we experience an absolute obligation towards compassion, resistance, justice, and hope that grips our lives and holds us to a new vision for all humanity."[27]

In these situations, in relationship to the modern homiletical crisis, a homiletic of the event highlights the *provocation* of the call to respond, to love and show compassion, but it doesn't substitute the finite actions of human beings for the unconditional call that solicits them, nor does it place infinite value on the actually existing forms of love and compassion that we already have. A homiletic of the event celebrates the times that human beings "make the love of God real"—as I have said, a homiletic of the event is a big fan of doing the truth—but it doesn't substitute the actually existing instantiations of love, hospitality, justice, and so forth for the unconditional call that provokes such actions.[28]

The same holds true in the face of death. If we recall the pastor in chapter 1 who said to a grieving family that in times of great sorrow, "we need somebody with skin to hold onto," it is possible for us to view the event harbored in the name of God, the event harbored in the name of love, as the event that calls us to one another in times of sadness and sorrow. Here, God is viewed as the call that solicits the presence of the loved one to "do the truth," to "make the love of God real," "to divide the abyss in half, to break open the tragic solitude, to divide the instant by sharing it between us," to usher in the time of the messiah.[29] Theologically speaking, this allows us to respond to the provocation harbored in the name of God and at the same time keep a safe distance between ourselves and God.

Even as a homiletic of the event emphasizes the importance of "doing the truth," it also recognizes that the messiah we hope and pray for never quite shows up—not if the future is to remain open—for there is always more truth to come, more truth to be done, lest the future close in on us. But instead of leading to an exhaustive sense of compassion fatigue and despondency—as is often the case in the modern homiletical

27. McClure, *Other-wise Preaching*, 133–34.

28. See Caputo, *Weakness of God*, 88.

29. Ibid., 250.

crisis—a homiletic of the event recognizes that the less the event harbored in the name of God is present, the less it is actualized, the more its call to exist, to be present, is intensified. In traditional language, this leads us to prayer and praise. When the messiah seems most absent, we pray for the messiah (the wholly other) to show up all the more. The less the messiah exists, the more the messiah insists, and the focus of a homiletic of the event celebrates the provocation of the call, of the "to come," recognizing that we never quite arrive but are always in pursuit (we are *after* God), and necessarily so.

Because the act of preaching is connected to the interpretation of texts within the context of communal worship, a homiletic of the event is always engaging texts that are made sacred by giving an ear to the poetics of the event they harbor. A homiletic of the event listens for the event that is harbored in sacred Scripture, the event that is testified to in Scripture, the event that calls to us and calls on us, that demands a response. By listening for the event harbored in these stories (as opposed to reducing them to a banal literalism), we are able to, in the words of Caputo, "stop thinking of Scriptures as handing over a string of supernatural assertions whose truth lies in their correspondence to supernatural facts too far off or too high up for us to see with our unaided natural eyes, as disclosing super-facts that would otherwise be withheld from humankind, and we start thinking of them as *invitations* to transform our lives."[30] Scripture (and religion as well) is true in the way that a poem is true, or a song is true, or a work of art is true. When interpreting Scripture in a homiletic of the event, when listening for the truth of the event harbored in Scripture (that is, the truth of the event that is called for in Scripture to come true), we are not listening for metaphysical propositions that definitively tells us How Things Are and What Is True, but we are listening for the event that knocks on our door through these stories, the event that comes calling, without having to wire up the call of the event to a Determinate Source. The call may or may not have a Determinate Source (about such things deconstruction cannot say a thing), but a homiletic of the event brackets the question of the source and listens for the event that is harbored in the poetics of the text, in the sacred names and languages that we have in-herited, that have been handed over to us, fully aware that the event stirs in other traditions and texts as well, for the event harbored in the name

30. Ibid., 119. Emphasis mine.

of God, in the name of the kingdom of God, can go by many names.[31] By approaching the interpretation of texts poetically, which is not an unfamiliar concept to progressives, we not only steer clear of the supernaturalism and magic associated with fundamentalism, but we also allow Scripture to speak in evocative and provocative ways that our love affair with the historical-critical method has declared off limits for far too long.

Deconstruction deals with texts, lives in the space between texts, and as such the Scriptures offer a wealth of possibilities for listening for the event harbored in the name of God. A homiletic of the event lends an ear to both Hebrew Scripture and Christian Scripture. In addition to hearing the kind of countertestimony that has been well developed by Walter Brueggemann and Anna Carter Florence,[32] we are invited into the upside-down world of the kingdom of God—a kingdom (or kin-dom) that parabolically disturbs the normalcy of civilization and invokes the madness of the event. In the Scriptures (not *sola* in the Scriptures, but in them nonetheless), we encounter the poetics of the impossible: "In the kingdom of God," Caputo writes, "things happen a lot more like the way things fall out in deconstruction—which has to do with events, and whose least bad definition, Derrida says, is an 'experience of the impossible'—than they do in classical metaphysics or natural law theories, which are too much taken with the princes and principalities of necessity, order, presence, essence, regularity, and stability."[33] In terms of biblical resonance, the provocation of the event that stirs restlessly in the name of God, in the name of justice, in the name of forgiveness, in the name of hospitality, and so forth, can be described in terms of the event that is harbored in the kingdom of God, that longs to come true, that groans to be born. When we long for the messiah to come, when we dream of all that is evoked in words like *justice* and *forgiveness* and *hospitality*, we find ourselves hoping and sighing and dreaming and weeping for the advent

31. Caputo writes: "A poetics does not record the strong force of hard facts; it describes the weak force of a call for the kingdom, or for justice, which is true even if the real world is unjust. That is why there can be more than one religious discourse, and why religions do not compete with one another in a zero-sum game in which the truth of one comes at the cost of the falsity of another. The idea of one true religion or religious discourse or body of religious narratives makes no more sense than the idea of one true poem or one true language or one true culture." Ibid., 118.

32. For this homiletical appropriation of Brueggemann, see Florence, *Preaching as Testimony*, 72ff. and Brueggemann, *The Word Militant*.

33. Caputo, *The Weakness of God*, 111.

of the kingdom of God to be born, to come true, to disturb and displace the kingdoms of this world. Our hearts beat for the kingdom of God, but we recall that the name of God goes by many names and can hardly be confined to any one religion, or even to religion *per se*. I like the way David Buttrick puts it, though I wouldn't be opposed to adding a bit of a spectral twist to his words: "Listen to Jesus speaking of kingdom-come in the Beatitudes. In God's new social order the hungry will be fed, yes, and the poor will be raised up, yes, and the powerless empowered. And those who grieve for the way of the world will find their delight. Peacemakers will triumph, and those who are persecuted will celebrate. So whenever and wherever you see beatitudes beginning to come true, there is where you will find the presence of an unseen, astonishingly modest God."[34]

It follows that the truth of a homiletic of the event is a poetic truth, not a metaphysical or representational truth. To borrow James Cone's felicitous words, our preaching bears witness to "a poetic happening, an evocation of an indescribable reality in the lives of the people."[35] The truth of our preaching isn't based on whether or not we accurately describe facts of the matter (propositional truths), but rather that our lives bear witness to the event that groans to be born, that wishes to come true, that wants to make itself felt. In this sense, a homiletic of the event is similar to Anna Carter Florence's testimonial homiletic, for it harbors the transformational event that is "testified" to in our experience, "by being borne out or confirmed in our lives," to draw on language used by Caputo. As such, our sermons can be viewed as a poetic way to "give interpretive life and breath to an event, to something that is alive within our sacred names, something going on within us."[36] In following Florence's insights related to testimony, our lives do not *prove* the event; rather, our lives are *sealed* to the event, sealed to the narrated and confessed freedom the event proclaims.[37] A homiletic of the event is a circumfession, for we have

---

34. Buttrick, "*Homiletic* Renewed," 115.

35. As quoted in Lowry, *The Sermon*, 36.

36. Caputo, *The Weakness of God*, 118.

37. Florence is drawing on poststructuralist theologian Mary McClintock Fulkerson. In the paraphrase, I basically changed the word *testimony* to the word *event*. The actual quote is this: "Our lives do not prove the testimony; rather, our lives are *sealed* to the testimony, sealed to the narrated and confessed freedom the testimony proclaims—which is the Word as perfectly open sign." See Florence, *Preaching as Testimony*, 97.

been cut by something wondrous, we know not what, and we are forever sealed to it, *s'il y en a.*

Postmodern preachers must keep in mind that the plurality of the event that stirs restlessly in the name of God cannot be contained to the singularity of individual expressions that bear witness to the event. To borrow the standard critique of the "New Homiletic,"[38] it is naïve to assume there is a "common human experience" to go on, to assume that the event is universal in scope. While I do short-circuit the insights of Caputo and Craddock in the next section in order to show that the structure of the event is connected to a basic structure of human experience (which is not to be confused for common human experience), the event calls and recalls in a *multiplicity* of ways, and the way that different people hear and heed the event is significantly influenced by social context and location. As such, when preachers celebrate the event harbored in the name of God—when we seal our lives to the event and bear witness to it—we do so by celebrating as many truths as possible. It is a *communal* proclamation of prayer and praise. As Caputo writes: "If the truth be told, and I would like to speak the truth, I would say with St. Augustine, who said let there be as many senses of Scripture as possible, so long as all of them are true, that I would like to have as many *truths* as possible, so long as all of them are true. . . . I am so much in favor of truth that I wish to multiply it, not subtract from it by confining it to the straight and narrow. More precisely, I am defending the plurality of truth and the truth of plurality."[39]

A homiletic of the event also shares some points of commonality with David Lose's critical fideism. For Lose, preachers can't prove the claims that are made in sermons, but can rather attest to their pragmatic usefulness: "What I advocate," Lose writes, "is a critical fideism that, while it cannot prove the truth of its ultimate claims, nevertheless seeks to make a case in the public arena for their utility and soundness."[40] While Lose

38. I put "New Homiletic" in quotes because it is not nearly as new as the name makes one think. As Dale Andrews has shown, it has much deeper roots in African American preaching traditions that stretch back much further than the mid- to late-twentieth century. See esp. his comments in *The Renewed Homiletic*, 96.

39. Zlomislić and DeRoo, *Cross and Khôra*, 17.

40. Lose, *Confessing Jesus Christ*, 40. A key difference between Lose and Caputo is based on pragmatic soundness (this is similar to the difference Caputo shares with Richard Rorty, so it's not altogether surprising that Lose consistently draws on a modified form of Rorty's pragmatism). For more on this, see ch. 6. See also Willimon, *Conversations with Barth on Preaching*, 64.

is more interested than Caputo in securing (penultimate) foundational truth (more about this in the next chapter), on the following point both Lose and Caputo agree: By their fruits you shall know them. In Caputo's words, "The truth of a religious discourse is whether a living tradition forms around it; its reality testifies to its rationality. . . . A religious discourse discloses or illuminates something about the event, about being born and dying, making love and giving birth, having hope and being filled with despair, being lifted up with joy or weighed down by suffering. The crucifixion and the resurrection are deep and overarching symbols of the rhythmic birth and death and rebirth that we call our lives, and the deeper such symbols sink their stakes into our conscious and unconscious life, the more enduring and compelling the narratives that embody them."[41] Poetic truth bears witness to transformational truth.

To summarize: A homiletic of the event can be understood as a proclamation of *prayer* because it has to do with "hearing, heeding, and hearkening to a provocation that draws us out of ourselves," which is not to be confused for a conversation with a Super Being in the heavens, or a Super Something behind the scenes, where we ask for divine intervention from a God who hears our prayers and decides whether or not to respond.[42] A homiletic of the event can be understood as a proclamation of *praise* because it celebrates the event, solicitation, and provocation that is beyond our own manufacture and all of our best efforts, the transformative event harbored in the name of God that disturbs both ourselves and our world, that makes being restless, that calls us to do the truth, *facere veritatem*. It is an eschatological proclamation of praise for the "to come," which is to be distinguished from a proclamation of praise for what has already been given.[43]

A homiletic of the event can be understood as a proclamation of prayer and praise for the *wholly other* precisely because the words and references in our sermons are irreducibly deconstructible. We bear witness not to a determinate God that we can name but rather to the spectral event harbored in the name of God that is beyond naming, the name that

---

41. Caputo, *The Weakness of God*, 118–19.

42. Caputo and Vattimo, *After the Death of God*, 57.

43. This is a technicality that serves to differentiate the positions of Derrida and Marion. A homiletic of the event hitches a ride with Derrida's emphasis that the promise harbored in the structure of the "to come" is never given. As such it has more in common with the Jewish structure of the messianic than with Christian neoplatonism. See ch. 11.

resists naming. The name of God is irreducibly translatable, and as such it is always beyond what we can imagine or foresee, which is precisely what puts us in pursuit of it all the more. Our sermons bear witness to the event, which is undeconstructible, but the words and images we use are always deconstructible, including the words and images in the texts we interpret. If we could adequately conceptualize the wholly other, then it wouldn't be wholly other but would rather be a finite object we could grasp, which is not all that worthy of praise unless we are content worshiping grandiose proclamations of our best selves and our best ideas on our best days. In a homiletic of the event, everything turns on the aporia of the impossible, on what we can't speak of, on the transformative event, the spectral structure of the messianic, lest we reduce the event harbored in the name of God to our own conceptual frameworks for understanding, and thus negate its provocative call and transformative possibility as the "wholly other" that disturbs what is.

In a homiletic of the event, the preacher's words (contra the traditional reading that "the preaching of the Word of God is the Word of God") do not constitute the Word of God, but are rather viewed as a proclamation of prayer and praise for, and in response to, the spectral/weak force of the call, the "word of God" that disturbs the heart of being, that makes being restless, that is the heart of a heartless world. And though it is a weak call, it carries an exceptionally strong appeal and claim on our lives.

A homiletic of the event celebrates and affirms the event that stirs beneath, that is harbored in, the name of God. For it is the event that makes us restless, it is the event that our hearts are responding to, it is the event that sends us out in search of what it is that we love when we say we love our God, all the while with the understanding that the name of God is a limit concept, "the most famous and richest name we have to signify both an open-ended excess and an inaccessible mystery,"[44] and that the event harbored in the name of God can go under many names.

A homiletic of the event consists of two yes's; the first yes is the call, the second yes is the response: "The power of that call, we might say, is the first yes, a solicitous yes, the yes that calls for confirmation. We in turn confirm, respond, answer. That is the second yes, *oui, oui.*" A homiletic of the event celebrates the provocation of the call, and, at the same time, inspires listeners to confirm, respond, and answer, to do the truth, *facere veritatem.*

---

44. Caputo and Vattimo, *After the Death of God*, 53.

OTHER-WISE INSENSITIVITIES?

So far in this book I have argued that overcoming the modern homiletical crisis—which includes the task of overcoming metaphysics—would be greatly helped by shifting the way progressives imagine and talk about God. At different points along the way, I can well imagine readers critiquing the homiletic I am pursuing by saying that while I may very well be advocating theological postmodernism, I am falling prey to an outdated mode of modern communication. After all, I haven't paid much attention to matters of style, and homileticians would not simply say that the modern homiletical crisis can be fixed by the preacher finding the "right" theological method and then telling listeners about it from the pulpit, and rightly so. Homileticians, especially those drawn to what is increasingly referred to as "other-wise preaching," encourage preachers to be attentive to conversations that take place in a variety of contexts, and not in a way that simply imagines or projects what the preacher thinks the positions of "others" are (as Doug Pagitt has shown so well, the last thing we need from the pulpit is more "speeching").[45] Instead of more speeching, it's possible for the other-wise preacher to be understood as host and guest of conversations with others, which are usually played out publicly (for better or worse) in monological sermon form. This is representative of various homiletic turns toward the listener that have become quite prominent. Listeners are not passive recipients of a singular message, for they are already part of an ongoing conversation that has its *arche* well before the preacher steps into the pulpit.

While most of this book is concerned with theological questions at the root of the modern homiletical crisis more than with questions related to sermon preparation and structure, it goes without saying that questions of sermon preparation and structure overlap with theological questions. That is an assumption that I make from the start. I affirm the concerns raised by other-wise homileticians. Because I have paid far more attention to theology than anything else, allow me to make a homiletic of the event's relationship to other-wise preaching a bit more explicit by making four brief points.

First, postmodern theology, as McClure demonstrates so well, prioritizes an openness to its "others," and a homiletic of the event follows suit.

---

45. See Pagitt, *Preaching in the Inventive Age*. The definitive book for other-wise preaching remains McClure's *Other-wise Preaching*.

One of the wonderful results of the folk postmodernism described in chapter 3 is that it leads progressive preachers to value, as Ron Allen describes, "collegiality, conversation, and respect for plurality and difference."[46] As much as possible, a homiletic of the event pays attention to the various perspectives and experiences of listeners, all the while recognizing, with Levinas, that the "other" constitutes a shore we will never reach. This is assumed from the get-go. A homiletic of the event considers the mutual meaning-making that takes place between preacher and congregation, as well as the conversation we find ourselves in. These ethical convictions, I hope, will inevitably come out not only in the "Sunday morning sermon," but in the preparation process as well. Which leads to the second point: Postmodern preachers should follow the insights of other-wise homiletics by making an even more intentional effort of drawing on collaborative approaches to preaching, including more radical forms of conversation and dialogue. We can take a cue from Derrida here, for a number of his texts are cast in the form of dialogues, of columns divided by space and lines, of messages given and received. When describing why Derrida uses this style of presentation, Steven Shakespeare notes how "it is not clear in these cases that there is one master voice or narrative that carries the day at the end of the text. Rather, we are invited into the space of an open-ended conversation." Even in interviews, Derrida often invites the interviewer to be part of his responses. The style Derrida uses ("the way those texts are performed") is not indifferent to what those texts are about: "As Kierkegaard might have put it, the 'how' and the 'what' are inseparable. This too has major implications for how theological questions are approached," to which I would add, "in a sermon."[47] In a sermon we too are performing a text,[48] and collaborative approaches to preaching allow for open-ended conversations that go hand-in-hand with the event that never quite arrives, is never fully present, that resists singularity, that comes over us in a multiplicity of ways (as stated above, a homiletic of the event is a fan of a plurality of truths, provided all of them are true). A homiletic of the event is an irreducibly open-ended *communal* act of invocation, prayer, and praise, and preachers are responsible for inviting others into the sermon in healthy and respectful ways. Collaborative

46. Allen, Blaisdell, and Johnson, *Theology for Preaching*, 10.

47. Shakespeare, *Derrida and Theology*, 7. See also Willimon, *Conversations with Barth on Preaching*, 95–96.

48. See Childers, *Performing the Word*, and Ward, *Speaking from the Heart*.

approaches to preaching help put a check on power and privilege, even when sermons are delivered by a pastor in a robe in a pulpit, and they help remind the preacher that his or her experiences are not necessarily representative of everyone who has gathered for worship. The preaching moment as generally structured in mainline settings—pulpit elevated and up front, congregants on benches listening to one speaker—is hardly ideal, and while collaborative approaches to preparation and structure still don't fully invite conversation and dialogue (nothing present is perfect), they are a step in the right direction.[49]

At the same time, there is still something to be said for the evocative power of the preaching moment, even within the traditional structure, and I am not ready to write it off quite yet. While we all know that there are plenty of sermons out there that lay an egg (show up to hear me preach on any given Sunday and there is always that chance!), I dare say that good preaching harbors the possibility for transformation as much as any current art form does, including music, film, and theater. Indeed, there's not a chance in the world I would be a pastor if I didn't think that the act of preaching harbors the possibility of transformation. If a preacher intentionally takes into consideration concerns related to power, privilege, and social location in the process of preparing and structuring the sermon, it is quite possible for the preaching moment, even in a traditional monologue setting, to be transformational, inviting, inventive, and respectful of preaching's "others."[50]

49. For all of the talk related to "postmodern" conversational sermons, such approaches remain mostly theoretical, *especially* in mainline settings, and as such they at times can come across as disingenuous. Aside from the more radical, truly conversational sermons found in places like Solomon's Porch in Minneapolis or VOID in Waco, Texas, most "conversational" sermons are still in the form of a pulpit monologue that carries with it all of the attendant symbolic and historical trappings (especially in relationship to authority and privilege). Similarly, most dialogical sermons that take into consideration the perspectives of others have retained monological forms of delivery. Even though this has long been an accepted convention among preachers and homileticians, it still strikes me as lacking. I tend to think Marlene Ringgaard Lorensen is right when she states: "The notion of dialogue is being used in so many ways that it tends to become senseless" (Lorensen, "Carnivalized Preaching," 2).

50. I am guessing that most readers of this book likely preach in established settings where a sermon delivered in monologue form is the expected norm, so most of the sample sermons I provide in part two are set up in such a way that collaborative concerns related to preparation and structure have been taken into consideration, even as the preaching moment plays out in the form of one person (the pastor) engaging the many (the congregation). I am partial to the collaborative approaches to preaching described

Third, a homiletic of the event must be very clear in distinguishing theological language from anthropological language, especially in relationship to the modern homiletical crisis. It seems to me that one of the most misunderstood aspects of other-wise preaching is the belief that it leads to the domestication of theological otherness, which is not always the case. When other-wise preachers stress the importance of engaging preaching's "others" and being open to them, it is usually understood solely in anthropological terms. As Lorensen observes: "A significant theological critique of other-wise preaching practices is that the collaborative co-authorship of the congregation threatens to dismiss divine agency."[51] This is picked up in Ron Allen's description of other-wise preaching: "Theologians of otherness note that each person, each community, each culture, indeed each element of creation is a distinct entity with its own identity and particularity. . . . Theologies of otherness insist on respecting the particularity of others—individuals, communities, cultures, and elements of nature. By honoring such distinctiveness, we allow the richness of difference and diversity to permeate and shape the world more and, therefore, to enrich our own lives."[52] While fully valuing the conventional sense of "others" as stated by Allen, a homiletic of the event goes one step further by highlighting the event harbored in the name of God, which is *theologically* restless with what is stirring in the name of God. In contrast to the more determinate "others" that are part and parcel of other-wise preaching (i.e., perspectives that are other than our own, whether in individual or cultural form, even though we never fully understand the perspectives of others, even though we even remain a question unto ourselves!), a homiletic of the event bends an ear not simply to others that already exist (entities), but to the spectral lure of the wholly other that does not exist (God does not exist, God insists). The event that is stirring in the name of God, the event that groans to be born, is the subject matter of the sermon's affirmation and desire, not the more determinate others that are already on the plane of being. The more "determinate" others, as reflected in Allen's description, are not the subject matter of a sermon's affirmation and desire. In a homiletic of the event, the subject matter is God, or the event harbored in the name of God, which can go by many

in John McClure's *The Roundtable Pulpit* and Lucy Atkinson Rose's *Sharing the Word.* O. Wesley Allen's *The Homiletic of All Believers* also provides a nice collaborative approach.

51. Lorensen, "Carnivalized Preaching," 11.

52. Allen, *Thinking Theologically*, 61–62.

names. While the event harbored in the name of God might very well lead us to be open to the more "determinate" others—that may be the event that groans to be born, to "come true," that we are called to confirm—the purpose of the sermon is not to be reduced only to considerations of how a text leads us to respect more determinate others.[53] A homiletic of the event consists of both call and response—not just response, not just call. A homiletic of the event celebrates excess and mystery, the unconditional and undeconstructible, the eschatological longing for the messiah, for the impossible, none of which is a determinate entity (on the plane of being).

Fourth, at the risk of losing my street cred with other-wise homileticians, there is a certain structure to experience, what constitutes experience as experience, that, dare I say, all of us share. I beg you to hear me out on this one before casting the first stone. Let's start with a quote from Caputo:

> Instead of distinguishing "religious people," the ones who go to church on Sunday mornings, from non-religious people, the ones who stay home and read *The Sunday New York* Times, I would rather speak of the religious *in* people, in all of us. I take "religion" to mean the being-religious of human beings, which I put on a par with being political or being artistic. By "the religious," I mean a basic structure of human experience and even, as I hope to show, the very thing that most constitutes human experience as experience, as something that is really happening.[54]

But so as to not worry us too much, or send us into premature cardiac arrest, Caputo quickly offers a disclaimer: "And once again, we need to remind ourselves, the religious sense of life would never mean just one thing for everybody, as if it had some sort of common ahistorical, universal, transcendental structure. I try to swear off thinking like that about anything." What Caputo has in mind when he talks about "the very thing that most constitutes human experience as experience" is the structure of the messianic, the longing for the impossible. What all of us have in common—provided we have life—is the future. We live in the mundane, foreseeable, conventional future, where nothing is really going on. But

---

53. *Pace* Allen. Here Caputo's commentary on Levinas is apropos for McClure's homiletic as well: "Our major debt to Levinas is that he has translated God into an event, and our major complaint with him is that he has constricted the event to a strictly ethical category that undermines its excess (since the event contained within this name has to do with more than obligation to others)." See Caputo, *Weakness of God*, 271.

54. Caputo, *On Religion*, 9.

the very thing that constitutes experience as experience is when the un-foreseeable future comes over us and shatters the horizon of our pres-ent and opens up a new way of being. This is the time of the messiah, the event that groans to be born, the truth-event of Christianity. And it's what makes our hearts beat. As Derrida writes: "The future is that which—tomorrow, later, next century—will be. There is a future which is predictable, programmed, scheduled, foreseeable. But there is a future to come (*l'avenir*) which refers to someone who comes whose arrival is totally unexpected. For me, that is the real future. That which is totally unpredictable. The Other who comes without my being able to anticipate their arrival. So if there is a real future beyond this known future, it's *l'avenir* in that it's the coming of the Other when I am completely unable to foresee their arrival."[55]

While the event very well may come over us in different ways (it doesn't have "some sort of common ahistorical, universal, transcen-dental structure"), all of us deeply long for it, whether we consider our-selves religious or not. While I find most of the criticisms hurled at the New Homiletic to be legitimate—I would never argue for some sort of Common Human Experience—I tend to think Fred Craddock is more right than wrong when he states,

> I used to work so hard at being relevant. I think now more about what is really going on, and I notice Flannery O'Connor can write about southern Protestant illiterate preachers and stir a genuine conversation among Jewish people sitting on the porch in the Adirondacks. What do they have in common? One thing: life. Adults, educated adults, sat in theaters, while upon the screen a strange little creature called E.T.—he was sort of greenish brown and had either two or three fingers. I mean, greenish brown with two or three fingers from another planet, and American adults sat there crying and said to each other, "This is the third time I've come to see this." Now do not tell me people cannot make shifts. Maya Angelou came out of the cotton patch of Arkansas and moved the elite of New York. What do they have in common? Life.[56]

55. Derrida, *Derrida* (DVD).

56. Craddock, "Inductive Preaching Renewed," 54. For ethically responsible ap-proaches to narrative preaching and the New Homiletic, see esp. Long, *Preaching from Memory to Hope*, 13, 18–26. I love the idea in the New Homiletic that preaching is an event to which we give testimony, and I think it is possible to do this by celebrating the multiplicity of the event that stirs restlessly in the name of God. Another helpful ap-proach to these concerns can be found in Eunjoo Mary Kim's trans-contextual approach

I am not sure I would go so far as to say, with Craddock, that "even in the multicultural context, beneath the surface people are more alike than they are different," and, to be sure, Craddock is analyzing *contextual* life in the United States, with all of its history and particularities. I would not begin to try to extend his analysis to some sort of Universal Experience of How Life Is. I don't advocate trying to definitively name the Essence or Meaning of Life, but prefer leaving such questions open, and irreducibly so. We are, as Augustine put it, a question unto ourselves, and, to add a motif from Caputo and Derrida, the answer to the question "Who are we?" is "We do not know who we are. That is who we are." What is the Secret to life? That there is no secret. Yet even amid the contingencies that shape our lives, that are forged in time and circumstance, that are irreducibly plural, we do share one thing: life—the secret that we do not know what life means, the secret that there is no secret. Further, there is a hunger and a restlessness for the event harbored in the name of what goes by many different names in many different cultures, that is evoked in words and in languages, that stirs in our limit concepts, with the word *God* functioning as perhaps the most famous of all the limit concepts, at least in the West. The lives of those in the slums of Calcutta and in the opulence of Orange County are not the same—but the experience of a different future that is unforeseen, that comes over us, that makes our lives restless, constitutes experience as experience, though in very different ways that are inevitably intertwined with culture and circumstance.

* * *

As preachers and congregants build meaning together over the long haul, I don't claim that a homiletic of the event is the only approach to preaching that progressives should implement. In fact, I often think it best to incorporate insights from a theology of the event into a variety of already established preaching methods, all with an eye toward the insights of collaborative, other-wise homiletics. A homiletic of the event can be helpful for teaching sermons, narrative sermons, testimonial sermons, confessional sermons, conversational sermons, as well as sermons of celebration and perhaps even exhortation. Sometimes we need to be prophetic, sometimes pastoral, sometimes a bit of both. A homiletic of the event doesn't view prophetic and pastoral aspects of preaching as mutually

---

to preaching. See Kim, *Preaching in an Age of Globalization*.

exclusive. Mary Donovan Turner's homiletic captures this beautifully. When describing "preaching as disruption," she notes the ways that the disruptions of the Hebrew prophets were often part of the healing process. Instead of dividing prophetic and pastoral preaching concerns in opposite camps, as is often the case, she doesn't so easily distinguish them from one another. I don't know if she had the structure of the messianic in mind when she wrote it, but she captures a love of the impossible quite well when she says: "Aren't we as preachers always hoping and/or longing that something will be *different*?"[57]

More than anything, I encourage preachers to listen to the religious themes stirring in the postmodern return of religion and to consider ways to preach *after* God in a variety of contexts and locations, incorporating and developing a number of methods. I concur with Ron Allen's observation: "respect for diversity and Otherness that is inherent in the heart of postmodernism undercuts any suggestion of a single postmodern way of preaching."[58] For preachers who don't find it difficult to speak of God's activity outside of the actions of human beings, or for those who don't have much difficulty believing in a supernatural God of being, then the insights of a homiletic of the event may not be all that helpful. But for progressives who do struggle to preach after God as "other," or are uncomfortable using God language in the pulpit, a homiletic of the event may be beneficial indeed. Perhaps the greatest challenge of preaching in a post-Enlightenment context is figuring out how to convey the deeply religious longing stirring in the postmodern return to religion—the desire for the event harbored in the name of God—with religious images and words that carry so much baggage for so many people. This is what I have tried to do with the sample sermons in part two, but I will leave it to you to decide if my attempts have been successful or not.

But before moving on to the second part of this book, there's one last thing that needs to be cleared up: the accusation that postmodern deconstruction means whatever one wants it to mean, which, from a Derridean perspective, couldn't be further from the *truth*.

---

57. Turner, "Disrupting a Ruptured World," 135. Emphasis mine. See also Tisdale, *Prophetic Preaching*.

58. Allen, *Preaching and the Other*, 2.

6

The Risk of Preaching

The fact that most attacks on postmodernism have been aimed at either generalities or caricatures of the movement, rather than at specific writers or the texts representing their arguments and positions, suggests that the clash is far more one of apparel than of substance.

—Carl Raschke[1]

Deconstruction . . . is not negative, even though it has often been interpreted as such despite all warnings. For me, it always accompanies an affirmative exigency, I would even say that it never proceeds without love.

—Jacques Derrida[2]

WHEN ONE READS LITERATURE related to postmodern homiletics, one of the themes that is explored most frequently relates to the way that postmodernism ushers in a loss of certainty, which makes preachers feel more than a little bit anxious. All of our knowledge, postmodern theorists tell us, is filtered through particular interpretive lenses. There is no God's-eye perspective. When Nietzsche said, "there are no absolute truths, only interpretations," he was very clear in stating that he too was making an interpretation.[3] While this approach is often appre-

1. Raschke, *Next Reformation*, 23.

2. Derrida, *Points . . . Interviews, 1974–1994*, 83.

3. For an excellent introduction to the interpretation that everything is an interpretation, see Vattimo's comments in Caputo and Vattimo, *After the Death of God*, 27–39.

ciated—especially among historically marginalized and/or oppressed groups—it's also viewed as threatening to our cherished institutions, not the least of which include our homiletical ones. Few homileticians are comfortable with the idols of modernism—particularly those that relegate progressive sermons to moral exhortations in which God becomes, for all practical purposes, "humanity said loudly." But at the same time, most homileticians are hesitant to embrace the more radical expressions of postmodern theory, including non-foundational approaches to deconstruction. This leads Ron Allen to conclude that even while "the modern goal of absolute and universal certainty is not achievable [the postmodern emphasis] on the relativity and particularity of all awareness leaves the believer on the edge of chaos."[4] Anna Carter Florence aptly describes the anxiety preachers feel in the midst of transitioning from modern to postmodern approaches to preaching by comparing the security of Egypt with the uncertainty of the wilderness:

> A wilderness holds within itself the promise of Canaan, and that promise keeps many of us going. But a wilderness also entails the hard work of exiting Egypt, and *this* is where the real wandering comes in. To leave behind the powers and authorities of a former existence, an enslaved and enslaving existence, is slow and painful and impossible to accomplish in a few months . . . It takes years— maybe forty of them—to leave yourself in order to find yourself. The process is not unlike the years of therapy that might accompany a recovery from depression. And this, I suspect, is probably why there is such resistance to postmodernism in some quarters: not all of us want to face Egypt, let alone leave it. We also do not particularly relish the exposure of our own homiletical fleshpots: if there is food in those pots, and we can count on it, so what if the price is remaining in slavery? Isn't the Egypt we know better than the liberation we don't?[5]

Because negative views of postmodern theory and deconstruction remain fairly pervasive in homiletical circles (even if we don't want to go back to Egypt), they demand a response. Throughout most of this book, I have intentionally focused on the affirming religious implications of

---

Caputo also offers a nice introduction in *What Would Jesus Deconstruct?*, 40ff. From a homiletical approach, see Lose, *Confessing Jesus Christ*, 22.

4. Allen, Blaisdell, and Johnston, *Theology for Preaching*, 59.

5. Florence, *Preaching as Testimony*, xiv–xv.

Derrida's later works, particularly his ethico-political-religious writings, mostly because they are the ones that Caputo draws on most frequently in his own work with Derrida, especially when developing a theology of the event.[6] While Derrida's later writings are influenced by deconstruction every bit as much as his earlier works, it is his earliest formulations of deconstruction that are most frequently under attack by homileticians. The negative homiletical reception of his early thought explains why his later works were—with very few exceptions—neglected, domesticated, and sometimes even treated with scorn. In the following section, I respond to several criticisms that Derridean-influenced postmodernism consistently receives from a variety of homileticians. I argue that in large part these criticisms not only perpetuate outdated stereotypes associated with Derrida, but, more importantly, they also fail to recognize the affirmation at the heart of deconstruction.

DECONSTRUCTION IS NOT DESTRUCTION

In the late 1960s, Derrida burst onto the philosophical scene and introduced us to what is now popularly referred to as deconstruction. Derrida has been widely misunderstood—perhaps more than any other contemporary figure—and though he is heralded as one of the towering intellectuals of the twentieth century, he hasn't received very much love from the church, at least not until recently. As is well known, deconstruction is threatening and challenging to our conventional assumptions, hence the strong reactions against it. As Mark C. Taylor and numerous others have described, deconstruction is set up around the notion that any structure—be it religious, political, or economic—is "constituted and maintained through acts of exclusion. In the process of creating something, something else inevitably gets left out."[7]

While Derrida is known for deconstructing "texts," the applicability of deconstruction, as Derrida's own work shows, stretches well beyond what is conventionally implied by the word *texts* (early on, deconstruction

---

6. Beginning especially with Derrida's 1989 essay "The Force of Law."

7. Taylor, "What Derrida Really Meant." Deconstruction exposes the way our perceptions are constructed by the privileging of certain items over and above others. For instance, as New Testament scholar Mark Given writes, "Logocentrism is Derrida's shorthand term for the Western privileging of 'speech over writing, immediacy over distance, identity over difference, and (self-) presence over all forms of absence, ambiguity, simulation, substitution, or negativity.'" See Given, "Paul and Writing."

was especially examined in relationship to architecture and art). When Caputo engages deconstruction, he often examines its function in relation to theology and biblical faith (he likes to describe deconstruction as the hermeneutics of the kingdom of God). This is why Caputo consistently uses Christian language when asking what is called forth in the name of the kingdom, even though he could just as easily ask what is called forth in the name of justice, hospitality, forgiveness, and so on, which he has done in numerous other contexts. In relationship to Christianity, deconstruction shows us that the actually existing forms of Christianity always fall short of all that is harbored in the name of Christianity. Deconstruction keeps our valued traditions open and alive, all in an effort to release the event that is promised in the name of our traditions, to set free the event that is restlessly stirring and longing to come true in our traditions, so that our traditions might have a future and not be allowed to harden over.

It's often assumed that deconstruction is something that we do. In pop culture, when we talk about "deconstructing" something, it usually means we are reevaluating our assumptions about a given idea or belief or object. For a simple example, consider how those who identify with the emergent church often talk about the ways they are in the process of "deconstructing" the church and/or Christianity. Here, deconstruction is viewed as somewhat synonymous with reevaluating or reassessing the church. It is something that *we* do—something that *we* have mastery over, that *we* are in charge of. However, as our conversation in chapter 4 pointed out, our efforts of reevaluating or reassessing or "deconstructing" are forged in *response* to the event. When we read texts, when we listen to what is called forth in our cherished traditions and symbols and words, we are responding to the event that overcomes and solicits us. We are not simply creating or manufacturing it. We are not the ones who "deconstruct."

As Steven Shakespeare and others show, Derrida doesn't view deconstruction as a technique that we can master and then bring to a text, but rather it is more of "an inherent dynamic of language and meaning. It is something that happens, and that reading and writing engages with, without us ever fully grasping it." To read deconstructively, according to Derrida, "means something like being attentive to an event, an unexpected arrival, that interrupts, contradicts and dislocates what appeared to be settled and fixed. It is important to note that deconstruction does not simply create this event, as if it were a matter of projecting our own wishes and fantasies upon a text." We don't deconstruct texts; rather, texts deconstruct themselves, precisely because of the event that they harbor, that can't be contained in words and texts. In deconstruction, words and texts contain what they cannot contain. From this perspective, "the event, the other, what is happening or being testified to or announced in the text, these have a certain priority in provoking the response of deconstruction. In this sense it is absolutely right to see deconstruction as *threatening*, because it is inhuman, no longer in the control of a human subject."[8] All of which is another reason deconstruction, as a repetition of the religious, has so much in common with biblical faith.

Because people interpret from different social locations, interpretations don't necessarily point to reality but generally shore up one's own place in the operative power structure. The ways we use words and symbols is connected to our social location/position and as such lack objectivity. Deconstruction points out the ways that languages and symbols are contingent on cultural usage and are unable to accurately "represent" universal reality. This leads Anna Carter Florence to compare deconstruction to therapy because it "permits us to uncover the masked priorities and power dynamics of a text that may warp its authority structures, and so create ingrown systems that lead to oppression and suffering."[9]

In relationship to the event that is harbored in words and texts—the event that overcomes and solicits us, that is not of our own doing—it's important to point out that in deconstruction, the meaning of a word doesn't point to some external reality outside of the text (recall Derrida's famous dictum "There is nothing outside of the text"[10]). Instead, meaning is created by the way words refer to other words, with a recognition that they always fall short of naming "the thing" (think about how definitions work in a dictionary: words are defined only in relationship to other words). To recall the example of democracy described in chapter 4, the event harbored in the name of democracy doesn't exist, it insists. All of our actually existing forms of democracy fall short of all that is harbored in the word *democracy*. We can try to define the ideals of democracy by using words that highlight mutuality and justice and egalitarianism and

---

8. Shakespeare, *Derrida and Theology*, 25.

9. Florence, *Preaching as Testimony*, xv. McClure's homiletical appropriation of Levinas's deconstructive thought shows that ethical concerns are most in peril when systems of totality harden over, for it is precisely then that "other" voices are silenced.

10. Derrida, *Of Grammatology*, 158.

such, but we recognize that we are in pursuit of the event harbored in these words, to which all of these words fall short. These words contain what they cannot contain. Words and texts are deconstructible, whereas the event they harbor is undeconstructible. We are in pursuit not of what exists, but of the event that insists. The event is not present, it is spectral. This is why, from a strictly linguistic standpoint, language is open-ended and inventive. The meanings of words do not completely give of themselves; there is always a "trace" that remains beyond what a word is able to give. The meaning of a word is always deferred because its meaning is dependent upon other words. We are interested in the event the words harbor, not the words themselves.

Linguistically speaking, emphasis isn't placed on *what* a word or symbol means but rather on *how* a word or symbol means. As John McClure describes, the meaning and truth of words lie more in their use than in their reference, and "the assumption that language serves an ontological function, that it discloses the being of things, can only be partly maintained, if at all. Instead of referring to Being or to the Ground of Being, words, at best, are traces of that which always remains otherwise than Being. Mostly, words refer to other words themselves."[11]

---

11. McClure, *Other-wise Preaching*, 79. For about as straightforward an introduction to deconstruction (more formally known as poststructuralism) as you can get, see Caputo's *What Would Jesus Deconstruct?*, 143–46 n. 10. For a fuller yet still very accessible introduction, see Caputo's *Deconstruction in a Nutshell*. In relationship to homiletical methods and figures, McClure's *Other-wise Preaching* is the place to go. McClure writes: "Prior to asking [linguistic] questions about reference, representation, or symbolic disclosure, one must ask critical questions about how a particular fact of value is being used with the interactive, face-to-face framework (discourse) that constitutes human-to-human reality. Issues of location, power, position, grammar, and paradigm, therefore, are crucial in the process of determining both facts and values. There is a direct relationship between one's social location, practices of knowing, and instruments of knowledge and whatever one calls 'truth,' whether that truth is conceived quantitatively (facts) or qualitatively (values). This is sometimes called a 'non-foundationalist' epistemology. This is because there is a movement away from building a knowledge base on universal foundations, whether they be biblically derived first principles, experientially derived existentials, perceptions, or hard-core commonsense notions." In relationship to the contemporary landscape of homiletics, particularly the seminal influence of David Buttrick, McClure observes: "I suspect that one of the reasons for Buttrick's success is his underlying modernist commitment to a unifying consciousness and a concomitant belief in the referential power of symbols. For Buttrick, when preachers work with biblical symbols and signs, they may not be working with unitary thematics, but they are still working with reliable language that faithfully leads a conscious subject to the point where symbols begin to give back that to which they point. The deep deconstructionist

The idea that language doesn't represent reality but rather shapes reality—which is connected to the postmodern critique of metaphysics that acknowledges that we are continually trafficking in interpretations—led most of the initial theological encounters with postmodern theory and deconstructive philosophy to be primarily critical in tone.[12] Derrida's critics perceived him to be, in the words of Taylor, "a pernicious nihilist who threatened the very foundation of Western society and culture." By insisting that truth and absolute value were subject to interpretation, it was believed that he "undercut the very possibility of moral judgment.

---

conviction that, in large part, symbols and signs refer to each other as in a house of mirrors has not yet seized the homiletical imagination in Buttrick's model" (McClure, *Other-wise Preaching*, 16). Buttrick emphasizes "the dramatic, performative function of consciousness" and "fails to fully anticipate the arguments of later structural linguists and poststructuralists that language is opaque and that subjects and meaning are created in large part by positionality within the language system itself. He assumes that preachers and hearers are autonomous, *partly* language-created, but *mostly* language-creating/using subjects." See McClure, *Other-wise Preaching*, 86, 88. For a more technical discussion of these linguistic issues, see esp. Derrida, *Speech and Phenomena, and Other Essays on Husserl's Theory of Signs*, 102–4.

McClure also distinguishes the way popular homiletical methods differ from non-foundationalism. Non-foundationalists "are not interested in the way that words represent (Broadus), disclose (Tillich and the New Homiletic), 'bring out' (Buttrick), or prehend (Allen) a core reality, but with how language, in fact, constitutes reality" (McClure, *Other-wise Preaching*, 99–100). This has led to several obstacles that homileticians have tried to overcome. Those who represent the New Homiletic turned to experience, narrative, parable, etc., but, as McClure observes, this can lead to potential abuses of power that accrue from the "soft-hermeneutic" approaches employed within the New Homiletic: "These increasingly other-wise homileticians urge caution, lest one potentially reify homiletic meanings that emerge more through positionality within the language-system (and thus from dynamics of power and symbolic capital) than through any secure relationship between language and Being. The patent distrust of ontology by deconstructionists is slowly leading a new generation of homileticians to distrust appeals to common human experiences of the sacred as well as to be suspicious of the tendency to impute meaning and generalized sacramental qualities to nearly everything. For these homileticians, God should not become too accessible, too easily located, too easily associated with symbols elevated to kerygmatic status within the tradition . . . or associated with symbols that may derive their meanings from subtle juxtapositions with what are largely hegemonic forms" (McClure, *Other-wise Preaching*, 80–81).

12. Robbins, "Hermeneutics of the Kingdom of God." Robbins explains that deconstruction was closely identified with the radical death-of-God theologies of the 1960s, and Taylor's early assertion of deconstruction as "the 'hermeneutic' of the death of God" led many theorists to seek "a new theological paradigm for what was thought to be a rapidly secularizing culture, a form of theological thought for those uncertain in, if not outrightly suspicious of, their faith."

To follow Mr. Derrida, they maintain, is to start down the slippery slope of skepticism and relativism that inevitably leaves us powerless to act responsibly."[13]

I suppose it was inevitable that this critical tone spilled over into the homiletical enterprise and has (for the most part) remained to this day.[14] When Ron Allen highlights postmodern insights for preaching, he generally describes two types of postmodern approaches: deconstructive and constructive. He associates deconstructive postmodernism with thinkers like Derrida and Michel Foucault, and constructive postmodernism with postliberal and revisionary schools of theology.[15] Like many critics of

13. Taylor, "What Derrida Really Meant." Caputo extends this observation: "You will believe me, then, although I will also document it, that Derrida and 'deconstruction' . . . have been blamed for almost everything. For ruining American departments of philosophy, English, French, and comparative literature, for ruining the university itself (provided that they are ruined), for dimming the lights of the Enlightenment, for undermining the laws of gravity, for destroying all standards of reading, writing, reason—(and 'rithmetic, too)—and also for Mormon polygamy. Derrida even gets a finger (pointed at him) for the nationalist wars in Central Europe and for Holocaust revisionism, even as he has been accused, if it is possible to be guilty of all these things at once, of an apolitical aestheticism, for being a flower child of the 1960s and still being read in the 1990s, a quasi-academic Timothy Leary inviting us to tune into textuality and drop out of reality." See Caputo, *Deconstruction in a Nutshell*, 41.

14. According to Scott Black Johnston, Taylor's interpretation of deconstruction as the hermeneutic of the death of God "casts the role of the preacher in an alarming light. For if Taylor is correct, Derrida has opened a chasm between the pulpit and the pews across which meaning and truth are unable to travel." This scenario, Johnston writes, "would banish preachers to a homiletical Babel in which God is dead and our words have become futile signs wandering in a labyrinth from which there is no exit." See Allen, Blaisdell, and Johnston, *Theology for Preaching*, 74. See also Eslinger, *Narrative and Imagination*, 77. What has generally been missed in homiletic circles is the more recent interpretation of deconstruction not as the hermeneutic of the death of God, as in the early work of Taylor, but as the hermeneutic of the kingdom of God, as expressed more recently in Caputo's writings. (For the record, as mentioned above, Scott Black Johnston, who pointed to the difficulties preachers face in relation to Taylor's interpretation of deconstruction as the hermeneutic of the death of God, is actually, so far as I can tell, the first homiletician to catch the affirming import of deconstruction, as seen in the quote of his I shared in ch. 2 when he compared the insights of Derrida and Barth.) Along with Florence's *Preaching as Testimony*, Charles Campbell's homiletical appropriation of Hans Frei's work seems to me the most friendly reading of Derrida. See Campbell's *Preaching Jesus*, 51, 40 n. 37.

15. In both his early and more recent books related to preaching and postmodernism, Allen follows David Ray Griffin and Huston Smith for this reading. See their *Primordial Truth and Postmodern Theology*, as well as Allen, Blaisdell, and Johnston, *Theology for Preaching*, and Allen, *Preaching and the Other*.

"deconstructive postmodernism," Allen argues that such a hermeneutic is for the most part unhelpful for preaching because it is both *negative* and *relative*. While he concedes that deconstructive postmodernism has the potential to offer a few "positive functions for preachers," it is, in the end, quite "problematic." For Allen, the greatest shortcoming of deconstructive postmodernism is that it doesn't offer the possibility for preachers to make sufficient truth claims, and as such it is unable to offer a consistently viable approach to preaching.[16] How is it, Allen wonders, that a "method" that lacks a firm foundation can provide ethical norms that can be trusted? Moreover, how can preachers who affirm the positive role of deconstruction enable the congregation to sort out complex moral dilemmas? "When serving as a community's only interpretive activity," he writes, "deconstruction leaves a community without a symbolic universe because every symbol has been deconstructed. The center of the community's life is a void. Or, perhaps it is more accurate to say that the community's life does not have a center. Consequently, a community is left in uncertainty and perhaps chaos. As a student reflecting on such matters once said, 'Since everything has been deconstructed, any behavior is possible and permissible.'"[17]

Even David Lose's important book on preaching in a postmodern context is hesitant to espouse the implications of the breakdown of metaphysics and the subsequent loss of a determinate center. If there is no truth, only interpretation, and if postmodernism subjects every truth claim to an ever-suspicious critique, then homiletics finds itself in a dire situation:

> The shadow side of postmodern antifoundationalism and its constructivist view of reality is that in attempting to free discourse from the restraints of an imposed order it inadvertently renders us mute by robbing us of the power of conviction. That is, apart from at least some *sense* that there exists a universal standard of the good, the true, and the beautiful (apart, that is, from some conviction of foundational truth), can one claim any sense of universal

16. Allen, Blaisdell, and Johnston, *Theology for Preaching*, 17–20. It's disappointing that some biblical scholars, most notably Stephen D. Moore, do nothing but perpetuate this stereotype by offering deconstructive readings that are nonsensical and impossible to follow.

17. Allen, *Preaching and the Other*, 70. For a brief assessment of what Allen views as the strengths and weaknesses of deconstruction, see his "Preaching and Postmodernism," 5–7.

rights to defend or extend? While postmodernists aver that local criteria are sufficient (indeed, are all that exist), far too many situations demand judgments of greater force and cultural dexterity.

. . . Driven by its dread of totalizing modernist truth-claims and metanarratives, postmodernists seek to alleviate their anxieties by encouraging an endless plurivocity of local narratives and perspectives. Ironically, the resulting cacophony nearly silences all claims to truth, making it extremely difficult to offer constructive critique or proclaim a universally liberating word. Ultimately, one is left in the unhappy position of having to choose, as Dennis Olson puts it, between the "Tower" of modern foundationalism or the "Babble" of postmodern relativism.[18]

But to approach postmodern philosophy and Derridean-influenced deconstruction in such a way is to leave at halftime and not stick around for the entire game. Derrida gives long speeches, and it would behoove us not to leave at intermission. What has been missed in homiletical circles is the much more positive appropriation of deconstruction that has been widely recognized over the last several years. What Derrida's critics haven't recognized, Caputo insists—and this is one of the reasons Derrida once said he has been read less and less well for over twenty years—is "that the destabilizing agency in his work is not a reckless relativism or an acidic scepticism but rather an *affirmation*, a love of what in later years he would call the undeconstructible."[19]

The most fundamental misunderstanding to beset Derrida and deconstruction is the mistaken impression that is given of the kind of anarchistic relativism in which "anything goes." On this view, texts mean anything the reader wants them to mean; traditions are just monsters to be slain or escaped from; the great masters of the Western tradition are dead white male tyrants whose power must be broken and whose name defamed; institutions are just power-plays oppressing everyone; and language is a prison, just a game of signifiers signifying nothing, a play of differences without reference to the real world. Thus the dominant reaction that Derrida provokes among his critics, who do not content themselves with simply disagreeing with him, is indignation.[20]

18. Lose, *Confessing Jesus Christ*, 28–29.

19. Caputo, "Jacques Derrida (1930–2004)." Emphasis mine.

20. Caputo, *Deconstruction in a Nutshell*, 38. Raschke importantly notes: "When postmodernism attacks the correspondence theory of truth, or the view of thought that the American philosopher Richard Rorty portrays as a 'mirror of nature,' it is not relegat-

Despite popular misconceptions, Derrida did not think that "we must forsake the cognitive categories and moral principles without which we cannot live: equality and justice, generosity and friendship. Rather, it is necessary to recognize the unavoidable limitations and inherent contradictions in the ideas and norms that guide our actions, and do so in a way that keeps them open to constant questioning and continual revision. There can be no ethical action without critical reflection."[21] Unlike the dominant tenets of modernism, Derrida understood that religion is impossible without uncertainty, and in order to be healthy, it must not be closed off. While this worries contemporary interpreters, this is not bad news, nor is it without precedent in the history of the church. In a deconstruction, Caputo has said, "our lives, beliefs, and practices are not destroyed but forced to reform and reconfigure—which is risky business. In the New Testament this is called *metanoia*, or undergoing a fundamental change of heart."[22] This is the endless task imposed upon the church, and in this sense deconstruction represents the long history of the church and its way into the future.

Derrida was well aware of the stereotypes that surrounded his work, and he frequently found himself in the odd position of defending positions that he simply did not hold. One time an interviewer asked him, "What's the most widely held misconception about your work?" to which he replied: "That I'm a sceptical nihilist who doesn't believe in anything, who thinks that nothing has meaning, and text has no meaning. That's stupid and utterly wrong and only the people who haven't read me say this . . . Anyone who reads my work with attention understands that I insist on affirmation and faith and that I'm full of respect for the texts I read."[23]

Steven Shakespeare notes that over the years, Derrida became annoyed at having to continually displace the idea that he had abandoned all truth claims. In a rather blunt response to the philosopher John Searle, Derrida took issue with the idea that "the deconstructionist (which is to say, isn't it, the sceptic-relativist-nihilist!) is supposed not to believe in

---

ing knowledge, like Cain, to exile in some distant land of Nod. It is calling attention to the finite boundaries of human knowledge and meaning so that God can continue to speak." See Raschke, *Next Reformation*, 31.

21. Taylor, "What Derrida Really Meant."

22. Caputo, *What Would Jesus Deconstruct?*, 27.

23. See Dick and Kofman, *Derrida*, 121–22.

truth, stability, or the unity of meaning." In what might come as a surprise to deconstruction's homiletical detractors, Derrida went so far as to say that "this definition of the deconstructionist is *false* (that's right: false not true) and feeble; it supposes a bad (that's right: bad, not good) and feeble reading of numerous texts, first of all mine, which therefore must be read or reread. Then perhaps it will be understood that the value of truth (and those values associated with it) is never contested or destroyed in my writings, but only reinscribed in more powerful, larger, more stratified contexts."[24]

Shakespeare is one of many contemporary interpreters who recognize that Derrida doesn't simply abandon truth, but seeks to trace the complexity and paradoxes that attend all of our attempts to express or define truth. "It is ironic," Shakespeare comments, "that a philosopher often associated with the idea that we can make texts mean whatever we like should so often have felt compelled to challenge misreadings of his work."[25]

Another common accusation hurled at postmodernism is that it simply repeats what it condemns, and is thus hoist by its own petard. It's often said that postmodernism's incredulity toward the metanarrative has become nothing other than a new metanarrative itself.[26] Sometimes such

24. Derrida, *Limited Inc*, 146. *Pace* David Bartlett, who has observed the ways that poststructuralists and deconstructionists play with images and puns in a given text. Bartlett makes the assumption that such interpretations don't necessarily take historical-criticism seriously. See Bartlett, *Between the Bible and the Church*, 142. However, interpreters like Caputo have repeatedly considered the "original context an indispensable first approach to the meaning of a text" (personal correspondence). From Caputo's perspective, interpretive methods and derived meanings ought not be viewed as an aloof, "anything goes" kind of relativistic enterprise. He (along with many other postmodern thinkers) just doesn't think that there can be one "right" reading of a text any more than there can be one "right" interpretation of a painting, play, or poem. Plus, he is interested in the spectral event that texts harbor. See Caputo's *Radical Hermeneutics*. Even Michel Foucault, who is known as perhaps the most rugged of all the postmodernists, pseudonymously writes that "a systematic skepticism toward all anthropological universals—which does not mean rejecting them all from the start, outright and once and for all, but that nothing of that order must be accepted that is not strictly indispensable." See Foucault, "Foucault."

25. Shakespeare, *Derrida and Theology*, 2.

26. Cf. Pablo Jiménez's comments in "A Response to David Buttrick," 118. While valuing several aspects of postmodernism, he names a handful of its dangers, including the "fragmentation of truth [and] attitude of incredulity" toward the metanarrative. By drawing on the work of Justo González, he says that postmodernity has created a new

accusations are hurled at Derrida, but more times than not they are cast in more general directions. Whatever the case, it's important to highlight that not only does Derrida not oppose what he calls a metanarrative of emancipation, but he recognizes that we can't simply escape all talk of metaphysics and foundations (that would be naive), for we would end up getting caught in the same problems from which we are trying to escape.[27] Derrida simply highlights that all of our attempts to make meaning are irreducibly open-ended and deconstructible. One can't help referring to words and images and symbols ("common, intelligible language"[28]) in the attempt of being faithful to the uncontainable, undeconstructible event that is harbored in the name of all of our deconstructible words and images and symbols, for they are all that we have. If the event we are trying to describe is worth its salt, then it is irreducibly deconstructible, and our concepts will always fall short—this due to the excess of the event. As Shakespeare describes: "Derrida doesn't simply reject or make great rhetorical claims about leaping out of past forms of thinking. Nor does he accept them as given. He inhabits them, probing their logic and their limits, and always looking out for what any organization of thinking, any theory or creed is suppressing. No system of thought is self-contained and self-evident. It always presupposes something. It always opens out onto an otherness that it cannot contain."[29]

Perhaps most worrisome for homileticians who engage Derrida's work is the concern that deconstruction's "deferral of meaning" will usher in a "post-modern 'malaise'" that "devolves into a 'deferral of

---

metanarrative that, paradoxically enough, asserts that there are no metanarratives. From a similar perspective, David Lose writes: "Ironically, the postmodern flight from totality renders only another, even if inverse, form of totality" (see Lose, *Confessing Jesus Christ*, 27). Ron Allen has a related concern: "some postmodern thinkers operate out of a center of thought that is structurally similar to the very singularity with which they accuse moderns. . . . From this point of view, postmodernism's absolutizing of diversity and relativity is itself a new authoritarianism" (Allen, *Preaching and the Other*, 20). Because Jiménez, Lose, and Allen are judicious in their attempts to not characterize all postmodern thinkers as the same, their concerns here may not necessarily relate to Derridean-influenced deconstruction, which is what I am most interested in.

27. See Shakespeare, *Derrida and Theology*, 12. Lose recognizes as much. See *Confessing Jesus Christ*, 43.

28. See Derrida's comments on prayer in Sherwood and Hart, *Derrida and Religion*, 30.

29. Shakespeare, *Derrida and Theology*, 12.

responsibility.'"[30] Here it is helpful to recall the aporia at work in Derrida's extensive ethical analyses, which always have as their driving force the undeconstructible "justice to come" (recall the way the event harbored in the name calls and recalls, but is not present, lest we diminish or confine it). For example, in terms of ethical worries about a "deferral of responsibility," Caputo reminds us that "the call for a justice to come is seen to go hand in hand with the urgency of justice now, with the absolute intolerance with anything in the present that would pass itself off as justice or that would make us complacent with the sorry state of the present."[31] In other words, when one has an ear for the spectral event harbored in the name of justice, in the name of the kingdom of God, the effect of the deferral of meaning does not lead to a lack of responsibility but drives responsibility all the more. The less the messiah exists, the more the messiah insists. Laws exist, but justice calls. We begin by the impossible. If laws were not deconstructible—if they had a fixed, determinate meaning that would not budge—then we would be in real trouble, for laws would soon become monsters that menace justice, as any cursory look at history will show.[32] "When something is said to be 'deconstructible,'" Caputo writes, "then, contrary to the received view, that is not bad news—in fact, if Derrida were of a more evangelical frame of mind, he might even call it 'good news'—for that means it has flexibility and a future, and it will not be allowed to harden over."[33] Deconstruction does not leave the "believer on the edge of chaos," as Allen describes, but is precisely what puts the hunger for justice (for the event harbored in the name of justice, *s'il y en*

30. Lose, *Confessing Jesus Christ*, 28. Deferral of meaning is the idea that we can never pinpoint exactly what a word or text means because its meaning is always connected to other words, for words only mean something in relationship to other words, and, for Derrida, language is always open-ended. Meaning is always "to come," which is to say, deferred. Caputo expresses this idea by saying that what is really going on in things, what is really happening, is always to come: "Every time you try to stabilise the meaning of a thing, try to fix it in its missionary position, the thing itself, if there is anything at all to it, slips away." See Caputo, *Deconstruction in a Nutshell*, 31.

31. Caputo, personal correspondence.

32. See Caputo, *What Would Jesus Deconstruct?*, 64.

33. Caputo, *Weakness of God*, 28. Derrida comes close to doing this very thing when he calls some of his critiques of Christianity both *"evangelical* and heretical." See *Gift of Death*, 109, emphasis mine. In relationship to homiletics, Anna Carter Florence writes: "One could even say that the deconstruction of preaching is a kind of repentance, of turning around and looking again at our beloved practices of proclamation and seeing them as if for the first time." See Florence, *Preaching as Testimony*, xv.

a) in motion, for deconstruction is done where the prophets are not far away, for it turns on an eschatological desire beyond desire, a hope against hope, for what eye has not seen and ear has not heard. To be clear: When advocating for deconstruction,

> *Derrida does not advocate outright chaos.* He does not favor a simple-minded street-corner anarchy (nothing is ever simple) that would let lawlessness sweep over the land, although that is just what his most simplistic and anxious critics take him to say. . . . [D]econstruction is not a matter of leveling laws in order to produce a lawless society, but of deconstructing laws in order to produce a just society. To deconstruct the law means to "negotiate the difference" between the law and justice, where the law is thought to be something finite, and "justice" calls up an uncontainable event, an infinite or unconditional or undeconstructible demand. . . . To feel the sharp tip of what deconstructing the law means, imagine if some relativistic deconstructor somewhere were reckless enough to say that the law concerns the ninety-nine, while justice goes off in search of the missing one![34]

Deconstruction's attention to what has been left out does not destroy meaning and replace it with some sort of anything-goes relativism, but is rather done in order to affirm the undeconstructible and keep the future open, to keep the future from closing in on us, to keep the future from being in peril. It is precisely deconstruction's love for the "wholly other," for the event, that keeps us in pursuit of the unconditional, the undeconstructible, not what shuts it off. In sum, from an ethical standpoint, it is our love for the event that is harbored in the name of justice that keeps us from allowing any current form of justice to pass itself off for all that is evoked and provoked in the name of justice.

Still yet, homileticians repeatedly worry that the loss of metaphysical foundations is responsible for ushering in a postmodern ethical malaise that leads to a slippery slope relativism in which it is impossible to make ethical claims or harbor ethical convictions. This comes out most clearly in the comment I shared from one of Ron Allen's students: "Since everything has been deconstructed, any behavior is possible and permissible." Allen and others wonder how, without a metaphysical foundation, it is even possible to determine ethical norms. He writes: "most postmodern

---

34. Caputo, *Weakness of God*, 27. Emphasis mine. See also Caputo, *What Would Jesus Deconstruct?*, 63–69.

writers assume that social repression is bad. But thoroughgoing postmodernism provides no real ground for that judgment. Indeed, while most postmodernists known to me incline toward justice and tolerance, in fact, they have no real *warrant* by which to object to injustice, intolerance, and even violence." Allen then turns to an attention-grabbing example: "If a community believes that a woman who engages in sexual intercourse outside of marriage should be stoned to death, a postmodernist-to-the-core can hardly disagree. Such a thinker is committed to recognizing the relativity of all thought and behavior and to respecting the worldviews of communities beyond one's own."[35] Here it is important to point out that, for Derrida and Caputo at least, the very notion of the justice "to come" (the event that is harbored in the name of justice) refers structurally to the *vulnerable*, to the *victim*, not the producer of the victim: "It would never be the case that the 'other' one to come would be Charles Manson, or some plunderer or rapist," Caputo writes. "The very notion of the to-come refers to the one who is not being heard, who is silenced, victimized by the existing structures. It will always be the case that someone is being injured by the present order, so that the worst injustice would be to say that present order represents perfect justice."[36] Deconstruction is done in a space where the prophets are not far away.

Of course, interpreters are quick to argue that postmodernists are caught in a circular argument: How can one be against violence yet at the same time be unable to say why violence is any worse than, say, love? Such reasoning leads Allen to lay out the core convictions of a belief system that make it possible for him to say that love is to be preferred to violence: "For example, I believe that one of *the* core Christian convictions is that God loves all people unconditionally and desires for all people to live together in relationships of love. Some cultures stone people to death. Some Others within my own culture advocate the death penalty. Putting another person to death contradicts the notion of God's unconditional love for all . . . I am morally obligated to oppose such a move."[37] This is all very well and good, and I think it is a safe bet that Allen and I harbor very similar ethical perspectives. However, I would simply point out that

35. Allen, *Preaching and the Other*, 20–21.

36. As a response to Kearney's essay "Desire of God," 131. Here we recognize significant affinities with McClure's appropriations of Levinas. Furthermore, Caputo is upfront about the problem of evil. See esp. Zlomislić and DeRoo, *Cross and Khôra*, 340.

37. Allen, *Preaching and the Other*, 41.

just because he wishes to ground his moral obligations by appealing to the core conviction that God loves all unconditionally, and that love is to be preferred to violence, it is only possible for him to do so through faith, not knowledge, which is a point Derrida drives home time and again. All of us—whether we consider ourselves postmodern or not—wander in the desert of undecideability, the desert where faith is born and decisions are made, as well as where the possibility for evil lurks. Much as we might try, there is simply no escaping the desert of undecideability. Preachers who want proof and ontological stability for their proclamations need to vacate the pulpit in favor of the laboratory, and even there they will encounter the inescapable web of interpretation. It is impossible to say that forgiveness or love is to be preferred to retribution or hate, whether one claims "core Christian convictions" or not. Foundational Truth Claims such as these, despite all of our best attempts, simply cannot be proven. This isn't to say they aren't true, but it is to say we are walking by faith, not by sight, every single one of us. Here Lose's reprise of Luther is apropos: "To dissent from confessing those things that one cannot prove, Luther contends, 'would be nothing but a denial of all religion.'"[38] Plus, to point out what seems to be fairly obvious: it is the desire to secure the ground of foundations that generally leads to violence, not the other way around. In what I view as the most concise and accessible introduction to postmodern ethics available, Gianni Vattimo writes:

> It is like what Dostoevsky wrote a century ago, that, if forced to choose between Christ and the truth, he would choose Christ. Contrast this sentiment with what Aristotle had to say about his teacher Plato: "Amicus Plato sed magis amica veritas" (Plato is a friend, but truth is a greater friend). Throughout the ages inquisitors have sided with Aristotle rather than Dostoyevsky on this sentiment. The result is that, although not all metaphysics [read: foundations] have been violent, I would say that all violent people of great dimensions have been metaphysical. If Hitler only hated the Jews of his particular neighborhood, he might have burned up their homes. But how much more dangerous he was because at a certain point he theorized about the general nature of all Jews and thus felt justified in his efforts to exterminate them all. I do not think it is difficult to understand this. Nietzsche is very explicit in this sense. According to him, metaphysics is itself an act of violence because it wants to appropriate the "most fertile regions,"

38. Lose, *Confessing Jesus Christ*, 234.

hence of the first principles, in order to dominate and control. The first lines from Aristotle's *Metaphysics* more or less confirm this when he says that the wise is the one who knows all. The wise knows all by knowing its first cause and is thereby thought able to control and determine all its effects. Our tradition is dominated by the idea that if we only had a stable foundation we could move and act more freely. But philosophical foundationalism does not promote freedom. Rather, it is for the purpose of obtaining some desired effect or of consolidating some authority. When someone wants to tell me the absolute truth it is because he wants to put me under his control, under his command. Is it any wonder, then, that we hear the refrain "Be a man" or "Do your duty" whenever it is those who are in power send others off to war?[39]

From Vattimo's perspective, postmodern ethics are really not that strange or unorthodox at all. Rather, he says, they promote the most Christian of notions, namely "charity," which he interprets not in the limited sense of almsgiving, but as love. As Vattimo shows, a postmodern deconstructive approach to ethics is deeply rooted in the Christian tradition, and has much more to do with biblical faith than with metaphysical foundationalism. Vattimo reminds readers that if you read "the gospels or the fathers of the church carefully, at the end, the only virtue left is always that of charity. From Saint Paul we learn that the three greatest virtues are faith, hope, and love, 'but the greatest of these is love.' Even faith and hope will end at one point or another. As Saint Augustine instructs, 'Love and do what you want.'" In contrast to the Western philosophical enterprise, the "truth" of love cannot be contained to any metaphysical foundation, no matter how much we might wish to fall back on one. This is the beauty of its excess. To paraphrase St. Augustine, "If love is the measure, the only measure of love is love without measure." Or, as Jean-Luc Marion writes, "as soon as we try to define [love], or at least approach it with concepts, it draws away from us."[40] In relationship to the event, to what is stirring in the name of love, to what is calling in the name of our "core Christian

39. In Caputo and Vattimo, *After the Death of God,* 43–44. Perhaps it shouldn't be surprising that Derrida, a French Algerian Jew living in the wake of the Second World War, was particularly sensitive to the kinds of either/or oppositions that fostered killing certainties. When that which is other is left out, it becomes all too easy for those in power to move toward totalizing systems of domination. Like Levinas and Vattimo, Derrida resists the violence of metaphysics.

40. See Marion, *Prolegomena to Charity.*

convictions," we are never sure who or what is doing the calling, or where the call comes from: "We have a sense, a faith, a hope in something, a love of something we know not what, something that calls on us."[41] And the passion of the call, according to Caputo, is intensified by its *undecideability*, not by its definitive identity:

> That we who have been wooed by a weak theology express some diffidence about the provenance of the call is not a temporary defect in our account that we hope to remove at a later date, perhaps in a new revised second edition, when we are feeling stronger and the System is complete. The hiddenness of the source is actually *constitutive* of the call, part of its positive phenomenal makeup, a positive function of its weak force, and a permanent feature of our anarchic and weakened theological condition. For if we could identify it further, or definitively, if we would get on top of it, master it, make it our own, then we would not be "called" upon, but would be simply musing over what we want to do. If God were a giant green bird, Kierkegaard once quipped, and regularly and conspicuously appeared thus in the town square, there would be much less skepticism about him, and of course a proportionately less passionate faith. In the hermeneutic situation from which I set out, we are all constituted as the recipients of a call about whose origin we cannot comment with assurance, a call floating out over the abyss of the radical hermeneutical fix we are in. The call is itself constituted by being heard, and its being heard is in turn constituted by our responding, by our heeding and not simply hearing, or by our hearing as heeding.[42]

Interpreters who wish to secure firm foundations—and, honestly, who can blame them for wanting to do so?—tend to respond to the call by trying to wire it up to a metaphysical Source. We experience love, so we think there must be a Source of love. We experience a new lease on life, so we think there must be Someone who gave it to us. In other words, when we experience the event that is harbored in the name— when we experience the impossible—we try to identify it with an Essence or Source or Presence. And in the wake of transformative experiences, one can see why this happens. Indeed, this is the faith and hope of the more determinate religions, which can be contrasted with the faith and hope of Derrida, which is more secular and less determinate.

---

41. Caputo, *What Would Jesus Deconstruct?*, 49–50.
42. Caputo, *Weakness of God*, 114.

I am not necessarily valuing one more than the other, except to say that the will to power is usually related to the desire to maintain a hold on metaphysics, which is a lesson given to us not only by Nietzsche and Vattimo but also by the biblical prophets who railed against idolatry. What religion is responding to—as well as what religion without religion is responding to—is the call of the event. *Events happen.* Now whether or not we can identify the Source of the event, deconstruction cannot say a thing. No matter what one's core convictions might be, it is equally impossible to *prove* whether there is an underlying Presence of Love to the cosmos, or whether the cosmos couldn't care less. All of us are trafficking in interpretations, and are ultimately dwelling in the desert of undecideability.[43] We walk by faith, not by sight.

Again, we must keep in mind that even though postmodern approaches to nonfoundationalism are often referred to as fatalistic or nihilistic, Nietzsche showed us in his own provocative way that nihilism is actually rooted in the desire to secure metaphysical foundations, not the other way around. Attempts to secure metaphysical foundations are disguised attempts to maintain ownership of the call, and our objective grasp of the call and mastery over the call kills the call (recall the apotheosis of modernity that we discussed in chapter 3, which leads to the modern homiletical crisis). Nietzsche concluded that Christianity's desire to secure foundations was really Greek metaphysics in disguise ("Platonism for the masses"): "Even though we have spoken reverently, religiously, and 'metaphysically' for two thousand years of the eternal Deity," Carl Raschke explains, "our God has been slowly 'dying' [because] the herd craves the metaphysical comfort of God and the moral certainty of theology all bundled up in the popular Platonic fiction." Raschke then appeals to postmodernism: "The philosophical trends now decipherable as postmodernism have rested on the premise that metaphysics must not be condoned, but must be 'overcome' in order to contend with the inherent nihilism of the metaphysical enterprise itself."[44] From a postmodern perspective, the attempt to secure metaphysical foundations for ethical

---

43. For a detailed analysis, see esp. Zlomislić and DeRoo, *Cross and Khôra*, 187–96.

44. Raschke, *Next Reformation*, 46–48. From the standpoint of preaching, according to McClure, several of the most common approaches "retain much of the veneer of foundationalism (universalism, dialectics, hierarchialism, and referentialism) that is found in the New Homiletic and in parts of [David] Buttrick's work, a foundationalism that other-wise homiletics resists." See McClure, *Other-wise Preaching*, 89–95.

action is not the source of responsible ethical action but rather of a debilitating nihilism, the sickness unto death.

A MORE RADICAL CONFESSION

I have enormous appreciation for the confessional homiletic developed by David Lose, and in many respects it shares a deep affinity with a homiletic of the event. Lose is very forthright in saying that we can't prove the truth of our claims in a metaphysical or foundational sense, and that the truth of our proclamations can only be evidenced in their pragmatic usefulness. What I would encourage Lose to consider, however, is that a deconstructive critique does not stand in the way of constructive assertion, as he maintains, but rather can be put in the service of constructive assertion.[45] Indeed, it is the affirmation at the heart of deconstruction—the love for the event harbored in the name of God—that allows preachers to pursue a homiletic of confession in its most radical form. Deconstruction is not antithetical to constructive Christian proclamation, but rather it is the repetition of the religious and can be seen to go hand in hand with a confessional homiletic:

> This is not the way it was supposed to turn out. . . . Much to the horror of the secularizing deconstructors, the notorious "free play of signifiers," which frees us from the shackles of the transcendental signified, and the famous saying, "there is nothing outside the text," which set off a Dionysian dance on the grave of the old God, has taken the form of the *kenotics of faith*. The deferral of presence turns out to imply messianic waiting and expectation, and the deconstruction of presence turns out to be not a denial of the presence of God but a critique of the idols of presence, which has at least as much to do with Moses' complaint with Aaron as with Nietzsche.[46]

Critical fideism, which is the hallmark of Lose's confessional homiletic, is (to state the obvious) rooted in *faith,* not knowledge, and it is precisely the undecideability in the space of not knowing that constitutes faith as faith. In contrast to the quests of modernism, Derrida's deconstructive thought, following Nietzsche, "exposes us to the 'secret' that there is no 'Secret,' no Big Capitalized Secret to which we have been wired

45. See Lose, *Confessing Jesus Christ,* 62.
46. Caputo and Scanlon, *God, the Gift, and Postmodernism,* 4–5.

up—by scientific reason, by poetic or religious revelation, or by political persuasion. We make use of such materials as have been available to us, forged in the fires of time and circumstance."[47] While Cartesian forms of metaphysics long for definitive knowledge, Derrida offers a more humble approach that confesses our *lack* of knowledge, that confesses our limitations. In some deep way, Derrida observes, we do not know who we are or what the world is. But on Caputo's reading, "That is not nihilism but a quasi-religious confession, the beginning of wisdom, the onset of faith and compassion. Derrida exposes the doubt that does not merely insinuate itself into faith but that in fact constitutes faith, for faith is faith precisely in the face of doubt and uncertainty, the passion of non-knowing."[48]

If we wish to implement a homiletic of critical fideism, based on faith as opposed to knowledge, then there is no other choice than to wander in the desert of undecideability. To be clear, I am not saying that Lose claims that our assertions about faith can be proven in a metaphysical/foundational sense. What I am pointing out is that postmodern deconstruction does not invite "paralysis," as he implies,[49] but rather constitutes the repetition of the religious, the kenotics of faith, that should be part and parcel of a critical fideism, provided that the fideism part of the equation is taken seriously. Thus, for Christians to "offer postmodernists the means by which to move beyond merely deconstructive critique to constructive assertion," as Lose exhorts, is to miss the point of what is going on in deconstruction, at least from the perspective of the Caputo-Derridean hybrid that I am working with. Deconstruction is about making a confession, or, better, a *circumfession*, in which we fess up to being cut by something we know not what, when we have no choice but to walk by faith and not by sight, when knowledge fails and faith is all we have to go on. Derrida writes: "If we read, if reading was simply seeing, we would not read. When I say we read in the dark, I do not mean that we have

47. Caputo, "Jacques Derrida (1930–2004)."

48. Ibid. Elsewhere Caputo comments: "Suffice it to say that by defending the idea of *différance,* Derrida meant to say that we make sense under conditions that threaten to undo the sense we make, and that our beliefs and practices enjoy only a provisional unity and tentative stability that is in principle liable to unravel at the most inconvenient times. I think Derrida is right about this. From a religious point of view, I think this does not undermine faith but explains precisely why we need faith, we believers and nonbelievers (or believers-otherwise) alike, and why in every believer there is a bit of an unbeliever (and conversely)." Caputo, *Weakness of God,* 25.

49. Lose, *Confessing Jesus Christ,* 61.

to read without seeing anything, but that the essential feature of reading implies some darkness. That is what distinguishes reading from seeing, from perception. You can transfer this law to the relationship between knowledge and faith."[50]

Instead of inviting homiletical paralysis, deconstruction loosens the homiletical tongue to move toward constructive assertion, to preach after the event harbored in the name of God. Deconstruction isn't antithetical to religion or to faith, but is the repetition of religion and faith. Deconstruction doesn't usher in nihilism and meaninglessness, contrary to the popular distortion, but affirms the unconditional and undeconstructible, what Christians might call the Holy. Deconstruction doesn't shut things down, it gets things going. Deconstruction is affirmation, not destruction. In Derrida's essay "Des Tours de Babel," he compares the history of theology, in both its Jewish and Greek forms, to the tower of Babel.[51] To be able to identify a foundationally secure name for God based on absolute knowledge would constitute, for Derrida, "pure presence." It would be the metaphysically correct "name," and would be knowable to human beings through common (pragmatic?) sense. But the tower of Babel—"the tower upon which the history of metaphysics and theology has sought to place the capstone with the name of names engraved upon its shining, alabaster surface—that tower has been sent hurling down." In Derrida's words, God "sows confusion among his sons."[52] Here, the confusion of language is the confusion of grammars, which serves the purpose of keeping the name of God safe, so that it might be honored as the name above all names. The name resists pure presence (knowledge) in order to be affirmed, not destroyed: "If postmodernism is vilified by philosophers and theologians today as 'sowing confusion,'" Raschke notes, "then from a biblical perspective it is on the side of the angels." The "Babble" of postmodern relativism, as described by Olson and referenced by Lose, misses the import of deconstruction's passion for the truth: for the unconditional, for the undeconstructible, for the impossible. Deconstruction is not out to destroy the name, but to save the name.

---

50. Discussion in Kearney's "Desire of God," 133.

51. Here I am following Raschke's reading of Derrida. See Raschke, *Next Reformation*, 114.

52. Derrida, *Acts of Religion*, 105.

The Risk of Preaching 163

THE RISK OF PREACHING

Generally speaking, when we examine why homileticians hesitate to affirm deconstruction, it is usually for at least one of two reasons: (1) Deconstruction is viewed as destruction, or (2) it is risky to venture into the unknown, where knowledge fails and faith is all we have to go on, which is where deconstruction takes us.

As I have tried to show, the first reason—that deconstruction is destruction (or an anything-goes relativism that lacks a passion for the truth)—is mistaken. If the truth be told, deconstruction turns on a desire for the truth, has a passion for the truth, is madly in love with the truth that is evoked in the event harbored in the name of God, which goes by many names. To be sure, the truth of the event is not the same kind of truth one tries to locate in a metaphysical principle, but rather is true in its phenomenological appeal and claim on our lives as the call and solicitation that overcomes us, that disturbs our lives and our world, and its work on us is never complete. Contrary to all of the bad press Derrida and company have received, deconstruction has a passion for truth. The truth of the event groans to be born, to come true, to make itself felt, *inquietum est cor nostrum*.

But the second reason preachers are hesitant to affirm deconstruction—that it is risky to venture into the unknown—well, that one I can't dispel, as much as I wish I could, for my sake as well as for yours. The event harbored in the name of God is not without risk; indeed, it is all about risk. With every promise there is also a threat; such is the "nature" of an open-ended world in which weak calls aren't confused for strong forces, to which the cross of Christ bears witness. It would be safer for us to avoid all this talk of the event by spicing up our sermons with lots of feel-good stories from Max Lucado, which I like as much as the next chap, or perhaps even go back to the security of Egypt by preaching sermons that are about ourselves, our same boring selves. We could draw up boundaries that confine us to the possible and do our best to insulate ourselves from the in-coming of the wholly other, of the event harbored in the name of God. We wouldn't have to run for cover, and we'd probably get a lot more sleep at night.

A homiletic of the event is to preach without guarantees, with prayers and tears that are forever after the event harbored in the name of God. The spectral call of God is a *weak* call with a strong appeal, but it doesn't have the strong force of a Big Being to back it up.[53] We hope and sigh and dream and weep for the event to come true, to be born into our world, for the event to transform our very existence, to experience the impossible, but the event only has the power of a weak *perhaps*, not a strong *guarantee*. It is a provocative perhaps to be sure, full of promise and hope, but not one that offers any set-in-stone assurances or apologetics (no wonder Caputo says it doesn't have a decent hymnal). Ultimately, with all due respect to a homiletic of critical fideism, a homiletic of the event is not pragmatic, mostly because the Spirit of God is not pragmatic, and those whom God calls don't lead very pragmatic lives. The call of God is a disturbance to the normalcy of civilization—indeed, to the normalcy of our lives. Caputo compares deconstruction to a poker game, a wager, a bet that the future is always worth more:

> Whether it is or not, whether things turn out well or not. It breathes the air of a bet on the future, a calculation of the incalculable, rolling the dice on the impossible. On that point, I have said, deconstruction is like a prayer where you damn well (if I may say so) better be careful of what you are praying for because you may get it, which is a venerable axiom of the spiritual masters. Deconstruction is love because the impossible is the only thing you can truly love. If in order to avoid taking a risk, you decide to love only the possible, then you take the risk of coming up with something that barely deserves the name of love and of ending up as what Johannes Climacus called a mediocre fellow. Everything in deconstruction is subordinated to the wager, the risk, which proceeds from love, a love of the game, a love of the future.[54]

When we step into the pulpit, we are betting that the future is worth more. We are risking our lives on the advent of the in-coming of the "wholly other," the impossible, and we can never be sure what is going to happen. If we are looking for safety, or if we want determinate guarantees, we need to remind ourselves that we preach in the shadow of the cross, with spilled blood and a broken body just a few steps away. We are haunted

53. For all of the differences I have expressed in relationship to Ron Allen in this chapter, here it is important for me to point out that in a certain sense the lure of the event and the lure of process theology are quite similar (Allen is a process homiletician). Both are responding to the power and appeal of a weak call. Readers interested in poststructuralism/deconstruction and process theology might especially like Catherine Keller's *Face of the Deep*.

54. Caputo, "Return of Anti-Religion," 52.

by a very holy ghost that will not rest in peace and will not give us peace. We are fools for Christ or damned fools—two awesome and awe-ful possibilities.[55]

55. I conclude part one by recalling the language of Thomas Long from *Preaching from Memory to Hope*, 37.

PART II

Preaching After God

7

On (Not) Planning for the Future

THE SECOND PART OF this book, beginning with this chapter, provides several lectionary-based sample sermons developed in relationship to themes located within the postmodern return of religion. The title of each chapter is also the respective title of each of the sermons. I offer a few introductory comments in each chapter in order to set up the content of each chapter's sermon.

All of the sermons, with the exception of the one in this chapter, were preached at Brentwood Christian Church (Disciples of Christ) in Springfield, Missouri, where I have been a pastor since 2003. Brentwood is a medium-sized, Protestant-liberal congregation in the heart of the Bible Belt. Springfield is home to several colleges and universities with roots in fundamentalist expressions of Christianity, and it's also the site of the world headquarters of both the Assemblies of God denomination and Bass Pro Shops Outdoor World. It's about forty-five miles north of Branson, Missouri, the popular tourist destination that has carved out a niche in the Ozark Mountains as the place where nationalism meets Christianity, and both are equally venerated. Glory be.

Yet even with such conservative roots, Springfield is (thankfully) also home to Missouri State University, with a student population of approximately twenty thousand, as well as Drury University, a prestigious liberal arts college historically rooted in the liberal United Church of Christ and Disciples of Christ traditions. There are also two major hospitals that serve as the largest employers in the area.

Given this context, those who attend Brentwood are usually, though not exclusively, coming from one of two backgrounds: (1) those who are leaving the fundamentalist churches of their childhood/youth and are looking for a more progressive approach to faith (I first became interested in the whole emergent church conversation simply because so many evangelical expatriates were making their way to Brentwood, and while the designation "emergent church" now sounds so passé, the dynamic of young evangelical expatriates exiting their former churches and finding a home at Brentwood is stronger than ever); and/or (2) professors, students, or well-educated professionals who want to connect with a progressive Christian congregation. While there are a handful of participants at Brentwood who grew up in the denomination, the vast majority of participants come from a hodgepodge of backgrounds: fundamentalist, Unitarian, Quaker, Assemblies of God, Mennonite, mainline, agnostic, etc. To borrow from a couple of our well-known slogans, Brentwood is known as "Springfield's Bible Belt Alternative" that seeks to engage Christianity in a way that "values both the mind and the heart." We give people a place to wrestle with questions of faith, and we tend to attract a bunch of folks who aren't quite sure what to make of Christianity and/or God. Some are on the verge of exiting Christianity altogether; others are looking for a fresh approach to Christianity. The one thing we are told most often regarding our worship service is that our welcome statement, which we read toward the beginning of worship each Sunday, is what people appreciate the most and what brings them back. While there are various aspects of the welcome statement that participants find meaningful, the phrase that most resonates with them is the concluding line: "If you believe in God some of the time, or none of the time, or all of the time, you are welcome here."[1]

As a preacher, I value several different approaches to preaching, as described in chapter 5. In relation to my gifts for preaching, I often find conversational sermons based on a collaborative homiletic to be the most

---

1. The entire welcome statement, as well as several other liturgical resources structured with believers, agnostics, atheists, and evangelical expatriates in mind, can be found in Snider and Bowen, *Toward a Hopeful Future*. In addition, the second half of Peter Rollins' *How (Not) to Speak of God* provides wonderful alternative liturgies that resonate with a similar demographic, especially those who are not drawn to established church contexts.

fruitful, though I also love Frank Thomas's approach to preaching as celebration (so long as it takes into consideration other-wise sensitivities).

These sermons—which were initially written in order to be spoken, not read (and unfortunately don't allow readers to experience inflection, rhythm, pacing, etc.)—represent just a few examples of the ways I have drawn on the postmodern return of religion as a remedy to the modern homiletical crisis. For the most part, the sample sermons I chose to include are the kinds that can be preached in established church settings, mostly because I am anticipating that the majority of my readers will be from established church settings. However, because they were developed with my own preaching style and context in mind, it's best not to simply copy them off and preach them as written, though you are welcome to borrow as much or as little as is helpful. More importantly, they are a means of getting the ball rolling so that preachers can consider helpful ways to draw on the themes stirring in the postmodern return of religion in their own particular contexts and in relation to their respective style of preaching. I hope what follows provides a bit of what Anna Carter Florence calls "direction," not "directions": "I have learned that giving direction is not the same as giving directions. Directions (notice the plural) can verge on the formulaic: follow these steps, and you will have a sermon. Direction (singular) is more akin to guidance. . . . [It's important to take] seriously that each situation will have its own struggle for forms that work and structure that holds. Each sermon will have to work its purpose out afresh. Offering direction rather than directions honors the act of preaching without idolizing any portion of it."[2]

* * *

As mentioned above, the sermon in this chapter is the only one that wasn't preached at Brentwood (though I later adapted it for use at Brentwood). It was originally preached at Drury University's baccalaureate worship service. The text is from the Fifth Sunday after the Epiphany in Year A, though that is not the day that I preached it. Here I am trying to accomplish a couple of interrelated things. The first has to do with the context and location of the sermon: It was preached to students and faculty at Drury, who tend to be quite liberal. Several who attended were graduates of Drury's department of philosophy and religion, and few of them

2. Florence, *Preaching as Testimony*, 134–35.

were content with the claims made in what Caputo or Derrida might call the more determinate religions. Given this context, I thought it would be interesting to try to preach a sermon that didn't use the word *God*, yet still turned on the unconditional event harbored in the name of God. Second, I developed this sermon with this book in mind. I wanted simply to show readers how basic ideas from the postmodern return of religion—in this case, the structure of the messianic—can be incorporated into a sermon without having to do a bunch of homiletical gymnastics. The themes explored here (namely, the two futures that Derrida and Caputo describe) can be adapted for preaching in a pretty straightforward sense, as this sermon attempts to show.

YEAR A: FIFTH SUNDAY AFTER THE EPIPHANY (1 COR 2:1–12)

On an occasion like this it probably isn't a terrible idea to talk about the future. At this point in time, so many thoughts are focused not just on the sense of accomplishment that you feel, but on what lies ahead: trying to find the right job, figuring out whether to go to grad school or not, deciding whether to stay in Springfield or to move to another community. There are so many things to take into consideration, so many things to plan for. And it's remarkable how quickly we have to get to work making our plans.

One of the few sitcoms that my wife and I make an effort to watch every week is *Community* on NBC. Those of you who watch it know it's about a group of friends who attend community college together. It's kind of a quirky show, but really, really funny. We're getting worried, though, that the show is going to go off the air because, really, how many seasons can you produce of a show about a two-year community college, at least with the same group of students? Life moves too quickly. We're guessing that in season three or four of *Community* some of the students will have to move on, to find out where their future is going to take them beyond college.

The future doesn't slowly arrive, does it? It has a driving force all its own; we are constantly responding to the future, readying ourselves for the future, trying to make plans for the future.

The philosopher Jacques Derrida talks about two different kinds of futures, one we can call the expected future and the other we can call the unexpected future. The expected future is the future we pay most of our attention to. It is the relatively foreseeable future that we can wrap our minds around. It's the future that we plan for, because for the most part we can know what to expect. We make important plans for the expected future. We think about what kind of job we wish to pursue, what kind of income will make us happy, and we wonder how in the world our student loans will get paid back!

In the expected future, we are responsible for paying attention to investment plans, pension plans, insurance plans, all kinds of things you are either already paying attention to or are getting ready to pay attention to. The expected future is the future we can and should prepare for. It is the future in which we live and move and have our being. The expected future demands our best efforts, always and uncompromisingly, and we're foolish not to plan for it.

Yet there is a different future—what can be called the unexpected future—that is a far cry from the conventional, expected future. In the unexpected future, we are taken by surprise, overcome by a dream or experience or longing that takes us where we could never have imagined going, that keeps us hoping and sighing and dreaming for a life that is not beholden simply to what we can think or imagine, what *we* can plan for, but is open to what we, in all of our best efforts, cannot quite make out. The unexpected future is the dream of a future that is not dulled by what eye has already seen and ear has already heard. The dream of an unexpected future takes us by surprise and breaks into our lives and world when we least expect it (like a thief in the night); the dream of an unexpected future shatters the conventional horizons of all of our reasonable expectations and best-laid plans. The dream of an unexpected future makes our hearts beat, our voices sing, our feet dance.

The expected future is content with the conventions that already exist; the unexpected future dreams of what is to come.

The well-known preacher Tony Campolo tells a story about a couple who went to watch the musical *The Man of La Mancha*. In the middle of the show, the wife started whispering emphatically to her husband, "Stop that! Stop that! You're embarrassing me!"

The husband was a well-dressed man with all the symbols of upper-middle-class propriety—he clearly had planned well for the expected future—but he was sitting in his theater seat, weeping uncontrollably as the man on the stage, Don Quixote, was singing "To Dream the Impossible Dream." He was singing about beating the unbeatable foe and striving to go where the brave dare not go. He was singing to the audience that the world would be richer because one man, bruised and covered with scars, still strove with all the courage he had to reach an unreachable star. This man was crying because somewhere along the way he had lost his dreams. This man was crying because somewhere along the way, he had lost his vision.[3] This man was crying because somewhere along the way, he became content with making conventional plans for a conventional future, and he had forgotten the promise of the unforeseeable future, the unexpected future, the impossible future, what eye has not seen and ear has not heard. And sitting right there in his theater seat, weeping uncontrollably, this man was in the process of being born, *again*.

Our hearts beat for a future that we can't see coming, that surprises us like a thief in the night, that is beyond what eye has seen or ear has heard or the human mind has conceived. As John Caputo has written,

> The borders of the expected future are safe but flat, sure but narrow, well defined but confining, and they stake out the lines of an unsalted and mediocre life, without a passionate hope, where nothing really happens and all present systems will do just fine. If at the end of our lives we find that all our hopes have been sensible and moderate and measured by the horizon of the expected future, if we have never been astir with the impossible, then we shall also find that on the whole life has passed us by. If safe is what you want, forget religion and find yourself a conservative investment counselor.[4]

I recently read a book with a title that immediately grabbed my attention: *Great Philosophers Who Failed at Love*. It documented a bunch of wonderful thinkers down through the ages, from ancient Greeks to modern Germans—many of them I'm sure had tenure and were quite well published—who waxed eloquently about the idea of love, the meaning of love, the value of love, *yet never risked their lives for the sake of love*. To love is to risk, for love draws us beyond what we can wax eloquently about—whether in Greek or German or Shakespearean English; love draws us out and solicits us from afar, carrying us to a future that is beyond our best-laid plans, to the unforeseeable and unexpected, beyond what eye has seen or ear has heard or the human mind has conceived. For that is where everything interesting in life *happens*.

3. This story is adapted from Campolo, *Let Me Tell You a Story*, 70.

4. Caputo, *On Religion*, 14.

One preacher had the audacity to say that Socrates got it wrong: it is not the unexamined life that is not worth living, but rather it is the uncommitted life that is not worth living. Descartes, too, was mistaken with his famous "I think therefore I am," *Cogito ergo sum*. Nonsense. It should've been *Amo ergo sum*, "I love therefore I am." And love, like faith, demands a risk, a venture into the unknown.[5]

Life happens when the dynamic power of love takes us to places we never could have dreamed of going on our own, to what eye had not seen, and ear had not heard, and the human mind had not conceived. Amen.

5. Coffin, *Credo*, 5.

8

Nourished by Our Hunger

THIS SERMON WAS PREACHED on the tenth anniversary of 9/11. It also follows the structure of the messianic, only in a more Augustinian sense of the restless heart. In following the thought of Richard Kearney, it views desire for God not as mere lack but as excess.[1] While the lectionary texts for this sermon can be found in Year C (Seventh Sunday of Easter), I went ahead and adapted them for use on the tenth anniversary of 9/11. In order to provide juxtaposition, I added the passage from Mark. All of the sample sermons in subsequent chapters were preached on the actual Sunday designated in the lectionary readings. If one wishes to preach a sermon such as this one on the Seventh Sunday of Easter in Year C, then one can change the imagery as needed.

YEAR C: SEVENTH SUNDAY OF EASTER (REV 22:12–14, 16–17, 20–21, SUPPLEMENTED WITH MARK 1:1–15)

Have you ever heard the expression "There is a hole in our heart that can only be filled by God"? It's pretty popular around here; I've heard it count-less times. The hole in our heart usually refers to our lack, our hunger, our thirst—that which we don't have—and we think about God's arrival as that which fills this void, satisfies it, quenches it. It's a nice image and all, but this morning I'm more interested in reversing this image, turning it inside out, setting it upside down.

---

1. See Kearney, "Desire of God." Inverting the God-shaped hole in one's heart is an idea I adapted from Rollins, *How (Not) to Speak of God*, 50ff.

And I'd like to talk about this God-shaped hole in our heart—this image of lack, of hunger, of thirst—within the context of the coming of the messiah. Most messianic language is structured around the hunger and longing of things to come. When we pray for the messiah's arrival, we're praying for that time and place that we don't have words for yet deeply long for; we're praying for that indescribable realm of love and justice, compassion and peace; we're praying for God's kingdom to come, for God's will to be done, on earth as it is in heaven.

We have to acknowledge, of course, that one of the oddities surrounding Christian belief in the messiah is that no sooner do we Christians proclaim that the messiah has come than we're praying for the messiah to come again. The book of Mark begins by proclaiming the messiah's arrival ("the time is fulfilled, the kingdom is at hand"), yet the book of Revelation—and thus the end of the entire Bible—concludes by praying for the messiah to come yet again. It's like the messiah *was* present and *had* arrived, yet now the messiah has gone missing, AWOL, absent (Jesus has left the building). Christians celebrate the messiah's presence yet at the same time mourn the messiah's absence. It's like Christianity needs to make up its mind already: Has the messiah arrived—as in the book of Mark's proclamation—or is the messiah still "to come," as in the book of Revelation's prayer?

One of the problems is that we tend to think about these things along either/or lines: *Either the messiah has arrived, or the messiah has not arrived; either the kingdom is here, or the kingdom is not here.* And if it's not here yet, then—depending upon one's perspective—it will either come one day in the future, or it will not come at all. It will appear one grand and glorious day, or it will never appear at all. It's messiah or no messiah. Kingdom or no kingdom. This or that. Now or later. Either/or.

But what if in the Bible we encounter a much more radical approach to all of this? What if Mark's proclamation *of* the messiah, and Revelation's prayer *for* the messiah—what if they somehow depend upon one other? What if the trace left in the aftermath of the messiah leaves our hearts forever hungry to catch glimpses of the messiah yet again?

Today we pause to remember that tragic September morning ten years ago, when airplanes were flown into the twin towers, when the World Trade Center came crumbling down. I don't know where you were on September 11th—I remember turning on the news just as the second plane hit the South Tower—and I can't remember all that went through my mind. But as I watched the sky fall that day, I thought one thing for sure, and that's that the kingdom was not here; God's will was not being done on earth as it is in heaven; *the indescribable realm of love and justice, compassion and peace, was nowhere to be found.* If the coming of the messiah meant that the time had been fulfilled and the kingdom was at hand, then I had picked the wrong messiah.

Yet at the same time, on that same day, amidst the wreckage and ruins of Ground Zero, there were cups of cold water given and received; there were warm blankets placed on damp, ash-strewn bodies; there were perfectly good lives lost so that others could be saved. In the midst of the wreckage, on the site of the ruins, where the kingdom was absent ("my God, my God, why have you forsaken me?")—it was precisely there, in that place, that the kingdom somehow emerged, like a flower growing through broken, cracked cement; like a small tree springing forth from the trunk of a hollowed-out old oak tree; like a stone being rolled away from a tomb.

Walter Benjamin says that praying for the messiah to come is not about praying for an arrival way off in the future, at the end of time or even outside of time, because, he says, *the heart of every moment—the heart of every moment—contains the little door through which the Messiah may enter.*[2]

When we hope for the kingdom to arrive and for the messiah "to come," it's not so much a prayer for what might arrive one day way off in the distant future, something that none of us will live to see, but it's rather about praying for the kingdom to come now, in the midst of our lives and in the midst of our world, even—perhaps especially—in the midst of the ruins. It's a prayer that doesn't require our patience as much as it requires our passion. As John Caputo says, the call for the messiah-to-come goes hand in hand with the urgency of justice now, with the absolute intolerance with anything in the present that would pass itself off as justice or that would make us complacent with the sorry state of the present.

All of which gets us back to the God-shaped hole in our heart that we talked about before. What if the hole in our heart is a void—a void that, instead of being filled, puts us in pursuit of God all the more? What if the glimpses and traces of the kingdom that we so fleetingly saw in Jesus, glimpses and traces so beautiful that many couldn't help seeing in

2. See Kearney, *God Who May Be*, 46.

him the messiah, the incarnation of their hopes and dreams, the embodiment of the kingdom—what if these glimpses and traces (which we locate in Jesus but don't confine to Jesus) don't so much fill the God-shaped hole in our heart as make it bigger and bigger, larger and larger, pointing to that which we most deeply long for, yearn for, hunger for, and want to see come into our lives and our world again, and again, and again, infinitely, ceaselessly? What if we imagine the hole in our heart not so much as what gets filled, but rather as the void left in the aftermath of the messiah, the void that compels us to call upon the messiah time and again?

What if, as Richard Kearney suggests, this hunger for God is no mere deficiency or lack, as we've often been led to believe, but instead is its own reward? As the psalmist says, "Those who seek the Lord lack no good thing." What if such desire is not some gaping emptiness or negation but an affirmative "yes" to the summons of that which we know not what, that which we desire beyond desire, that which we pray for, long for, hope for? What if this hole in our heart is not a symptom of deficiency but of excess; what if it is not to be mourned but to be celebrated? *What if we are nourished by our hunger?*

Such a desire leads to an odd paradox at the heart of Mark's proclamation of the messiah and Revelation's prayer for the messiah: On the one hand, it's like the messiah had to come—otherwise we wouldn't know what we are waiting for. But on the other hand, the messiah can't possibly be here—otherwise we wouldn't still be waiting.

Many of us have caught traces of our heart's longing in the kingdom inaugurated by Jesus—in sharing and receiving cups of cold water, in breaking bread with friends and strangers, in loving our neighbors and (crazy enough) our enemies—and as we catch these glimpses, these traces, we become dissatisfied with anything less; these glimpses keep us hoping and praying and dreaming and weeping for the messiah to come not once but again, and again, and again; not to come way down the road in the far-off future, at the end of time or beyond time, but today, this week, *now*, with the name of the messiah, the name of God, being what we desire with a desire beyond desire and a hope against hope, that exceeds what we can put into words. In the aftermath of the messiah, in the trace that tears our hearts and leaves a void, we are forever left inviting, calling, and longing, hoping, sighing, and dreaming—and thankfully so.

The God-shaped void in our hearts leaves us forever after God, forever restless, forever weeping and praying for the messiah to come again, and again, and again. When our world is shattered and hope seems lost, we pray for the messiah to enter, not just once, but a thousand times:

Into a world where religion is marked more by hatred than by love, we pray,

"Come, Lord Jesus."

Into a world where heartache and sorrow is all too often the norm, we pray,

"Come, Lord Jesus."

Into a world where fear drives more decisions than clarity of thought, we pray,

"Come, Lord Jesus."

Into a world where the rush to violence silences calls for peace, we pray,

"Come, Lord Jesus."

Into a world where reconciliation seems impossible, we pray,

"Come, Lord Jesus."

"The Spirit and the bride say, 'Come.' Let everyone who hears say, 'Come.' Let everyone who is thirsty come. 'Surely I am coming soon,' says the Lord. 'Surely I am coming soon'" (Rev 22:17).

In moments of our lives when hope feels lost, when our ways have worn thin, and we are in need of a different world to be born: "Come, Lord Jesus, come!"

Amen.

9

Implicitly Speaking

THIS SERMON WAS PREACHED on Pentecost Sunday, 2008, and so it focuses on the racial undercurrents that were escalating in regard to presidential candidate Barack Obama in general and his relationship with Rev.
Jeremiah Wright in particular. Through a modified deconstructive analysis, I tried to highlight the implicit and explicit dynamics of racism that
are still quite prominent in the United States today. I then drew on the
conventional reading of Pentecost as the inverse of the Tower of Babel,
while also trying to convey to listeners that the "principalities and powers" that govern our world—that is, the normalcy of civilization in the
early part of the twenty-first century in America—are still beholden to
norms that are predicated on male Eurocentrism. Oddly enough, these
norms need to be scattered in a manner reminiscent of the event that
took place in the narrative of the Tower of Babel (God needs to sow some
confusion here, God needs to disrupt these norms), so in a certain sense,
even as this sermon celebrates the inverse of the Tower of Babel (people
understanding one another), it also prays for the event of disruption that
took place at the Tower of Babel to take place again.

DAY OF PENTECOST (ACTS 2:1–11)

Within the context of both Pentecost Sunday and the dynamics of race in
America, I would like to talk to you today about that which is explicit, and
that which is implicit. By explicit, of course, I mean that which is obvious,
out in the open, for all to see. By implicit, I mean that which is subtle, hidden, lurking just beneath the surface. For instance, when the Bible says

that women should be silent in church and submit themselves to their husbands—that is an explicit way of reflecting patriarchal assumptions. It's obvious, out in the open, for all to see. Without even casting judgment on whether such assumptions are good or bad, they are obviously, explicitly apparent. On the other hand, when the Bible talks about two different people in a story, and perhaps only one of them is named, then it is often the case that the named person is a man and the unnamed person is a woman. In this case, we sense implicit patriarchal assumptions—they are subtle, hidden, lurking just beneath the surface. The explicit is that which we tend to cast judgment on, but the implicit is that which we rarely notice.

To use another example: the National Socialist movement of Hitler's Germany promoted the idea of a master Aryan race—one that possessed greater strength, intelligence, and ability than any other in the history of the world. In the 1936 Olympics—held in Berlin—Hitler wished to display the superiority of Nazi ideology for all the world to see.

So it brings us great satisfaction to remember that African-American track and field star Jesse Owens brought home four gold medals, because for us the idea of a master race is explicitly abhorrent, and we cast judgment upon it. It's obvious, out in the open, for all to see. *Of course* there's no such thing as a master race with greater strength and intelligence and ability than any other!

But implicitly, things are a bit different. In the same year that Jesse Owens freely entered German restaurants of his choice and used whatever public form of transportation necessary in Berlin, he was denied those very choices in the segregated Deep South of his home country.

There is the explicit, and there is the implicit.

Explicitly, we know there's not a master Aryan race. But just last year a good friend of mine, in polite company, sitting next to me on a couch during an NFL football game, said that blacks don't make very good quarterbacks because they don't analyze things well and they have trouble communicating with their white teammates.

There is the explicit, and there is the implicit.

The explicit states the obvious, yet the implicit often goes unnoticed. Recall the founders who held that "all men are created equal, that they are endowed by their Creator with certain unalienable Rights." These founders still managed to count slaves as only three-fifths of a person. Perhaps this irony is most readily seen in figures like Jefferson, Washington, and

Madison, all of whom are on record for believing that slavery was explicitly abhorrent and wrong, and that the slave trade should be abolished as quickly as possible—yet at the same time those words were penned, each of them owned slaves, profited from them, and refused to give them up (until they died, at least).

There is the explicit, and there is the implicit.

Explicitly, I am a preacher standing here today speaking on the dynamics of race in America, and much of what I want to say is that any kind of racism—explicit or implicit—is, if not equal in degree, still threatening to the well-being of our society, both individually and collectively.

But implicitly, I am a preacher standing here today speaking on the dynamics of race in America who carries the baggage and prejudices of being a white man conditioned in and by our culture, and such implicit bias and prejudice—that which subtly lurks beneath the surface—can't help influencing my own experiences and perspectives. This is a sensitive topic to talk about, to be sure, not least of all because of our own prejudices, biases, and fallibility, all of which lead to limited vision and perspective.

Scholars often talk about the implicit nature of our observations and feelings—most of which are constructed more on cultural conditioning than on the use of reason. In other words, there are things that we cognitively, reasonably, explicitly know—that there is no such thing as a master race and that slavery is wrong—yet our cultural conditioning, the way we operate, also leaves one prone to feel that African-Americans don't make very good quarterbacks—even though the last several years have produced Donovan McNabb, Steve McNair, and Vince Young, not to mention many others.

We see this operating on several different levels, some more serious than others. Stand-up comedian Chris Rock has a great bit on this. Back in 2000, when Colin Powell was vying for the Republican presidential nomination, one of the regular compliments given Powell was that "he speaks so well." To paraphrase Rock's routine: "'He speaks so well.' *Like that's a compliment!* 'Speaks so well' is not a compliment! What voice were you expecting to come out of his mouth? What did you expect him to sound like? 'I'm gonna drop me a bomb today . . . I'll be prez-o-dent!'"[1]

1. Chris Rock, "Colin Powell, black president." (Please note: This video contains explicit language).

It's like last year, when Sen. Joe Biden said that Barack Obama had a real chance to be elected because he was the first African-American man running for president so "clean and articulate."

Has anyone ever said something to you like, "You know, I was having lunch today at Applebee's, and I've got to tell you, I just had the nicest black waiter." What does being black have to do with that? What did they expect? That a black waiter was going to come up to their table and say, *"Give me your order! I said, give me your order!"*

There is the explicit, and there is the implicit.

Explicitly, we know that *Mein Kampf* is a racist book—obviously—but sitting at home on my bookshelves is Britannica's fifty-four-volume series Great Books of the Western World—and every single one of the fifty-four classic, seminal volumes was authored by a Eurocentric white male.

Explicitly, we know that lynching is a travesty of justice. But implicitly, lurking just beneath the surface, is the reality that on average African-Americans get harsher sentences than whites for committing the exact same crimes; and often, whites who commit more serious offenses get probation while persons of color committing less serious offenses are given jail time.

Explicitly, we say that all children are equal, school segregation is wrong, and that every child has a right to an equal education. But implicitly, we share in a system where poor people—no matter their color—are not given the same access to an equal education, so that there is a greater discrepancy today in terms of school segregation by economic class than there was in 1954 when the Supreme Court's ruling on Brown v. the Board of Education began the process of desegregating public schools.

Explicitly, we valorize Martin Luther King Jr. as one of our nation's greatest heroes, and well we should. But implicitly we valorize the pre-1964 King and leave the post-1964 King—the one who consistently critiqued not just racial inequality but also economic inequality, who provocatively critiqued the Vietnam War, and who called the United States "the greatest purveyor of violence in the world today"—we leave this King, this post-1964 King, lying dead on a hotel balcony in Memphis, Tennessee.

There is the explicit, and there is the implicit.

Over the last few months, there has been all kinds of explicit controversy surrounding Rev. Jeremiah Wright and his now infamous five-second sound bites. I have heard Rev. Wright preach on two occasions in person, and there is much that I respect about the man and much that, as you can imagine, has caught my attention as of late.

While some of his comments have been ripped by the media and taken way out of context—no surprise there, it happens all the time—and few have taken the time to watch or read more than just a tiny bit here or a tiny bit there over the course of his thirty-plus years of speaking, there are certain things he says that I have trouble agreeing with.

And there are some comments that simply cannot be condoned, such as the following: "It was the disobedience and rebellion of the Jews . . . that gave rise to the opposition and persecution that they experienced beginning in Canaan and continuing to this day"—opposition and persecution that includes the Holocaust. I also find it inexcusable to demonize the Catholic Church, calling it "the great whore of Babylon . . . the antichrist, and a false cult system."

Quotes like these are, in my opinion, egregious and indefensible, and I cannot support those who make them. However, the quotes I just read to you didn't come from the lips of Rev. Jeremiah Wright. Instead, they came from the lips of Rev. John Hagee, the megachurch pastor in Texas who believes that all-out war in the Middle East will bring about the rapture, and that peace treaties between Israel and Palestine go against God's endtimes will. John Hagee, by the way, is not one of Barack Obama's spiritual guides; he is one of John McCain's, of whom McCain said he was "proud and honored to have his support."

Yet somehow, someway, even though Hagee said that the Jews brought persecution on themselves, including the Holocaust, and that the Catholic Church is the great whore of Babylon, McCain did not face the same pressure to separate himself from John Hagee as Barack Obama did from Jeremiah Wright.

There is the explicit, and there is the implicit.

Frank Schaeffer, the son of the late religious-right leader Francis Schaeffer, writes:

> Every Sunday thousands of . . . white preachers [following in my father's footsteps] rail against America's sins from tens of thousands of pulpits. They tell us that America is complicit in the "murder of the unborn," has become "Sodom" by coddling gays, and that our public schools are sinful places full of evolutionists and sex educators hell-bent on corrupting children. They say, as my dad often did, that we are "under the judgment of God." They

call America evil and warn of imminent destruction [and say that God allowed 9/11 and Hurricane Katrina in order to punish us]. By comparison, [Wright's] "controversial" comments were mild . . . He said that God should damn America for our racism and violence . . . and that no one had ever used the N-word about Hillary Clinton. . . . But when my late father—Religious Right leader Francis Schaeffer—denounced America and even called for the violent overthrow of the U.S. government, he was invited to lunch with presidents Ford, Reagan, and Bush, Sr."[2]

Can you imagine what would happen if Jeremiah Wright had called for the violent overthrow of the US government? Do you think he would get invited to the White House for lunch?

There is the explicit, and there is the implicit.

I don't know about you, but I come from a biblical tradition that makes the implicit explicit, that lays bare the injustice of double standards.

In Matthew's Gospel, Jesus says, "Woe to you, scribes and Pharisees, hypocrites! For you [explicitly] tithe mint, dill, and cummin, and have [implicitly] neglected the weightier matters of the law: justice and mercy and faith. It is these you ought to have practiced without neglecting the others. You blind guides! You strain out a gnat but swallow a camel!" (Matt 23:23–24).

In the book of Amos, God cries out through the prophet, detesting the explicit forms of religion that forget the point of authentic religion. As Amos puts it:

I hate, I despise your festivals,
and I take no delight in your solemn assemblies.
Even though you offer me your burnt-offerings and grain-offerings,
I will not accept them;
and the offerings of well-being of your fatted animals
I will not look upon.
Take away from me the noise of your songs;
I will not listen to the melody of your harps.
But let justice roll down like waters,
and righteousness like an ever-flowing stream. (5:21–24)

In today's beautiful passage from the book of Acts, there were people from all nations present: There were Parthians, Medes, Elamites,

---

2. Schaeffer, "Obama's Minister Committed 'Treason.'"

Mesopotamians, Judeans and Asians; there were Egyptians, Libyans, Romans, Greeks, and Arabs. It was their known world.

I want you to hear me. That's like saying there were whites and blacks and Asians and Latinos, Africans and Native Americans and Iranians and Iraqis, Cubans and Mexicans and Palestinians and Israelis.

These people groups shared a rough-and-tumble history. Some had been the oppressors, others had been the oppressed. They were suspicious of each other, they didn't understand each other, they didn't necessarily like each other. But when God's Spirit broke out, things began to change.

When God's Spirit broke out, those who didn't understand each other, those who didn't trust each other, those who were uncertain about their future together—they began to understand each other, they began to hear how God was working in the midst of their differences, in the midst of diversity. For what is impossible with humans is possible with God. When God's Spirit breaks out, things begin to change.

I don't know about you, but I come from a tradition in which a slave-ship captain by the name of John Newton is transformed by the call of the Spirit to pen the hymn "Amazing Grace" and to work tirelessly for abolition.

I come from a tradition in which the call of the Spirit empowers a freed slave by the name of Sojourner Truth to refuse to cling to her bitterness and instead be used as an agent of change, transcending the boundaries of gender and race.

I come from a tradition in which the forgotten, despised Samaritan becomes the embodiment of God's transformative love.

I come from a tradition in which Christ breaks down every dividing wall of hostility.

I come from a tradition that celebrates the gifts of those from all nations and empowers God's people to ceaselessly work for justice.

I come from a tradition in which the Spirit does not rest until all of God's children—blacks and whites, Jews and Gentiles, Catholics and Protestants—will be able to join hands and sing, in the words of the old spiritual, "free at last, free at last, thank God Almighty, we are free at last."

I come from a tradition in which those with brown skin, black skin, white skin, yellow skin, and red skin have a place at the table—and the table is not complete without them.

I come from a tradition in which no person, no institution, no principality, no power, no place, and no time—however implicit or explicit—will keep the call of justice from flowing down like waters, and righteousness like an ever-flowing stream.

I come from a tradition that lays bare the injustice of the past and opens the door to a transformed future in which we can live as part of the restored, renewed, beloved community.

For when God's Spirit breaks out, things begin to change.

10

Impossible Gifts

To SET UP THE sermon in this chapter, it's necessary to provide introductory comments on Derrida's well-known analysis of the gift, which provides a wonderful structural example of the way we begin by the impossible.[1] On the surface level, giving a gift seems simple enough, until we consider the chain of events that is set off when a person attempts to give a gift. These dynamics are captured quite nicely in an episode from the sitcom *The Big Bang Theory*, which humorously depicts the anxiety Sheldon feels when he learns that his friend Penny has a Christmas present for him. Not only does Sheldon now know that he needs to get a gift for Penny in return, but he immediately worries about how much she spent on him. If he reciprocates with a gift that is more expensive than the one he receives, then it makes Penny look bad. But if he spends far less on Penny than she spent on him, not only does he look cheap but he also runs the risk of insulting Penny (by making her think he doesn't value her as much as she values him). In an effort to escape this "economy of exchange," Sheldon goes out and buys a bunch of bath and body gift baskets of all different prices and sizes and resolves to give Penny one of the baskets only after he opens her gift for him (so he can exchange value for value). It turns out, however, that Penny got Sheldon a napkin autographed by Leonard Nimoy, which, in Sheldon's eyes, is priceless. After opening his present, Sheldon rushes back to his bedroom (where he had stashed the gift baskets) and frantically brings out all of the baskets and gives every single one of them to Penny. Still he knows that isn't enough

1. For what follows, see Caputo, *What Would Jesus Deconstruct?*, 69–75.

to show his gratitude. Nothing is enough. So he does the unexpected—he gives Penny a hug. Those familiar with Sheldon's idiosyncratic character know that giving a hug is by far the most priceless gift he could give in return.

Notice the chain of events at work in this gift *exchange*: As soon as Penny gave her gift to Sheldon, her gift began to annul itself. Penny tried her best to give a gift to Sheldon, but as soon as he became aware of it, he was encumbered with a sense of debt that, in turn, he tried to discharge by finding an equal gift to give. So, along with receiving a gift from Penny, he also received a debt (this is why, Caputo notes, we speak of "owing a debt of gratitude" to someone). Sheldon wasn't simply given a gift, he was also put into debt, which is not what a gift is supposed to do, even when it is well intentioned. By contrast, Penny, who should be experiencing a lack since she gave something *away*, actually gets something in return, for she has added to her reputation for generosity and kindness. So in giving, she is actually receiving. Indeed, you can go so far as to say that by giving a priceless gift, Penny has come out ahead. This is the opposite of what she intended to do, but it is the consequence nonetheless. As Caputo summarizes, "The gift is supposed to be an act of 'giving,' but it has quickly turned into an economy, a matter of 'debts' and 'repayment,' of balance and payments. The idea behind a gift ideally ought to be to give a gift without return, to make an expenditure without the expectation of reciprocation." But the result is an economy of exchange. While the giving between Penny and Sheldon was an example of a beautiful exchange, sometimes the economy of exchange can rear its ugly head. This can be seen especially in relation to donors who make "gifts" (often to public officials or to organizations) but expect substantial *returns* on their investments. One needn't look any further than church board meetings (or stewardship committee meetings) in order to see how various church programs and ministries must have the indirect approval of the major "givers" in the church, for the donors are usually expecting something in return from their church when they give away such large sums of money. Strings are always attached, whether intended or not.

So, is there a way out of this circle of exchange? Derrida and Caputo say that it's possible for one to give a gift anonymously, so that the recipient doesn't know whom to thank, but then the recipient is blocked from discharging the debt and the giver will most likely congratulate oneself all the more for the nobility of giving anonymously.

So the receiver is still put into debt and the giver receives because of the nobility of their gift. What about giving the gift of an inheritance to one's children? After all, in this case, one wouldn't be around to receive expressions of gratitude from one's heirs. But it is likely that because one knows deep down that the beneficiaries of the inheritance will be profoundly grateful, one is repaid over and over again in one's mind by the prospect that one's heirs will prosper as a result of such generous giving. But what about the possibility of one's gift being met with cold ingratitude from the recipient? Well, that only makes the giver feel even better about himself; he congratulates himself all the more for being benevolent even when his giving is not appreciated.

When we analyze the structure of the gift, we see that the giver is the one who receives, and the recipient is put into debt. Which is the opposite of what is supposed to happen. As soon as the gift *presents* (gift/present) itself, it is annulled. This leads critics of Derrida to conclude that "the self-annulling character of the gift means that the gift is impossible." But that is to miss what Derrida is up to. "The conclusion," Caputo describes, "is not that the gift is impossible but that the gift is *the* impossible (it belongs to the vocative order), which is why we love it so and why we are mad about the gift with the madness of love itself, which dreams of the impossible. The aporia, *the* impossible, is never the end of action in deconstruction but the start, the condition of possibility of a genuine action, one with teeth in it." In other words, it is true that the economy of exchange is inescapable: when Penny gave her gift to Sheldon, she ended up on the receiving end and he was put into debt. *But the gift was still worth giving.* Indeed, the idea of the pure gift (what we might call the undeconstructible)—the attempt to give a gift to someone that makes a profound difference in her life, without expectation of return—is what gets things going, is what makes life priceless. "Appreciate the aporetic situation," Caputo writes, "but still *give*. It is impossible that the gift will not in one way or another be reciprocated, even as it is impossible to purge ourselves of every expectation of a return, for even were such purity of intention possible for our consciousness, there would be no telling what is going on in our unconscious. But still *give*, make the Kierkegaardian leap, seize the madness of the moment, and give, expecting no return—even though there will inevitably be a return." The event of the pure gift lures us, draws us, solicits us, makes us want to give a gift, even though it is impossible to do so. The gift Penny gave to Sheldon was profoundly meaningful even though it was caught up in the economy of exchange, even though it was impossible for her to give a pure gift without Sheldon feeling like he was in her debt. The lure of the gift is similar to the structure of the messianic. The gift calls from the vocative order—what doesn't exist—and drives us to try to make the impossible possible, *to experience the impossible*, which, again, Derrida calls the least bad definition of deconstruction. For Derrida, such impossibility does not stop us in our tracks but instead "stirs our desire, feeds our faith, and nourishes our passion; the impossible is such stuff as dreams are made of. It is just when we see that it is impossible that our hearts are set afire and we are lifted up above the horizon of pedestrian possibility. For Derrida, we must not lose our faith in the impossible, which is also our hope, our love, our faith in the gift."[2]

If we extend this analysis we notice that in deconstruction, the gift is closely related to love. We live in a society where business as usual consists of doing things for the payoff. Economies of exchange are everywhere around us: in churches, schools, hospitals, the law, the government, and so on. People are contractually bound to do certain things in order to receive certain things. For instance, I have a contract that stipulates the general tasks that I am supposed to do for the congregation where I work and, in turn, what the congregation is supposed to do for me. If I do such and such (the tasks of ministry), the church will do such and such (provide housing and a living wage). We are contractually bound to do certain things in order to receive certain things. It is all about an economy of exchange. But if such a contract constituted the vocational relationship I share with the congregation—the relationship that can't be put on paper—then the ministry that the congregation and I are involved in would be doomed from the start. As Caputo puts it, "We cannot do everything 'for the money,' for the payoff. There have to be things we do for the sheer love of them, things that are given to us to which we in turn give ourselves, where we break the chain of means-and-ends." While economies of exchange are all around us (they constitute business as usual, the normalcy of civilization), we must also consider what would happen if economies were all that we had, if nobody did anything without expecting to receive in return. The call of the gift saves us from such mediocrity. Even though giving a gift is *impossible*, the beauty of the gift lures us and draws us and compels us to give. We begin by the impossible. Christianity, like the gift,

2. Caputo, "Apostles of the Impossible," 205.

is about a love that exceeds the economy of exchange and the normalcy of civilization. Christianity is about a love beyond measure, in excess, a love that is never fully present (*parousia*), a love that always slips away and yet, in slipping away, paradoxically draws us in its train.[3] Can you imagine what kind of world we would live in if the deconstructible economies of exchange took precedence over the lure of the undeconstructible gift?

For example, I remember when my grandmother was in a nursing home. Some of her nurses would come in right on schedule and change her sheets, change her clothes, give her medicine, things like that—everything they were obligated to do in order to fulfill their contractual responsibilities. But some of her nurses would come in and do all of that—change her sheets, change her clothes, give her medicine—and then they'd pull up a chair, sit by her bed for a few minutes, gently hold her hand, smile, look into her eyes, and ask how she was doing. While economies of exchange are all that we have, we are driven by the gift. Our world can't be contained by rules or laws or principles, for our world is made beautiful by the call of love that transcends every law, every rule, every principle, every contract, every economy of exchange. In Caputo's words, "Economies are made fertile and productive by the gift by which they are ruptured and interrupted, punctuated, opened up, and expanded. Economies need gifts even as the gift goes beyond what is needed."

We can also consider the gift in relationship to for/give/ness. The madness of truly forgiving, with no strings attached—what Christians might call grace—is not only an exemplary dynamic at the heart of the kingdom of God as proclaimed by Jesus, but it also runs counter to virtually all economies of exchange that operate under the day-to-day normalcy of civilization (what *is*). When we forgive someone, certain strings are always attached: The person must feel bad for what they did, they must apologize, they must promise to change, they must be "worthy of forgiveness," and so on.

But if forgiveness is a matter of the gift (grace) and not an economy of exchange, then the only thing that can be truly forgiven is the unforgivable.[4] What then would it mean to forgive someone? Caputo says such forgiveness "would have to mean something uneconomic—like a gift—something unconditional, something unaccountable, something mad.

3. See Caputo, "Jacques Derrida (1930–2004)."

4. Caputo and Derrida are aware of the ethical dilemmas involved here. See esp. Zlomistić and DeRoo, *Cross and Khôra*, 225ff.

But the New Testament turns on just such unaccountables." In Scripture, we encounter a parabolic world where unconditional gifts are given and received, beyond economies of exchange. The radical forgiveness offered by Jesus, with no strings attached, is very well one of the things that got him into hot water.[5]

Derrida once said that he is "interested in Christianity and in the gift in the Christian sense,"[6] and while he consistently refuses to name what it is he loves when he loves his God, he does say, while reflecting on Kierkegaard, that he "interprets the divinity of God as gift or desire of giving."[7] In relation to the unconditional, undeconstructible gift of forgiveness—*impossible* forgiveness—I am reminded of the words Jesus spoke to his disciples: What is impossible for human beings is possible for God (see Luke 18:27). In Scripture, the kingdom of God calls for the event of forgiveness that is unconditional, beyond all of our economies of exchange. This impossible gift lures us, draws us, compels us. And when we experience the impossible, we are driven to our knees in thanksgiving and praise.

YEAR C: FOURTH SUNDAY IN LENT (LUKE 15:1–3, 11B–32)

Have you ever thought about the difficulty of giving a gift? Not just because so many of our friends already have everything they need, but because it seems impossible to give something away without getting something in return. The great theologian Thomas Aquinas once said that "a gift is literally a giving that can have no return." But this is hard to do! Most of the time, when we try to give a gift, we get something back.

Let's walk through this together. If there's going to be a gift, you need at least three things, right? You need the giver of the gift. You need the recipient of the gift. And, of course, you need the gift itself. Say that you give a huge sum of money to an organization as a gift, like one of the characters from the movie *Return to Me*. The man who made the donation was a retired senior citizen worth millions of dollars. He decided to donate tons of money to the Chicago Zoo in order to finance a new gorilla habitat. It

5. See Caputo, *Weakness of God*, 217.

6. Jennings, *Reading Derrida/Thinking Paul*, 84–85. Jennings states: "The gift in the Christian sense means here, it seems to me, the understanding of grace that Paul seeks to clarify especially in Romans."

7. Ibid. One must ask: Is Derrida speaking of himself here, or of his interpretation of Silesius?

was a very generous, gracious gesture. But throughout this movie, there are a lot of comedic moments involved because this man takes every opportunity to remind others just how generous and gracious his gift was. While at a dinner party, he asks those around him, "Perhaps you heard about my *sizeable* donation?" Then, toward the end of the movie, he gets to be one of the featured speakers at the dedication ceremony for the gorilla habitat (that's what you get to do when you give lots of money to a project). So he stands up in front of everyone with all of the cameras on him and opens his speech by saying, "We're not here today because of my *sizeable* donation." The idea is that he gave this money, this gift, but come on now—he's getting a little bit in return, isn't he? At least, he expected a little bit in return. But if it's a true gift, it shouldn't have any kind of return.

Maybe he could have made that gift a little better by making it anonymously. But after making our anonymous gifts, we'll sometimes say to ourselves, "Well, look at me. I gave this gift and I didn't even expect recognition. That's pretty classy on my part." Even those anonymous gifts sneak up on us, and we start to feel really good about ourselves. So we give the gift, but the gift is returned to us in the sense of making us feel like we did a pretty nice thing, a pretty honorable thing, a pretty noble thing. So we get something back.

Now let's think about how difficult it is to receive a gift. Let's say my friends Maurice and Susan want to take my family and me out for a birthday dinner. It's a gracious gesture on their part; they're not expecting anything in return, and I would gladly say yes. After dinner, I would guess that the check would be at minimum fifty dollars, depending upon where we go and what we order. While neither Maurice nor Susan would ask me to do anything whatsoever in return for this birthday dinner gift, I'll still be sitting at that table wanting to know how much the check is because I've got to at least leave the tip, right? You know how this is. My friends offered me a great gift, but now I feel indebted to them. Don't get me wrong, I'm glad they offered the gift, and feeling indebted to them isn't a bad feeling. I'm thankful for their kind gesture. So when it's Maurice's birthday, or Susan's birthday, I'll say to myself, "I should take the Bowens out for dinner!" I feel a responsibility to pay them back, so in a sense you could even say they are getting a little return on their gift, even though they didn't ask for a return, even though they didn't give expecting or desiring a return.

Have you ever received a birthday gift from somebody that you didn't expect? And then you immediately marked your calendar for when their birthday rolled around? Since they gave you something, you feel like you're indebted to them and that you need to return the favor. Often we go online to try to get a ballpark figure of how much they spent on us, so that whenever we return the favor at least we're in the same ballpark when it comes to value. To be sure, they didn't ask for anything in return, but their gift actually set in motion the dynamics for them to get something back. It's not surprising that the French word for present comes from the Latin word for chain, because gifts (presents) set this chain in motion! One philosopher calls this "the economy of exchange."

This is quite the dilemma. For there to be a possibility of a pure gift to be given, it's almost like the giver needs to give a gift without knowing they gave it and the recipient needs to receive the gift without knowing they received it. Which all sounds pretty crazy. Pretty impossible.

I think the most difficult of all gifts to give is the gift of forgiveness, and I'm not sure that it's possible for us as human beings to grant unconditional forgiveness. If we are going to grant somebody forgiveness, then, generally, they have to fall into line. There are conditions they have to meet. There are strings attached. If we are going to forgive them, they should feel sorry for what they did. They should admit that it was wrong. They should try to make restitution, to the extent that they can. And they should commit themselves to not doing it again, or trying not to do it again. And after they've met these criteria, these conditions, then we will give them the gift of forgiveness. But is that really a gift, if there are strings attached? Can it be a gift if it is conditional?

Isn't that kind of like going to the bank for a loan? If you have good collateral, good credit history, and a good income, then the banker will most likely give you the loan, *if you meet the conditions*. But if you don't hold up your end of the bargain, then they can revoke the loan. If you have a mortgage loan, for instance, when do you get the deed from the bank? After you have paid it all off, right? There are certain conditions that have to be met. And we see this a lot in terms of forgiveness.

There is a parable in Matthew's Gospel about a king who wants folks to come in and pay him what he is owed. So this one guy comes into his court and he owes him like a zillion billion dollars (at least that's how we might put it). It's a huge sum of money that this man couldn't possibly begin to pay back. So in his desperation, this man pleads to the king, "Please have mercy on me, please, please, please, have mercy on me, please!" And what does the king do? He forgives the man's entire debt. Remarkable. Unexpected. Impossible.

But no sooner does this man leave the king's court than he runs into somebody who owes him some money. It's a paltry, paltry sum of money compared to what he had been forgiven by the king. But instead of forgiving the person who owes him a little bit of money, he takes this man, grabs him by the throat, and demands that he be repaid right there, right then! The audacity! And then the king catches word of this. And you can imagine how it makes the king feel, right? The king calls this man back into his court and revokes his forgiveness. He imprisons this man until he is able to pay back everything he owed.

We can probably agree that the king had every right to do what he did, right? It's reasonable, it makes perfect sense, it holds up to all of our contracts and loan statements. Yet we also have to admit that, in this parable, the forgiveness granted by the king was conditional. It had strings attached. As soon as this forgiven man didn't extend the same kind of generous forgiveness to others, the original gift of forgiveness was revoked. The conditions were not met.

In Luke's Gospel, there's a story of a man who has two sons. And there's a younger son who wants his share of the property, his share of the family fortune, so he insults his dad and asks for it. And to make matters worse, after he receives his share of the family fortune, he goes off on a trip to an ancient Mediterranean Vegas and goes through his part of the family fortune faster than bailed-out AIG executives on a corporate retreat.[8] And he's sitting there with the pigs, eating their scraps, and it finally dawns on him: "You know, the hired hands, who work for my father, even they have plenty to eat. They've got food left over. So I know what I'll do. I will go back to my home and I will confess my wrongs." So you can hear this younger son practicing his line, because he knew that the conditions had to be met. He knew there was a lot at stake, and he didn't want to screw it up. So you can hear him practicing his line, "Father, father, I have sinned against heaven, and before you I am no longer worthy to be called your son. Father, I have sinned against heaven and against you. I am no longer worthy to be called your son." He knew there was a lot at stake, and conditions had to be met. Yet in this story, the son is coming up the road,

---

8. I preached this sermon in 2009.

back to his home, and his father sees him. And his father runs out to greet him. And before his son can get one word of repentance out of his mouth, before he can meet one condition, his father embraces him, kisses him, gives him his best robe, calls for a party, a celebration. Unconditionally, no strings attached.

Now the older son knew that this isn't how things worked. This son has to earn his keep, he's got to pay his dues, pay his debts so he can give back to his family table. "You mean to tell me," this older son says, "that my brother, who screwed up everything, who squandered all of his fortune and half the family fortune, that he gets his place back at this table, back at this home, no strings attached. Are you kidding me? That's not how this world works. Forgiveness isn't given—it has to be earned!"

In this parable, the Father forgives unconditionally, no strings attached, before his younger son can even begin to meet any of the criteria. Some scholars think that forgiveness like that is part of the reason Jesus got in so much hot water. It was too revolutionary, too much.

Remember when I mentioned the idea of giving a gift but not knowing it, and receiving a gift but not knowing it? It seems pretty crazy, but I wonder if forgiveness works that way? We live in this economy of exchange where there is always a balance sheet, a ledger being kept. The younger son knew what he had to do to get back into the good graces of his father. The older son knew the father had broken the rules by doing away with the balance sheet. We live our lives thinking our forgiveness is conditioned by that balance sheet.

A lot of times people will come by my office and tell me they are wondering whether or not they should forgive a certain person. In their minds, they're thinking about what this person has done, and they are wondering if the person deserves forgiveness, is worthy of forgiveness. They're making a calculation in their mind.

But I've come to believe that the miracle of forgiveness works a little differently than that. Ultimately, forgiveness isn't anything that we can give, because we always give with conditions, with strings attached, in an economy of exchange, calculated by us. I've come to believe that when forgiveness takes place, it's a miracle: it's beyond our own doing. And a lot of times it's a miracle because the person who gave the forgiveness and the person who received the forgiveness didn't even know they were doing so, and sometimes I suspect that the same people, both the "giver" and the "recipient," are giving and receiving at the same time, without even knowing it. And perhaps that's how it must be if there is such a thing as a gift.

I would like to tell you about another prodigal family, one that also has a checkered past.

It started in high school and college, when the daughter in the family made a bunch of decisions that disappointed her parents, and they responded in ways that disappointed her. She felt like they didn't listen to her, they felt like she didn't respect them. It's a story so many of us have heard; it's a story so many of us have lived.

Truth be told, she did regret a lot of her decisions. She knew she had let them down. There had been times when she could have stayed engaged in the conversation rather than storming off in a huff, times when she could have recognized they were doing their best. But she didn't know what to do about it. Things had gotten so bad, it just seemed easier to not spend time with them. She didn't know how to cross the great chasm between them.

Truth be told, the parents regretted a lot as well. They knew they had let their daughter down. There had been times when they hadn't *really* listened to her, when they had closed themselves off from her, when they hadn't paid attention to her perspective on things. But it seemed too late now, and they didn't know what to do.

One day, in perhaps the darkest moment of their relationship, as the dad sat in the drive-thru line at the bank, he was surprised to hear the teller say, "Congratulations! I hear you're going to be a grandpa!" The dad tried to hide his shock behind a smile, said "thank you" as he took his receipt from the carrier tube, and drove away. He felt the smile melt off his face as his heart pounded within his chest. His heart was broken. Had things gotten so bad that his own daughter wouldn't call him up to tell him he was going to be a grandpa?

The teller, who was a good friend of the daughter's, excitedly told her that evening, "Hey, I saw your dad and congratulated him. I bet your parents are so excited about becoming grandparents!" The daughter's stomach dropped. She knew that she should have told them; she should have called them with her good news.

Hearts were breaking and the chasm was growing. All three regretted the alienation they felt. They knew they had wronged one another. On the ledger sheet, things didn't add up. Each of them knew they had screwed up. And deep down, all three longed for reconciliation.

And what is remarkable—what is miraculous—is that these many years later, these three have grown back together as closely as anyone I know. To see the joy between the family as the father plays ball in the backyard with his grandson, you'd never know they went through a period where the daughter couldn't bring herself to tell her parents about his impending birth. To see the lively conversation around the dinner table during the holidays, you'd never know that meals were often eaten together in stony silence, if they were eaten together at all.

Perhaps most remarkable of all is that the three never stopped to calculate what was on the ledger sheet. Not once did they make calculated exchanges. Not once did they say, "Since you feel bad for what you did, I will forgive you," or "Since you have apologized, and you seem to really mean it, I guess I will forgive you." Never once did they make those calculated exchanges. Never once.

And yet they experienced forgiveness. The ledger sheets were miraculously thrown out. The relationship between the three was mended. It was a gift beyond their manufacturing. None of them knew they were extending the gift of forgiveness, and none of them knew they were receiving it, but all three experienced it. And it changed the very fabric of their beings, the very course of their relationship, the very meaning of their lives.

In the end, gifts are miraculous. We can't manufacture them. We can only respond to them, and most of the time we probably don't even realize we're doing so. That's why we don't call gifts—we don't call grace—"reasonable" or "calculable." No, we call grace amazing.[9]

9. See Caputo, *Weakness of God*, 225–31.

11

Lost in Wonder, Love, and Praise

THE SAMPLE SERMON IN this chapter draws on the theology of Jean-Luc Marion in relation to Moses' encounter with God at the burning bush. It is placed immediately following the analysis of Derrida's gift because Marion and Derrida share a handful of significant differences in their approach to religion and faith, and their respective interpretations of the gift offer a nice point of orientation for those trying to get a handle on what differentiates their perspectives.[1]

As we have already discussed at length, Derrida's deconstructive structure of the messianic is based on a hunger and longing for the "to-come," for what eye has not seen and ear has not heard. In deconstruction, the presence of the undeconstructible is always deferred, and necessarily so. Consider the sermon from chapter 8 that highlighted the way that the lack of the messiah's presence is precisely what nourishes the hunger for the messiah's presence all the more. For Derrida, if the messiah was to ever fully show up, the game would be over, for there wouldn't be anything left to pray and weep for. The hunger for the messiah to come is fueled by the messiah's absence, which can easily be seen in the history of Christianity's creeds and prayers that long for the second coming of the messiah. The less the messiah exists, the more the messiah insists. So the important point to communicate here is that in deconstruction, the "wholly other" never quite arrives but, by never quite arriving, sets us in its tracks all the more. In deconstruction we begin by the impossible, as

---

1. For what follows, see Caputo, "Apostles of the Impossible," 185–222. For an even more technical discussion, see Marion, *God Without Being*, and Marion, *Being Given*.

seen in the structure of the messianic in general (see chapter 4) and the gift in particular (see chapter 10). As such, we are unable to adequately comprehend the wholly other or speak of the wholly other. If we could adequately comprehend the wholly other, or speak of the wholly other, we would domesticate the wholly other, we would diminish the wholly other, we would "kill" the wholly other, mostly by reducing the other to the same (to what we can adequately understand and speak of). As Theodore Jennings observes, for Derrida, our faith in the gift, the wholly other, "takes us beyond knowledge, even if not beyond thought."[2]

Like Derrida, Marion is madly in love with the gift, with what we can never speak of. He too maintains that it is impossible to adequately comprehend and conceptualize the gift. However, Marion provides very different reasons for speaking about the impossibility of speaking—whether about the gift, about the wholly other, or about "God" (what do I love when I say I love my God?) For Marion, the reason we are unable to speak of the gift—the reason we are unable to speak of God—is not that the presence of the gift is perpetually deferred, as in Derrida, but rather that it is given with an overwhelming, saturating givenness that exceeds all of our frameworks for understanding. Such givenness overflows our comprehension and intellect. As Caputo describes, Marion "proposes a radical phenomenology of a saturating *givenness*, a phenomenological description of an event, or the possibility of an event, of bedazzling brilliance, given without being, visited upon us beyond comprehension, leaving us stunned and lost for words."[3] God is without being, for Marion, because a God of *being* is a concept within our own framework for understanding, and God exceeds every framework for understanding that we have. The reason we can't adequately understand or conceptualize God isn't that God's revelation is too little, but rather that it is too much. This is similar to the mystical theologians, as well as to figures like Luther and Barth, who maintain that God is revealed in hiddenness. It also has a lot in common with Anselm's auto-deconstructing claim that God is "something than which nothing greater can be thought."[4] Here the concept of God is not as the greatest conceivable being but the concept that exceeds all of our thinking and cannot be thought. Peter Rollins describes the con-

2. Jennings, *Reading Derrida/Thinking Paul*, 92.
3. Caputo, "Apostles of the Impossible," 185.
4. Davies and Leftow, *Cambridge Companion to Anselm*, 163.

nections between Anselm and Marion this way: "For Anselm, the concept 'God' must include the idea of how the object of the concept transcends every concept. As the contemporary philosopher Jean-Luc Marion writes, 'The root of the argument is not reliance on the concept but reliance on a non-concept, acknowledged as such.'"[5] But the acknowledgment of this non-concept, of the impossibility of speech, "is not the silence of banality, indifference or ignorance but one that stands in awe of God. This does not necessitate an absolute 'silencing,' whereby we give up speaking of God, but rather involves a recognition that our language concerning the divine remains silent in its speech. As Marion writes, 'The silence suitable to God requires knowing how to remain silent, not out of agnosticism (the polite surname of impossible atheism) or out of humiliation, but simply out of respect.'"[6] Our language and logic cannot express the inexpressible. That is why our response to the event of God leads us to be *lost* in wonder, love, and praise.

YEAR A: ELEVENTH SUNDAY AFTER PENTECOST (EXOD 3:1–15)

You have probably noticed that just about everything has a name. In this room alone, hundreds—if not thousands—of objects have names. There are books, candles, and microphones; there is bread, cup, and cross. And these general items have even more specific names: Some of the things generally named as a book are more specifically named as a Bible or hymnal; some of the things generally named as microphones are more specifically named as lapel mikes or podium mikes. We could go on and on with these examples, for virtually everything we are aware of has a name.

We use names to help classify, categorize, and comprehend everything we encounter. As philosopher Richard Rorty says, all "languages are tools for dealing with what is out there."[7] By helping us classify, categorize, and comprehend, language serves as a very practical and useful tool, perhaps the greatest invention of the human race.

And all of these names help us out in countless day-to-day experiences: Having different names for different things helps us know whether the exit on the highway is for a weigh station or for a rest stop; having

5. Rollins, *How (Not) to Speak of God*, 29.

6. Ibid, 41.

7. Rorty, *Philosophy and Social Hope*, xxvii.

different names for different things helps us when we ask our friends around the dinner table to pass the salt, guac, or queso—which is an issue of no small import to picky eaters like me!

Having different names for different things helps us order our world. Amanda and I have three children, and each has a different name: There is Elijah Cole, Samuel Micah, and Lily Grace. Not only does each of these names mean something different and valuable to us, but the names also help us order our lives. When I need to talk to Eli, I can call him by name, and, *hopefully*, at least within two or three tries, he will respond. Or when Sam wants to tell me about Lily, her name (and mine) offer simple points of reference: "Hey dad, Lily is crying!"

I would hate to think what it would be like around the house of former heavyweight boxing champion George Foreman, who named his first son George, his second son George, his third son George, not to mention his fourth and fifth sons—all George! This of course leads his wife and him to use other names to order their world, so their sons are known as George Jr., George the third, George the fourth, and so on.

While all names contain vast and varying levels of meaning that help us classify, categorize, and comprehend our world—as well as what is often very dear to our hearts like our family members and friends—we also have to admit that *names conceal as much as they reveal*—that what we see of our world, and what we see of others, is like seeing through a glass darkly or dimly, as St. Paul liked to say.

For as we give names to classify and categorize, to understand and know, we are forced to recognize, especially in our relationships with others, that the other person we know by name is also, as John Caputo says, "a shore we will never reach, another side for which we set sail in our little boats but one on which we never actually arrive." Those we know are also, paradoxically, those we don't know, for every other person—whether spouse, partner, child, relative, coworker, or friend—has a certain interiority that we can never fully reach or know.

By contrast, Caputo says, "We can lift the lid of a music box and peek inside to see what was hidden from our view, or we can look inside a clock to see what makes it tick, but no matter how hard we try, we can never fully look inside the mind and heart of another person." The more deeply we know an other, the more we realize just how much the fullness of who they are paradoxically eludes us. "For the relation with the other is a journey we never complete, the shore we never reach, where that incompleteness is not an imperfection but a testimony to the perfect excess of the other; it is not a loss but a source of endless novelty and discovery."[8]

In our relationships with others whom we call by name, we set out for a shore that we can never reach. And "to set out for a shore that we can never reach" Caputo says, "to be exposed to a secret that we can never fully know"—this is part of the joy, wonder, and mystery of being alive in our world. It is also, not coincidentally, "a description of a proper path to God," to the One whose excess must always remain beyond classification, category, and comprehension.

Now there are many names we use for God: In the most dominant Western traditions, we usually hear names like Yahweh, Lord, or Allah. But of course, we have to recognize that the word *God* is also just that: a word, a name, one that we use to try to describe, to try to order, to try to classify, categorize, and comprehend. But what if God, as God, eludes all of these efforts of ordering, classifying, and comprehending?

Perhaps God is the name *we give* for that which we know not what, for that which we deeply desire, for that shore we can never reach but are so hungry to find. Perhaps God is the name *we give* to that which is beyond any proper name, beyond classification, beyond category, beyond comprehension. Perhaps God is the name *we give* to that which we long for, yearn for, struggle for, yet that which we can never fully know. Perhaps, therefore, the Name of God is not a name we can ultimately give at all.

When Moses was tending his father-in-law's flock just beyond the wilderness, he encountered God in the burning bush. Moses had the blessed audacity to ask what name this God went by, and God responded without giving a proper name, but instead said, "I am who I am," which can also be translated as "I will be who I will be." In other words, I have no proper name; I escape your names, I escape your categories, I escape your classifications; I escape your boxes, I escape your limitations, I escape your conceptions: "I am who I am, and I will be who I will be."

To this day, in order to honor the magnitude and reverence of the Holy Other, Jewish people of faith refuse to pronounce the proper name that Jewish Scripture attributes to God. In equivalent English renderings of the Hebrew Bible, it would be like having the letters YHWH written

8. See Caputo, *What Would Jesus Deconstruct?*, 44–45.

without vowels, so the Holy Name of the Wholly Other cannot be pronounced and cannot be uttered. It is the name that we cannot say.

And this tradition has been honored in both Jewish and Christian circles down through the years: Justin Martyr, the second-century Christian saint, said that "no one can utter a name for the ineffable God." Saint Basil said that "knowledge of the divine involves sensing God's incomprehensibility." And Thomas Aquinas once wrote that "the highest human knowledge of God is to know that one does not know God"—God remains a shore that we will never fully reach. As Simone Weil beautifully and paradoxically describes, this "good which we can neither picture nor define is a void, but it is a void fuller than all fullness."

Such a tradition reminds us that all of our attempts to name God, to classify, categorize, and comprehend God, inevitably fail. It's why St. Augustine famously said, "If you comprehend it, it is not God." "I am who I am, and I will be who I will be."

And so, finally, we are left to pray with the mystic Meister Eckhart, who prayed for God to rid him of God—that is, for God to rid him of his own limited, idolic conceptions of God. We are left to pray with the modern theologian Paul Tillich, who prayed for what he called the "God beyond God," the One who is beyond all of our finite names and classifications, the one who must always elude our grasp—indeed, the very One who disrupts and shatters all of our preconceived boxes and limitations. "I am who I am, and I will be who I will be."

And with Catholic theologian Jean-Luc Marion, we affirm most wonderfully that though the Holy Other remains *incomprehensible*, that shore we can never fully reach, the Wholly Other does not remain *imperceptible*. For our impossibility of naming God does not come from a lack, but from a surplus, which neither concept nor name can organize or contain. It's not because the givenness of God is lacking, but because its excess overcomes, submerges, exceeds, and saturates the measure of each and every one of our concepts.[9]

"I am who I am and I will be who I will be."

In the end, it is the ineffable, saturated givenness of *that which we know not what* that calls us, draws us, and provokes us to go to a place we cannot know and yet at the same time cannot resist; it is that which we call the Holy Other, the God of our ancestors, the God beyond God,

---

9. See Caputo, "Apostles of the Impossible," 194–95.

the God that rids us of God, that leaves us hoping, sighing, and weeping, longing, yearning, and praying.

And, like Moses on the mountain of God, we find ourselves in front of a burning bush that is not consumed. Like Moses, we find ourselves on holy ground, where all we can do is take off our shoes in awe and in reverence, lost in wonder, in love, and in praise.

12

Grilled Cheesus
(Or, the Gospel according to Slavoj Žižek)[1]

I DON'T KNOW IF the writers of the hit television show *Glee* have ever heard of Slavoj Žižek, but the third episode of the second season ("Grilled Cheesus") provides a summary of Žižek's approach to religion and Christianity that is simply brilliant. *Glee* chronicles the ups and downs of teenage life as experienced by members of a high school glee club, and the episode "Grilled Cheesus" examines questions of faith and religion in times of great need. As I describe in the sample sermon, one of the main characters in the show (Finn) thinks that he sees the face of God in his grilled cheese sandwich. This leads him to pray for a handful of selfish wishes to come true, much in the same way that one makes wishes to a genie. To Finn's delight, his prayers to Grilled Cheesus (the nickname he gives to his sandwich) seem to be working. Every selfish request that he makes is granted. All the while, however, Finn's good friend Kurt is facing the very serious possibility that his father might die from a massive heart attack. Yet Finn's newfound belief in Grilled Cheesus doesn't lead him to care for his friend Kurt—instead, it makes him all the more self-centered.

Over the course of the episode, however, Finn slowly begins to realize that his prayers to Grilled Cheesus come true as a result of circumstance and coincidence rather than supernatural divine intervention. When he steps back and starts thinking about it, there are very strong and quite logical reasons that explain each of the events he has wished for (winning

1. The sermon title was simply "Grilled Cheesus."

208

the first football game of the season, getting to second base with his girl-friend, winning back his role as starting quarterback of the football team). He also comes to terms with the fact that his belief in Grilled Cheesus selfishly distances him from the very real concerns that others face (e.g., Kurt's worries and fears). While visiting with the high school counselor, Finn expresses disappointment in no longer having a direct line to God. He doesn't like thinking that there is no "big Other" (Žižek's phrase, not Finn's) giving meaning and purpose to the universe. The scene concludes with Finn's singing R.E.M.'s "Losing My Religion."

After Finn's confession of *disbelief*, viewers of the show are left to interpret what all of this means for him. Does his lack of faith lead to a downward spiral of meaningless nihilism? Or instead does it lead him to more fully embrace the concerns and matters of this world? In this sermon, I drew on the philosophy of Žižek in order to argue for the latter option. According to Žižek, the narrative of Christianity provides the framework in which the big Other dies (on the cross) so that something new can be born. It is our belief in the big Other, Žižek contends, that keeps us from embracing the material reality of our existence. Only when belief in the big Other *dies* are we free to more fully live. But instead of viewing the death of the big Other as contrary to the tenets of Christianity, he argues that the death of the big Other is central to Christianity's subversive proclamation. In the narrative of Christianity, Žižek says, even God becomes an atheist ("My God, my God, why have you forsaken me?"). The resurrection is then experienced among collectives that refuse belief in the big Other and, as a result, experience the transformation at the heart of Christianity. For Žižek, "The subversive kernel of Christianity . . . is accessible *only* to a materialist approach."[2]

The episode ends with Finn eating Grilled Cheesus, which further symbolizes his disbelief in the big Other. From a Christian point of view, one can interpret this as a radical eucharistic act in which the body and blood of Christ is consumed and the new community (collective) in Christ is born. As Matthew Gallion argues,

> the Eucharist becomes a ritualistic act of rebellion in which one recognizes the absence of God by consuming the material presence of God . . . [W]hen one recognizes the "reality" that Žižek sees behind the "big Other"—namely that there is no "big Other"—one

2. Žižek, *Puppet and the Dwarf*, 6. See also Kotsko, *Žižek and Theology*.

is free to partake in the material ritual of the Eucharist; when one loses faith in a pie-in-the-sky deity, one is capable to recognize the "real presence" of God, which comes in the form of absolute absence of the "big Other" and the total responsibility of human beings to become the incarnation of the Holy Spirit in society.[3]

With Žižek in mind, Gallion acutely observes, "Perhaps the problem with progressive sermons is that we merely pretend to talk about God rather than outright reject God altogether, which is what happens at the cross, Christianity's greatest stroke of genius."[4] From this perspective, the idea is that post-Enlightenment preaching comes across as shallow and inauthentic because it still cloaks itself in the trappings of belief in God, the big Other—and, according to Christianity, true transformation occurs when the big Other dies. If most progressive listeners are "functional atheists," to recall Thomas Long's phrase from chapter 1, progressive listeners shouldn't hide from it, but rather own it—indeed, even celebrate it—and do so in a *Christian* way. As Žižek would say, Christianity is a properly atheistic religion (in Christ's abandonment on the cross, Žižek tells us, even God became an atheist). Therefore, from Žižek's point of view, we should do away with any talk of the "wholly other."[5] While this might at first sound absurd, it is echoed in theologians such as Paul Tillich and Dietrich Bonhoeffer (Žižek would throw G. K. Chesterton into the mix as well, and Peter Rollins consistently draws on this theme). To recall Bonhoeffer's provocative quote from his *Letters and Papers from Prison*, written just before he was executed for being part of a plot to assassinate Hitler: "God lets himself be pushed out of the world on to the cross. He is weak and powerless in the world, and that is precisely the way, the only way, in which he is with us and helps us . . . the God who is with us is the God who forsakes us . . . Before God and with God we live without God."[6]

At the risk of oversimplification, we might say there are at least two opposing perspectives at work in the postmodern return of religion: the first affirms Nietzsche's critique of metaphysics yet at the same time turns

3. Gallion, "Eating God to Death," 4.

4. Personal correspondence.

5. This can be read as the inverse of Barth: "Nothingness is that which brought Jesus Christ to the cross, and that which he defeated there" (*Church Dogmatics*, III/3:305). For Žižek, the cross properly exposes the nothingness. Indeed, to "defeat" nothingness would be to betray the subversive kernel of Christianity and the work of Christ.

6. Bonhoeffer, *Letters and Papers from Prison*, 360.

on a celebration of the "wholly other" (Derrida, Caputo, etc.), which was an event Nietzsche never saw coming, while the second (Žižek, Rollins, etc.) affirms Nietzsche's critique of metaphysics and prescribes the death of the "wholly other," which in the narrative framework of Christianity takes place at the cross.

So how does a homiletic of the event navigate this crossroads? While I suppose it could be limited to the either/or described above, I choose to emphasize deconstruction's "wholly other" *along with* a radical reading of the cross. Following Caputo, who also develops a theology of the cross, this approach affirms the position proffered by Žižek but takes it one step further:

> Žižek is only half right to say that the perverse core of Christianity lay in Jesus' being abandoned and that what we should learn from his death on the cross is that there is no Big Other to save us, so we should get on with our lives. The other half, what Žižek leaves out, is that in this abandonment there lies the weak force of God. I agree that we should not think of God as a source of magical effects or as a master manipulator of mundane powers and that in that sense we should get on with our lives. But the divinity of the truly divine God is to be displayed neither in a display of magic by Jesus or his heavenly Father, nor in the secret hope that the Father is going to square the accounts for him in an afterlife and give these Roman soldiers their comeuppance in the world to come. The divinity is rather that his very death and humiliation rise up in protest against the world, rise up above power. . . .The perverse core of Christianity lies in being a weak force. The weak force of God is embodied in the broken body on the cross, which has thereby been broken loose from being and broken out upon the open plane of the powerlessness of God. The power of God is not pagan violence, brute power, or vulgar magic; it is the power of powerlessness, the power of the call, the power of protest that rises up from innocent suffering and calls out against it, the power that says *no* to unjust suffering, and finally, the power to suffer-with *(sym-pathos)* innocent suffering, which is perhaps the central Christian symbol.
>
> . . . If the kingdom Jesus preached were a kingdom of real power, he could, by a mighty roar—nay better, by a soft sword—from his mouth, spring the nails from his hands, thrust away the spears from the hands of the soldiers, heal the wounds of his flesh, and shatter the cross into a million splinters in a dazzling display of sheer might. But his kingdom did not belong to the world, to

the realm of meeting power with power. His strength was the weak power of powerlessness—my God, my God, why have you abandoned me?—not the real power of the world, and so he was killed, quite against his will and the will of his Father. But in the powerlessness of that death the word of God rose up in majesty as a word of contradiction, as the Spirit of God, as a specter, as a ghostly event that haunts us, but not as a spectacular presence.[7]

Even though Žižek's perspective leads to the radical responsibility of human beings, it is rooted in the transformational event that, to use Christian language, takes place at the cross. In relationship to the modern homiletical crisis, I contend that the transformational event should be the source of celebration in progressive sermons.

By drawing on the Words of Institution in 1 Cor 11:23–26, I preached this sermon on World Communion Sunday. While the storyline surrounding Finn is a primary component to this sermon, I also highlight the plot line that revolves around Kurt and his other friends, which is pivotal to this episode as well (Kurt is an atheist who has a difficult time accepting spiritual words of comfort and prayers from his theist friends). Along the way, I incorporate a bit of a Caputian emphasis on the event harbored in the name of love and compassion that leads to the reconciliation experienced between Kurt and his friends, even though they maintain very different cognitive beliefs about God. Thus this sermon is informed by both Žižek and Caputo.

WORLD COMMUNION SUNDAY (1 COR 11:23–26)

In a recent episode of the hit television show *Glee*, which is a dramedy (half drama, half comedy) about the ups and downs of teenage life as experienced by members of a high school glee club, one of the main characters, named Finn, accidentally burned his grilled cheese sandwich and on it appeared an image that looked strikingly similar to traditional pictures of Jesus. Even though Finn wasn't all that religious, he viewed Jesus' face on his sandwich as a sign from God. He carefully preserved the sandwich and gave it the nickname "Grilled Cheesus" (because really, what else can you call a grilled cheese sandwich with the image of Jesus burnt into it?).

At various points throughout the show, Finn bowed before Grilled Cheesus and prayed for certain things to come true: His first prayer to

---

7. Caputo, *Weakness of God*, 43–44.

Grilled Cheesus was for the high school football team to win their game, which they did. He later prayed for his relationship with his girlfriend to advance to the next level, which it did. Next he prayed to earn back his job as the starting quarterback on the football team, which he did. He was three for three on his prayers. Grilled Cheesus came through.

Yet at the same time that these somewhat superficial wishes were being granted, Finn's good friend Kurt was dealing with the very serious fear of losing his dad, which of course made for a much more solemn story line. At the beginning of the episode, Kurt's dad suffered a massive heart attack that put him in a coma. His dad was unresponsive. The doctors were unsure if he would wake up. Regular watchers of the show know that Kurt had already lost his mother at a very early age—the wounds of which he never fully recovered from—and the fear of being without both his mom and dad was more than he could face.

This episode juxtaposes Finn's selfish prayers to Grilled Cheesus with Kurt's very real fears of losing his dad. And much of the plot line revolved around the role that God plays in times of crisis. While Kurt's other friends from the glee club rallied around him and pledged their support to him, Kurt had a lot of difficulty accepting their prayers and spiritual words of comfort. In large part this was because Kurt didn't believe in God. For what kind of good God would allow the kind of suffering we see in our world take place? Kurt viewed God as a Santa Claus in the sky, a fairy tale, if you will (Finn's approach to Grilled Cheesus only added to his convictions about this!), and while he appreciated the thoughts of his friends, he didn't want their prayers.

This episode portrays one of the most unfortunate realities of human life: oftentimes, the beliefs that people have about God—whether God exists or not, whether God is true or not—separate us from one another rather than draw us toward one another—even, perhaps especially, in times of great need. As this episode progresses, the tensions between Kurt's beliefs and his friends' beliefs escalate to the point where Kurt goes so far as to kick them out of his father's hospital room because they had gathered around his bedside to pray for him. *For Kurt and his friends, belief was getting in the way of community.*

But then a couple of remarkable events took place, with the first happening in church, of all places. Kurt's best friend, Mercedes, invited him to go to church with her, and in an effort to mend their relationship, Kurt accepted. In one of the most beautiful moments of the show, as Mercedes sings Aretha Franklin's arrangement of "Bridge Over Troubled Waters," you not only anticipate the reconciliation that takes place between Kurt and Mercedes, but you also witness a change of heart in Kurt, a transformation, if you will.

To be sure, the transformative moment did not occur through Kurt's changing his beliefs about God to match Mercedes' beliefs about God, or Mercedes' changing her beliefs about God to match Kurt's beliefs about God. Neither of them changed their beliefs about God, as the episode makes clear. Instead, the transformative moment of reconciliation, of healing, of a changed heart—it was beyond all of their beliefs about God. Their beliefs were merely peripheral to the occasion of transformation. The transformation was beyond the ideas in their minds about who or what God is, or who or what God is not, and it was rather about the experience of drawing together in community (*or better, it was about the power that draws us together in community*), which is more powerful and transformative than otherworldly doctrines or creeds or beliefs can ever be. This power is not to be confused for the power of a magical Santa Claus in the sky that fulfills all of our wishes, like the God Finn prayed to for selfish gain, but rather it is about the power of the call of love and care and compassion that emanates from below, that draws us to one another in times of great need, even though none of us can fully explain—or even begin to explain—how or why. Indeed, it is the power of the call of love and care and compassion that transforms our lives, that claims our lives, that is worthy of celebration. Whether we believe in God or not.

Which in a roundabout way gets us back to Finn and to Grilled Cheesus. Over the course of this episode, Finn slowly took into consideration all that Kurt was going through, and he began to recognize that his prayers to Grilled Cheesus had been shallow, selfish, and superficial. He also started to think that what he at first took as answers to his prayers were probably more a product of circumstance and coincidence than anything else. It was a harsh realization for him to come to terms with the fact that he was using religion for personal gain, that his beliefs in Grilled Cheesus—his beliefs in God—were full of narcissistic self-interest, which distanced him from others. So he did the only sensible thing. At the end of the show, Finn took the sandwich out of the refrigerator, unwrapped it, and ate it.

Several critics of this episode said that even though the show touched on some serious themes, the plot line surrounding Finn's treatment of

Grilled Cheesus was silly, that it lacked conviction. Surely Finn must have had more depth, right? But in my opinion, the critics missed it.

Allow me to quote from St. Paul: "For I received from the Lord what I also handed on to you, that the Lord Jesus on the night when he was betrayed took a loaf of bread, and when he had given thanks, he broke it and said, 'This is my body that is for you. Do this in remembrance of me.' In the same way he took the cup also, after supper, saying, 'This cup is the new covenant in my blood. Do this, as often as you drink it, in remembrance of me.'"[8]

Finn ate Grilled Cheesus because he was no longer going to use religion for selfish gain. Finn ate Grilled Cheesus because he was no longer going to allow belief in a God "out there" to keep him from taking responsibility right here. In short, Finn ate Grilled Cheesus because he had been transformed. Finn ate Grilled Cheesus because he had been born, again.

At the heart of Christianity is the image of one whose death on a cross is a continual reminder that transformative faith is not about selfish gain, but rather is about the call to risk a life based on love, care, and compassion. Most striking of all is that in Christianity, the God who is "out there," the "Big Being" in the sky, that God comes to earth and dies, which is what we remember every time we eat the bread and drink from the cup. When we gather around this table, we don't so much proclaim a God who is "out there" or "up in the sky," like a cosmic Santa Claus at our every beck and call. Instead, we proclaim a God whose death transforms our lives, so that we too might be born, again. Not by selfishly praying to a Big Being Out There, but by living and loving right here, experiencing the kind of resurrection that is, quite literally, beyond belief.

8. 1 Cor 11:23–25.

Bibliography

Allen, David. "A Tale of Two Roads: Homiletics and Biblical Authority." *Journal of the Evangelical Theological Society* 43 (2000) 489–515.

Allen, O. Wesley. *The Homiletic of All Believers: A Conversational Approach to Proclamation and Preaching.* Louisville: Westminster John Knox, 2005.

———, editor. *The Renewed Homiletic.* Minneapolis: Fortress, 2010.

Allen, Ronald J. *Patterns of Preaching: A Sermon Sampler.* St. Louis: Chalice, 1998.

———. *Preaching and the Other: Studies of Postmodern Insights.* St. Louis: Chalice, 2009.

———. "Preaching and Postmodernism." *Interpretation* 55 (2001) 34–48.

———. *Thinking Theologically: The Preacher as Theologian.* Minneapolis: Fortress, 2008.

Allen, Ronald J., Barbara Shires Blaisdell, and Scott Black Johnston. *Theology for Preaching: Authority, Truth, and Knowledge of God in a Postmodern Ethos.* Nashville: Abingdon, 1997.

Andrews, Dale P. "Response to Eugene L. Lowry." In *The Renewed Homiletic*, edited by O. Wesley Allen, 96–100. Minneapolis: Fortress, 2010.

Augustine. *Confessions.* Translated by Henry Chadwick. Oxford: Oxford University Press, 1991.

———. *Teaching Christianity [De Doctrina Christiana].* Translated by Edmund Hill. The Works of Saint Augustine 1/11. New York: New City, 1996.

Barth, Karl. *Church Dogmatics,* III/3. Edited by G. W. Bromiley and T. F. Torrance, translated by A. T. Mackay and T. H. L. Parker. Peabody, MA: Hendrickson, 2010.

———. *Epistle to the Romans.* 6th ed. Translated by Edwyn C. Hoskyns. Oxford: Oxford University Press, 1968.

———. "Jesus is Victor." In *A Chorus of Witnesses: Model Sermons for Today's Preacher,* edited by Thomas G. Long and Cornelius Plantiga Jr., 73–81. Grand Rapids: Eerdmans, 1994.

———. *The Word of God and the Word of Man.* Translated by Douglas Horton. Cleveland: Pilgrim, 1928.

Bartlett, David. *Between the Bible and the Church.* Nashville: Abingdon, 1999.

Bennington, Geoffrey, and Jacques Derrida. *Jacques Derrida.* Translated by Geoffrey Bennington. Chicago: University of Chicago Press, 1993.

Benson, Bruce Ellis. *Graven Ideologies: Nietzsche, Derrida and Marion on Modern Idolatry.* Downers Grove, IL: InterVarsity, 2002.

———. *Pious Nietzsche: Decadence and Dionysian Faith.* Bloomington: Indiana University Press, 2008.

Bonhoeffer, Dietrich. *Letters and Papers from Prison*. New York: Touchstone, 1997.

Borg, Marcus. *The Heart of Christianity: Rediscovering a Life of Faith*. San Francisco: HarperCollins, 2003.

———. *Speaking Christian: Why Christian Words Have Lost Their Meaning and Power— And How They Can Be Restored*. New York: HarperOne, 2011.

Brooks, Gennifer Benjamin. "Response to Fred Craddock." In *The Renewed Homiletic*, edited by O. Wesley Allen, 55–58. Minneapolis: Fortress, 2010.

Brueggemann, Walter. *The Word Militant: Preaching a Decentering Word*. Minneapolis: Fortress, 2007.

Buttrick, David. *A Captive Voice: The Liberation of Preaching*. Louisville: Westminster John Knox, 1994.

———. *Homiletic: Moves and Structures*. Minneapolis: Fortress, 1987.

———. "*Homiletic* Renewed." In *The Renewed Homiletic*, edited by O. Wesley Allen, 105–16. Minneapolis: Fortress, 2010.

Campbell, Charles L. *Preaching Jesus: New Directions for Homiletics in Hans Frei's Postliberal Theology*. Grand Rapids: Eerdmans, 1997.

Campolo, Tony. *Let Me Tell You a Story: Life Lessons from Unexpected Places and Unlikely People*. Nashville: Thomas Nelson, 2000.

Caputo, John D. "Apostles of the Impossible: On God and the Gift in Derrida and Marion." In *God, the Gift, and Postmodernism*, edited by John D. Caputo and Michael J. Scanlon, 185–222. Bloomington: Indiana University Press, 1999.

———, editor. *Deconstruction in a Nutshell: A Conversation with Jacques Derrida*. New York: Fordham University Press, 1997.

———. "Jacques Derrida (1930–2004)." *Journal for Cultural and Religious Theory* 6:1 (2004). Online: http://www.jcrt.org/archives/06.1/caputo.pdf.

———. *The Mystical Element in Heidegger's Thought*. Athens: Ohio University Press, 1978.

———. "On Not Settling for an Abridged Edition of Postmodernism." In *Religion with Religion*, edited by J. Aaron Simmons and Stephen Minister. Pittsburgh: Duquesne University Press, forthcoming.

———. *On Religion*. New York: Routledge, 2001.

———. *The Prayers and Tears of Jacques Derrida: Religion without Religion*. Bloomington: Indiana University Press, 1997.

———. *Radical Hermeneutics: Repetition, Deconstruction, and the Hermeneutic Project*. Studies in Phenomenology and Existential Philosophy. Bloomington: Indiana University Press, 1987.

———. "Radical Theology Part I." No pages. Online: http://trippfuller.com/Caputo/09-01-09%20Radical%20Theology%20Part%20I.mp3.

———. "The Return of Anti-Religion: From Radical Atheism to Radical Theology." *Journal for Cultural and Religious Theory* 11:2 (2011). Online: http://www.jcrt.org/archives/11.2/caputo.pdf.

———. "Temporal Transcendence: The Very Idea of *à venir* in Derrida." In *Transcendence and Beyond: A Postmodern Inquiry*, edited by John D. Caputo and Michael J. Scanlon, 188–203. Bloomington: Indiana University Press, 2007.

———. *The Weakness of God: A Theology of the Event*. Bloomington: Indiana University Press, 2006.

———. *What Would Jesus Deconstruct? The Good News of Postmodernity for the Church*. Grand Rapids: Baker Academic, 2007.

Caputo, John D., and Gianni Vattimo. *After the Death of God*. Edited by Jeffrey W. Robbins. New York: Columbia University Press, 2007.

Caputo, John D., and Linda Martín Alcoff, editors. *St. Paul among the Philosophers*. Bloomington: Indiana University Press, 2009.

Caputo, John D., and Michael J. Scanlon, editors. *Augustine and Postmodernism: Confessions and Circumfession*. Bloomington: Indiana University Press, 2005.

———, editors. *God, the Gift, and Postmodernism*. Bloomington: Indiana University Press, 1999.

———, editors. *Transcendence and Beyond: A Postmodern Inquiry*. Bloomington: Indiana University Press, 2007.

Caputo, John D., Mark Dooley, and Michael J. Scanlon, editors. *Questioning God*. Bloomington: Indiana University Press, 2001.

Childers, Jana. *Performing the Word: Preaching as Theatre*. Nashville: Abingdon, 1998.

———, editor. *Purposes of Preaching*. St. Louis: Chalice, 2004.

Coffin, William Sloane. *Credo*. Louisville: Westminster John Knox, 2004.

Craddock, Fred. "Inductive Preaching Renewed." In *The Renewed Homiletic*, edited by O. Wesley Allen, 41–55. Minneapolis: Fortress, 2010.

———. *Tell It* (DVD). Disciples of Christ General Assembly, 2011.

Crossan, John Dominic. *God and Empire: Jesus against Rome, Then and Now*. New York: HarperOne, 2007.

Davies, Brian, and Brian Leftow. *The Cambridge Companion to Anselm*. Cambridge Companions to Philosophy. Cambridge: Cambridge University Press, 2004.

Deleuze, Gilles. *Difference and Repetition*. Translated by Paul Patton. New York: Columbia University Press, 1994.

Depoortere, Frederick. *Christ in Postmodern Philosophy: Gianni Vattimo, René Girard and Slavoj Žižek*. London: T. & T. Clark, 2008.

Derrida, Jacques. *Acts of Religion*. Edited by Gil Anidjar. New York: Routledge, 2002.

———. "Circumfession: Fifty-nine Periods and Periphrases." In *Jacques Derrida*, by Geoffrey Bennington and Jacques Derrida, translated by Geoffrey Bennington, 3–315. Chicago: University of Chicago Press, 1993.

———. "The Force of Law: 'The Mystical Foundation of Authority.'" In *Deconstruction and the Possibility of Justice*, edited by Drucilla Cornell et al., translated by Mary Quantaince, 3–69. New York: Routledge, 1992.

———. *The Gift of Death*. Translated by David Willis. Chicago: University of Chicago Press, 1995.

———. *Given Time: I. Counterfeit Money*. Translated by Peggy Kamuf. Chicago: University of Chicago Press, 1992.

———. "How to Avoid Speaking: Denials." In *Derrida and Negative Theology*, edited by Harold Coward and Toby Foshay, 73–142. Albany: State University of New York Press, 1992.

———. *Limited Inc*. Evanston: Northwestern University Press, 1988.

———. *Of Grammatology*. Corrected ed. Translated by Gayatri Chakavorty Spivak. Baltimore: Johns Hopkins University Press, 1997.

———. *Points . . . Interviews, 1974–1994*. Edited by Elisabeth Weber, translated by Peggy Kamuf et al. Stanford: Stanford University Press, 1995.

———. *Sovereignties in Question: The Poetics of Paul Celan*. Edited by Thomas Dutoit and Outi Pasanen. New York: Fordham University Press, 2005.

————. *Speech and Phenomena, and Other Essays on Husserl's Theory of Signs.* Evanston: Northwestern University Press, 1973.

————. "Violence and Metaphysics: An Essay on the Thought of Emmanuel Levinas." In *Writing and Difference,* translated by Alan Bass, 79–153. Chicago: University of Chicago Press, 1978.

Derrida, Jacques, and Gianni Vattimo. *Religion.* Stanford: Stanford University Press, 1996.

Descartes, René. *The Philosophical Writings of Descartes.* Vol. 2. Translated by John Cottingham et al. Cambridge: Cambridge University Press, 1985.

Dick, Kirby, and Amy Ziering Kofman. *Derrida: Screenplay and Essays on the Film.* Manchester: Manchester University Press, 2005.

Dostoevsky, Fyodor. *Notes from the Underground.* Indianapolis: Hackett, 2009.

Eslinger, Richard L. *Narrative and Imagination: Preaching the Worlds that Shape Us.* Minneapolis: Fortress, 1995.

Florence, Anna Carter. *Preaching as Testimony.* Louisville: Westminster John Knox, 2007.

Foucault, Michel. "Foucault." No pages. Online: http://foucault.info/foucault/biography .html.

Gallion, Matthew. "Eating God to Death: A Materialist Reading of the Eucharistic Imagery in John 6." Unpublished paper. Missouri State University, 2010.

Given, Mark D. "Paul and Writing." In *As It Is Written: Studying Paul's Use of Scripture,* edited by Stanley E. Porter and Christopher D. Stanley, 237–59. Society of Biblical Literature Symposium Series 50. Atlanta: SBL, 2008.

Gomes, Peter. *Sermons: Biblical Wisdom for Daily Living.* San Franscisco: HarperSanFrancisco, 2002.

González, Justo L. "A Hispanic Perspective: By the Rivers of Babylon." In *Preaching Justice: Ethnic and Cultural Perspectives,* edited by Christine Marie Smith, 80–97. Cleveland: United Church Press, 1998.

Graves, Mike. "God of Grace and Glory: The Focus of Our Preaching." In *What's the Matter with Preaching Today?,* edited by Mike Graves, 109–25. Louisville: Westminster John Knox, 2004.

Greenberg, Irving. "Cloud of Smoke, Pillar of Fire: Judaism, Christianity, and Modernity after the Holocaust." In *Auschwitz: Beginning of a New Era? Reflections on the Holocaust,* edited by Eva Fleischner, 7–55. New York: KTAV, 1977.

Griffin, David Ray, and Huston Smith. *Primordial Truth and Postmodern Theology.* Albany: State University of New York Press, 1989.

Hägglund, Martin. "The Radical Evil of Deconstruction: A Reply to John Caputo." *Journal for Cultural and Religious Theory* 11:2 (2011). Online: http://www.jcrt.org/ archives/11.2/hagglund.pdf.

Harris, Sam. *The End of Faith: Religion, Terror, and the Future of Reason.* New York: Norton, 2005.

Hedges, Chris. *I Don't Believe in Atheists.* New York: Free Press, 2008.

Hedahl, Susan. "Jesus Christ in the Sermon—Presence or Absence?" No pages. Online: http://www.workingpreacher.org/theologypreaching.aspx?article_id=432.

Heidegger, Martin. Interview by Rudolf Augstein and Georg Wolff. *Der Spiegel* (31 May 1976). No pages. Online: http://web.ics.purdue.edu/~other1/Heidegger%20Der%20 Spiegel.pdf.

Hodgson, Peter. *Winds of the Spirit: A Constructive Christian Theology.* Louisville: Westminster John Knox, 1994.

Hooke, Ruthanna B. "Response to Fred Craddock." In *The Renewed Homiletic,* edited by O. Wesley Allen, 58–62. Minneapolis: Fortress, 2010.

Jennings, Theodore W., Jr. *Reading Derrida/Thinking Paul: On Justice.* Stanford: Stanford University Press, 2006.

Jiménez, Pablo A. "Response to David Buttrick." In *The Renewed Homiletic,* edited by O. Wesley Allen, 116–19. Minneapolis: Fortress, 2010.

Kearney, Richard. *Debates in Continental Philosophy: Conversations with Contemporary Thinkers.* New York: Fordham University Press, 2004.

———. "Desire of God." In *God, the Gift, and Postmodernism,* edited by John D. Caputo and Michael J. Scanlon, 112–45. Bloomington: Indiana University Press, 1999.

———. *The God Who May Be: A Hermeneutics of Religion.* Bloomington: Indiana University Press, 2001.

Keller, Catherine. *Face of the Deep: A Theology of Becoming.* New York: Routledge, 2003.

Kierkegaard, Søren. *Journals of Søren Kierkegaard.* Translated by Alexander Dru. Oxford: Oxford University Press, 1948.

Kim, Eunjoo Mary. *Preaching in an Age of Globalization.* Louisville: Westminster John Knox, 2010.

Kotsko, Adam. *Žižek and Theology.* Philosophy and Theology. London: T. & T. Clark, 2008.

Kysar, Robert, and Joseph M. Webb. *Preaching to Postmoderns: New Perspectives for Proclaiming the Message.* Peabody, MA: Hendrickson, 2006.

Levinas, Emmanuel. *Of God Who Comes to Mind.* Translated by Bettina Bergo. Stanford: Stanford University Press, 1998.

Long, Thomas G. *Accompany Them with Singing: The Christian Funeral.* Louisville: Westminster John Knox, 2009.

———, and Cornelius Plantiga Jr. *A Chorus of Witnesses: Model Sermons for Today's Preacher.* Grand Rapids: Eerdmans, 1994.

———. "Funeral." In *The New Interpreter's Handbook of Preaching,* edited by Paul Scott Wilson, 385–90. Nashville: Abingdon, 2008.

———. "Imagine There's No Heaven: The Loss of Eschatology in American Preaching." In *Journal for Preachers* (Advent 2006). No pages. Online: http://www.ctsnet.edu/JournalforPreachers/index_files/PDFs/Advent_2006.pdf.

———. *Preaching from Memory to Hope.* Louisville: Westminster John Knox, 2009.

———. *The Witness of Preaching.* 2nd ed. Louisville: Westminster John Knox, 2005.

Lorensen, Marlene Ringgaard. "Carnivalized Preaching—in Dialogue with Bakhtin and Other-Wise Homiletics." *Homiletic* 36:1 (2011). No pages. Online: http://ejournals.library.vanderbilt.edu/ojs/index.php/homiletic/article/view/3438/164.

Lose, David J. *Confessing Jesus Christ: Preaching in a Postmodern World.* Grand Rapids: Eerdmans, 2003.

Lowry, Eugene. *The Sermon: Dancing the Edge of Mystery.* Nashville: Abingdon, 1997.

Manoussakis, John Panteleimon. *After God: Richard Kearney and the Religious Turn in Continental Philosophy.* New York: Fordham University Press, 2006.

Marion, Jean-Luc. *Being Given: Toward a Phenomenology of Givenness.* Translated by Jeffrey L. Kosky. Stanford: Stanford University Press, 2002.

———. *God Without Being.* Translated by Thomas A. Carlson. Chicago: University of Chicago Press, 1991.

———. "In the Name: How to Avoid Speaking of 'Negative Theology.'" In *God, the Gift, and Postmodernism,* edited by John D. Caputo and Michael J. Scanlon, 20–53. Bloomington: Indiana University Press, 1999.

——. "Is the Ontological Argument Ontological?" In *Flight of the Gods: Philosophical Perspectives on Negative Theology*, edited by Ilse N. Bulhof and Laurens ten Kate, 78–99. Perspectives in Continental Philosophy 11. New York: Fordham University Press, 2000.

——. *Prolegomena to Charity.* Translated by Stephen E. Lewis. New York: Fordham University Press, 2002.

McClure, John S. "Changes in the Authority, Method and Message of Presbyterian Preaching in the Twentieth Century." In *The Confessional Mosaic,* edited by John Mulder et al., 84–108. Louisville: Westminster John Knox, 1990.

——. "Deconstruction." In *The New Interpreter's Handbook of Preaching.* Edited by Paul Scott Wilson, 146–49. Nashville: Abingdon, 2008.

——. *Other-wise Preaching: A Postmodern Ethic for Homiletics.* St. Louis: Chalice, 2001.

——. *The Roundtable Pulpit: Where Leadership and Preaching Meet.* Nashville: Abingdon, 1995.

McFague, Sallie. *Super, Natural Christians: How We Should Love Nature.* Minneapolis: Fortress, 2000.

Negri, Antonio, and Michael Hardt. *Empire.* Cambridge: Harvard University Press, 2000.

Nietzsche, Friedrich. *The Gay Science.* Translated by Walter Kaufmann. New York: Random House, 1974.

——. *The Will to Power.* Translated by Walter Kaufmann and R. J. Hollingdale. New York: Vintage, 1967.

Northcutt, Kay. *Kindling Desire for God: Preaching as Spiritual Direction.* Minneapolis: Fortress, 2009.

Pagitt, Doug. *Preaching in the Inventive Age.* Minneapolis: Sparkhouse, 2011.

Placher, William C. *The Domestication of Transcendence: How Modern Thinking about God Went Wrong.* Louisville: Westminster John Knox, 1996.

——. *The Triune God: An Essay in Postliberal Theology.* Louisville: Westminster John Knox, 2007.

Plumer, Fred. "I Love Richard Dawkins!" No pages. Online: http://www.tcpc.org/library/article.cfm?library_id=1082.

Raschke, Carl. *The Next Reformation: Why Evangelicals Must Embrace Postmodernity.* Grand Rapids: Baker Academic, 2004.

Robbins, Jeffrey W. "The Hermeneutics of the Kingdom of God: John Caputo and the Deconstruction of Christianity" (6 February 2008). No pages. Online: http://www.metanexus.net/magazine/tabid/68/id/10298/Default.aspx.

——. "Religion for the Rest of Us." *The Huffington Post* (29 May 2007). No pages. Online: http://www.huffingtonpost.com/jeffrey-robbins/religion-for-the-rest-of-b_49796.html.

——. "Weak Theology." *Journal for Cultural and Religious Theory* 5:2 (2004). No pages. Online: http://www.jcrt.org/archives/05.2/robbins.pdf.

Robbins, Jeffrey W., and Christopher D. Rodkey. "Beating 'God' to Death: Radical Theology and the New Atheism." In *Religion and the New Atheism: A Critical Appraisal,* edited by Amarnath Amarasingam, 25–36. Boston: Brill, 2010.

Robinson, John A. T. *Honest to God.* Philadelphia: Westminster, 1963.

Rock, Chris. "Colin Powell, black president." YouTube video. No pages. Online: http://www.youtube.com/watch?v=DePjG71zttQ.

Rodkey, Christopher D. "Easter Sunday Sermon: 'Too Good to Be True!'" No pages. Online: http://itself.wordpress.com/2011/04/20/easter-sunday-sermon-too-good-to-be-true/.

Rogers, Thomas G. "Emerging Church Preaching." In *The New Interpreter's Handbook of Preaching*. Edited by Paul Scott Wilson, 298-300. Nashville: Abingdon, 2008.

Rollins, Peter. "Batman as the Ultimate Capitalist Superhero" (16 June 2008). No pages. Online: http://peterrollins.net/?p=49.

———. *The Fidelity of Betrayal: Towards a Church Beyond Belief.* Brewster, MA: Paraclete, 2008.

———. *How (Not) to Speak of God.* Brewster, MA: Paraclete, 2006.

———. *Insurrection: To Believe Is Human; to Doubt, Divine.* New York: Howard, 2011.

———. "Lessons in Evandalism Tour" (19 January 09). No pages. Online: http://peterrollins.net/?p=132.

———. "Religion, Fundamentalism and Christianity" (26 June 08). No pages. Online: http://peterrollins.net/?p=54.

Rorty, Richard. *Philosophy and Social Hope.* London: Penguin, 1999.

Rose, Lucy Atkinson. *Sharing the Word: Preaching in the Roundtable Church.* Louisville: Westminster John Knox, 1997.

Schaeffer, Francis. "Obama's Minister Committed 'Treason' but When My Father Said the Same Thing He Was a Republican Hero." *The Huffington Post* (16 March 08). No pages. Online: http://www.huffingtonpost.com/frank-schaeffer/obamas-minister-committed_b_91774.html.

Shakespeare, Steven. *Derrida and Theology.* Philosophy and Theology. London: T. & T. Clark: 2009.

Sherwood, Yvonne, and Kevin Hart. *Derrida and Religion: Other Testaments.* New York: Routledge, 2005.

Smith, Anthony Paul, and Daniel Whistler, editors. *After the Postsecular and the Postmodern: New Essays in Continental Philosophy of Religion.* Newcastle: Cambridge Scholars, 2010.

Smith, James K. A. "Between Predication and Silence: Augustine on How (Not) to Speak of God. Online: http://www.calvin.edu/academic/philosophy/virtual_library/articles/smith_james/Betwo72701.pdf.

Snider, Phil, and Emily Bowen. *Toward a Hopeful Future: Why the Emergent Church Is Good News for Mainline Congregations.* Cleveland: Pilgrim, 2010.

Spong, John Shelby. *Eternal Life: A New Vision: Beyond Religion, Beyond Theism, Beyond Heaven and Hell.* New York: HarperOne, 2009.

Stewart, Jon. *Earth (the Book): A Visitor's Guide to the Human Race.* New York: Grand Central, 2010.

Sullivan, Amy. In "Faith and Citizenship in America" podcast, Yale Divinity School (6 August 07). No pages. Online: http://itunes.apple.com/us/itunes-u/yale-religion/id341654959.

Taylor, Mark C. *After God.* Chicago: University of Chicago Press, 2007.

———. *Erring: A Postmodern A/theology.* Chicago: University of Chicago Press, 1984.

———. *Tears.* Intersections: Philosophy and Critical Theory. Albany: State University of New York Press, 1990.

———. "What Derrida Really Meant." *The New York Times* (14 October 2004). No pages. Online: http://www.nytimes.com/2004/10/14/opinion/14taylor.html?ex=1255492800&en=2f805b31ffoaa5e7&ei=5088&partner=rssnyt.

Thomas, Frank A. *They Like to Never Quit Praisin' God: The Role of Celebration in Preaching.* Cleveland: Pilgrim, 1997.

Tillich, Paul. *The Shaking of the Foundations.* New York: Scribner's, 1948.

———. *Systematic Theology.* Vol. 1. Chicago: University of Chicago Press, 1973.

Tisdale, Leonora Tubbs. *Prophetic Preaching: A Pastoral Approach.* Louisville: Westminster John Knox, 2010.

Turner, Mary Donovan. "Disrupting a Ruptured World." In *Purposes of Preaching,* edited by Jana Childers, 131–40. St. Louis: Chalice, 2004.

Ward, Graham. *Barth, Derrida, and the Language of Theology.* Cambridge: Cambridge University Press, 1995.

Ward, Richard F. *Speaking from the Heart: Preaching with Passion.* Eugene, OR: Wipf & Stock, 2001.

Westphal, Merold. "Overcoming Onto-theology." In *God, the Gift, and Postmodernism,* edited by John D. Caputo and Michael J. Scanlon, 146–69. Bloomington: Indiana University Press, 1999.

Willimon, William H. *Conversations with Barth on Preaching.* Nashville: Abingdon, 2006.

———. *Preaching and Leading Worship.* Louisville: Westminster, 1984.

———. "What's Next." *The Christian Century* (1 June 2010), 28–30.

Wilson, Paul Scott. *The New Interpreter's Handbook of Preaching.* Nashville: Abingdon, 2008.

———. "Preaching as a Theological Venture." In *Purposes of Preaching,* edited by Jana Childers, 141–56. St. Louis: Chalice, 2004.

———. *Setting Words on Fire: Putting God at the Center of the Sermon.* Nashville: Abingdon, 2008.

Žižek, Slavoj. *The Fragile Absolute: Or, Why Is the Christian Legacy Worth Fighting For?* London: Verso, 2000.

———. *The Puppet and the Dwarf: The Perverse Core of Christianity.* Cambridge: MIT Press, 2003.

———. *The Sublime Object of Ideology.* London: Verso, 1989.

Zlomislić, Marko, and Neal DeRoo. *Cross and Khôra: Deconstruction and Christianity in the Work of John D. Caputo.* Postmodern Ethics 1. Eugene, OR: Pickwick Publications, 2010.

Index of Names

Made in the USA
Lexington, KY
28 March 2014